MONEY GUI

One in three marriages ends in divorce; one in five women is the head of a household. By 1991, more than 60 per cent of married women will be in full-time paid employment.

Statistics like these show that the modern woman is the new dynamic in today's workforce, often the sole breadwinner, often single, and often trying to balance her own requirements with those of her family. And yet there is still little specific information which can help her on her financial course.

Now the MONEY GUIDE FOR WOMEN, written by two acknowledged professionals, gives sensible suggestions and reveals practical ways of managing and magnifying that hard-earned cash. Detailed chapters cover taxation, maternity rights, the financial implications of divorce, life insurance, and planning for health disabilities and retirement.

MONEY GUIDE FOR WOMEN is a comprehensive, sympathetic handbook – a unique reference tool that responds effectively to the needs of women living and working in the 1980s.

About the Authors

Nigel Smith was a lecturer at Lincoln College of Further Education before joining the staff of *Money Which?* magazine where he researched and wrote reports on all aspects of personal finance. He has appeared on radio and television talking about consumer issues and is a contributor to THE WHICH? BOOK OF MONEY, THE WHICH? BOOK OF SAVING AND INVESTING and THE WHICH? BOOK OF TAX. He is married with two daughters and lives near Cambridge.

Jill Greatorex has worked in financial journalism for six years on a variety of magazines, including *Which?* (published by the Consumers' Association) and has contributed to books and pamphlets on tax and employment law. She is a graduate in Social Sciences, with a special interest in trade union law and women's rights, insurance and investments. She is single and lives in London.

MONEY GUIDE FOR WOMEN

Nigel Smith and Jill Greatorex

With a Foreword by Audrey Slaughter

CORONET BOOKS
Hodder and Stoughton

First published in Great Britain in 1986 by Coronet Books

British Library C.I.P.

Smith, Nigel
Money guide for women.
1. Women – Great Britain – Finance,
Personal
I. Title II. Greatorex, Jill
332.024′042′0941 HG179

ISBN 0-340-39318-1

Printed and bound in Great Britain for Hodder and Stoughton Paperbacks, a division of Hodder and Stoughton Ltd., Mill Road, Dunton Green, Sevenoaks, Kent (Editorial Office: 47 Bedford Square, London WC1B 3DP) by Cox and Wyman Ltd., Reading
Photoset by Rowland Phototypesetting Ltd., Bury St Edmunds, Suffolk

Contents

FOR REFERENCE

Foreword

The statistics are daunting: one in three marriages end in divorce. One in five women are heads of households. One in seven women earn more than their partners. By 1991 – so few years away – more than 60% of married women will work full-time. It is clear that women are no longer working for 'pin money' – if ever they did so. Yet, the myth remains that most women will be swept off their feet by Mr Right, and live happily ever after without an economic cloud on the horizon. He'll take over from Daddy in shielding delicate Mrs Right from the harsh financial facts of life.

What a dangerous assumption. It has been the reason why so many women, faced with their husband's redundancy or divorce or some other cruel act of Fate, have had to set-to – perhaps in middle age – to earn a living with no more preparation than a few O-levels and a stint as a clerk before marriage.

Or it has been the reason why so many girls have been discouraged at school from pegging away at maths and science and chemistry which would open up wider career choices for themselves, because these were unfeminine subjects and men shy away from women with brains. The school swot always has scraped-back hair and horn-rimmed glasses and no man, of course, as Ogden Nash would have it, ever makes passes at girls who wear glasses.

In fact, if we ever face up to reality, we will realise that even if Mr Right *does* turn up and we do live happily ever after, a second paycheque is going to be the norm for a couple who want to have what is popularly known as 'the good life'. A second paycheque can ease the strain of making ends meet, and it can release a man from the struggle of climbing the ladder, perhaps forsaking work he does enjoy for work he may not but which he has hitherto felt pressured to take because it has meant more financial ease at home. The sole breadwinner has a lonely responsibility.

Married or single, the chances are that women today will go on working even if there is a short interruption for a family. The average 'career break' lasts a mere three to seven years – a tiny proportion of the average lifetime. This makes for a profound social change. The new dynamic is the number of women in the workforce, the ones who do not consider work as 'just a job' but a career. As a result, we are having to change and adapt our lifestyles. New markets are opening up. Time is at a premium.

With new-found economic independence, women are beginning to realise that managing their money well is *their* responsibility. It is, though, merely a beginning. Too many of us haven't yet appreciated that a salary cheque is more than an invitation to 'spend, spend, spend', which is why I welcome the work put into this book by Nigel Smith and Jill Greatorex.

They have taken the mystique out of managing money. Whatever your circumstances, *Money Guide for Women* caters for your needs. It is unique in its organisation of comprehensive information and although not all its contents will apply to you right now, you will be able to look up all the relevant financial information as and when you find yourself in different situations. Unless you have such information you can't act, and your hard-earned money will continue to dribble away uselessly through the holes of ignorance.

A few months ago we carried out a financial survey in *Working Woman* and were staggered to find how few of our readers were truly financially sophisticated. Surplus salary mounted up in current accounts, doing nothing but make banks richer and bank managers complacent. Though many were self-employed and worried that possible ill health could prevent them from earning, few had health insurance. Those women without dependants were talked into life insurance policies instead of pension plans or health insurance. The majority didn't know how to invest on the stock market though quite a few had building society accounts – a safe way of earning interest but not much prospect of capital appreciation.

In *Working Woman* we have always carried features on finance, but it was only after two of our sub-editors had been working on the pages for some months that they started to appreciate the significance of some kind of financial planning. They both promptly enrolled in an evening class run by a stockbroker and today they pore over the *Financial Times*, fascinated by the relevance of foreign news or volatile interest rates to the stock market and their own fortunes. Like so many of us, they hadn't realised that once you gain a little knowledge and learn your way around the financial pages, watching even a small investment grow (or, sadly, diminish) adds a vast amount of interest to previously dull financial reports.

One day, perhaps, school curricula will be expanded to include financial planning. Children will know how to weigh up the merits of renting or buying a house, the true cost of hire-purchase agreements, the real cost of overdrawing a bank account, the hidden snags in long-term savings plans and endowment mortgages, the sensible ways to use a credit card. They will know the meaning of cash-flow. One friend, proud of her careful budgeting, worked out how much her son's school fees were going to be and set so much aside each month. Unfortunately, she had to pay the school at the beginning of each term – not after she'd carefully hoarded her monthly sums. 'That's the difference between a profit-and-loss account and a cash-flow forecast,' her boss told her. If she'd been more aware – as well she might if she'd read this book some years ago – she might have taken out a school fees insurance plan which would have spread the load over an easier length of time.

Some of us are just not able to save, however much we earn. I'm certainly not. I share the same outlook as the little boy whose parents made him save all 'unexpected' money – tips from relatives, birthday money and so on, much to his disgust. When finally his grandfather gave him a whole fiver for being brave at the dentist's, he put it firmly in his pocket and said, 'You're not going to put this in the bank and waste it.' I have to pretend to myself that I earn less than I do by arranging for a set sum each month to be transferred automatically to a deposit account, just as if it were a firm commitment like a hire-purchase agreement. When it reaches a likely sum, I buy shares through the bank since I rarely have an amount large enough to make a stockbroker jump for joy at the prospect of me as a client. Strangely enough, I find it hard to spend 'capital', so once I have a little capital hoard, I use it quite productively and monitor my own investments. A friend, who has the same 'spend' mentality but is bored with the stock market's machinations, buys unit trusts on a monthly basis so that she doesn't have to watch them herself. Both of us have taken steps to guard against our own feckless temperaments in a fairly painless fashion. Another friend makes her investment antique furniture. Antique-hunting is her leisuretime interest. Her monthly saving eventually is invested in a piece of furniture which gives her pleasure to use but, because she has bought carefully and with knowledge, will inevitably appreciate.

Money has a mercenary ring; 'money doesn't bring happiness, you know,' people say sagely, and 'the love of money is the root of evil'. Of course money alone doesn't bring happiness, but then neither does poverty. I can't remember which Hollywood celebrity said, 'I've been rich and I've been poor, but I can tell you, rich is better', but they had a point. I don't think that, in this book, we are being urged to love money, merely to manage it well, make it our servant, give ourselves a little freedom and independence and comfort. After all, if I hadn't had a little money I would never have been able to start a magazine – something that has given me lots of interest, lots of friends, and employment to others. That can't be bad.

Audrey Slaughter,
January 1986

MANAGING YOUR MONEY

1

Getting the Best from Your Money

A number of people whom we told we were writing a book about personal finance for women asked us, 'What is so different about women?' In some areas there are obvious differences – in tax, pensions, maternity rights and social security, for example. But in addition to differences of fact, there are also many areas where a woman's interests are very different from a man's – for example, when a marriage breaks up, in planning for retirement, in making a will, in deciding on single or joint ownership of things you buy and who will pay which of the household bills, in insuring against poor health or death. Many books still assume that it is men who make most of the financial arrangements and decisions, completely ignoring the fact that there are now millions of households in which the woman is the only, or the main, earner or makes an essential contribution to a joint income. We hope, therefore, that you will get further with this book than with others you may have tried. In this short chapter we want to give you a very brief indication of some of the many aspects of personal finance which are dealt with in the book and which we hope you will find useful.

To start on a fairly mundane level, avoiding bank charges has in the past been a fairly challenging task, particularly if you have standing orders or direct debits or a joint account. The only safe way was to keep a fair amount of money in your account to make sure you did not go below the bank's level for free banking. But this was wasteful, because you got no interest on the money. In Chapter 2 we tell you about accounts which solve the problem with no effort on your part whatsoever. All the money you pay in goes into a building society account where it earns interest until it is needed; but you draw out from a bank account which is topped up automatically from the building society account whenever the balance falls below £100.

Credit cards are viewed in very different lights by different people; they are supposed to indicate wealth and status but to some people they are just temptations to get increasingly into debt. Used sensibly, however, they are invaluable aids to managing your spending efficiently. In Chapters 2 and 3, we suggest a number of ways in which a credit card will save you money and not cost you anything.

There are times when most of us find that the money coming in just will not meet the demands being made on it. The problem has become extremely acute for a great many families in recent years with high unemployment, an increasing number of one-parent families, cuts in public services and state benefits under attack. But a very basic problem that affects many of us is that, while we are paid weekly or monthly, the bills tend to be yearly, half-yearly or quarterly. In Chapter 2 we suggest ways of keeping very careful tabs on the money that is coming in and going out and in Chapter 4 we look in more detail at paths you may be able to take if you cannot manage on what money you have.

In more fortunate times, many of us will have money we do not want to spend straightaway and will think of saving and investing. Even when money is tight, it is essential to make provision for the future, whatever your circumstances. There is now an enormous number of financial institutions trying to attract the ordinary person's savings, and seldom stressing the features that are the most important considerations from your point of view. In Chapter 5, we tell you how to choose the most suitable of these for your needs.

One of the best investments that most people have made in the past is simply to buy their own homes. Property prices have outpaced inflation by a considerable margin, and although the monthly payments on a mortgage may initially seem a considerable drain on your pocket, they really are worthwhile. It is worth remembering that over the years many people get back all the money they pay for their homes. They buy their first home with a deposit of perhaps £5,000 and 60 monthly payments of £250, a total of £20,000. After five years they sell it and find they have £15,000 left after repaying the mortgage. They use this as the deposit on the next home, pay 60 more payments of £250 and move again five years later, this time having perhaps £30,000 left over. On the third move five years later they may well have £50,000 left after paying off the mortgage, which is equal to the amount they have paid in over the years. The combination of rising house prices and tax relief on the mortgage has allowed them to live rent-free for fifteen years. This is why everyone should think very seriously about buying their own home, especially if they would otherwise be renting for long periods. Even if you are a very mobile or unsettled person and end up letting your home for some of the time, the rental income is likely to far exceed any Capital Gains Tax you end up paying. We cover renting a home in Chapter 6 and buying and selling homes in Chapter 7, including the important business of getting a mortgage.

In Chapter 8 we deal with aspects of running a home that apply to both owners and tenants, including insuring the contents. You would be unwise not to insure your possessions, especially if you live in a city area where theft is now widespread. But did you know that some insurance companies charge over three times as much as others to cover the same property against the same risks? We tell you in Chapter 8 which insurance companies could save you £100 a year or more, simply because they do not have excessive rates for inner-city areas.

Having bought your home, we deal in Chapter 9 with aspects that will concern you over the years – insuring it, improving it and letting it out. We also look at the circumstances in which Capital Gains Tax may arise, and point out that the large bite which many people expect the tax to take may turn out to be a mere nibble.

We cover the important issues that arise when you share your home in Chapters 10 to 15. We look at your legal position if you live with someone as a couple, the ownership of things you share, the invidious snooping by DHSS investigators, and how to get the last laugh by arranging things so that you pay less tax than a married couple. But the following chapter shows how a highly-paid married couple can strike back by the wife asking for her earnings to be taxed as if she were a single person. In marriage there is not much choice as to how you can arrange your personal finances. But when a marriage breaks down there are endless possibilities and few reliable sources of information and advice on the money side, even though lack of money nearly always causes far more problems than the separation or divorce itself. So Chapter 12 gives a detailed coverage of the money problems that are likely to arise, the financial arrangements that need to be made, and managing afterwards. We give a whole host of suggestions for arranging things in the most efficient way – which together could increase your income very substantially.

As women are on average three years younger than their

husbands and live four years longer, a large percentage of married women can expect to have to deal with their husband's death and face several years of life on their own. In Chapter 13 we look at the arrangements that have to be made, and the effect on your home, your possessions and your finances. We tell you about the various sources of income you may be entitled to and how to claim them, and the long-term state benefits paid to many widows. We also describe the arrangements that have to be made regarding your husband's estate.

For those with children, Chapter 14 takes you from maternity leave and social security benefits through caring for children while you are at work, pocket money, saving up for private school fees, investing for children, student grants and how you can give a student child £140 at a cost of only £100.

In Chapter 15 we turn to the important question of protecting yourself and other people in your household from the risks which, however slight, could cause a major setback in your lives. Insurance is not the most exciting of subjects and it is so easy to find excuses not to do anything about it. But it is vital, and need not be expensive. The very cheapest type of life insurance, under which you get a large lump sum if you die within a certain period but nothing if you don't, is the most suitable for many people. We point out that while many couples have adequate insurance on the man's life, they have none at all on the woman's. If you have children, your partner could find himself in serious difficulties paying for people to carry out all the roles that you currently perform. Life insurance is cheaper for women than for men, and is a must. Almost as important is insurance which pays out an income if you have any long-term illness which prevents you from carrying out your usual roles (not to be confused with insurance which only pays towards hospital costs and medical bills).

Chapters 16–18 provide a detailed guide to earning money through having a job, earning money at home and starting your own business. Did you know that there is a government scheme which will pay you £40 a week for two years if you want to work for yourself? And it is fairly easy to get on to – details are in Chapter 18.

In Chapter 19 we take a long hard look at the future and planning for retirement. Pensions have rightly come back into the limelight and we assess which schemes are best for individual needs.

In Chapter 20 we cover all aspects of retirement – the effect of retiring early or late, ways of giving your pensions a last-minute boost, how to get a higher income in retirement, what happens if you carry on working, ways of getting an income from your home, how to escape from the infamous 'age-allowance trap', and where you should invest any spare money in retirement.

Many people wonder what it is all for when they think that half their money will go in tax when they die. Fortunately they are mistaken; for the vast majority of us there will not be a large tax bill when it is our time to go. But you do not have to be very wealthy for your heirs to have to pay some tax, so in Chapter 21 we look at ways in which you can reduce the tax that will be payable and any risks involved in doing so. Of course, one of the most important things is to make a will, and we give you a checklist of things to consider before deciding what you should leave to whom.

We have made a deliberate attempt in this book not just to explain how things work, but to judge everything from the point of view of the ordinary person with the problem. We do not imagine for one moment that you will regard this as a book to read from cover to cover. In fact we hope you will not, because we want you to use it, not just read it. We hope that when you have a problem you will refer to the appropriate sections before going to see a 'professional' adviser or making any decisions. You will almost certainly make a better decision by doing so. And we hope that you will pick up the book from time to time and think about the things which are not pressing but which are no less important – like your retirement, making a will, your children or other dependants and what arrangements you should be making for your future and theirs. In your life as a whole, these are the most important arrangements you will have to make, but as they are so often overlooked we have dealt with them in some detail in Chapters 15, 19, 20 and 21.

Finally, we hope that the information and advice in this book puts you more in control of your finances, that it makes you more secure and that it saves you money – leaving more of your hard-earned money to spend on what you want.

2

Managing Your Money

In this chapter we look first at what we want to achieve and at problems in managing money, then we put together a plan for making your money go further and work better for you, and finally we look in detail at the various types of account that are available and how they may be able to help.

Aims – and problems

No one should pretend that balancing the books is an easy matter for most people these days. A monthly budget is much harder to manage than the traditional weekly one. Running a current account from which much of the money is taken automatically through standing orders is harder than keeping a pot on the mantelshelf – and a joint account is particularly hard to keep track of.

So let us start by thinking what needs to be done to keep your head above water. Three things come to mind:

- to have enough ready money to meet the bills you are expecting
- to have some extra money you can get at quickly to meet any unexpected expenditure (an 'emergency fund')
- to have any other spare money invested where it will earn a reasonable return.

These objectives are really pretty obvious. But we might add two more:

- to be thinking about the future, and making sensible provision for yourself and your dependants (we cover these in Chapters 15, 19 and 21);

- to take advantage of the various accounts and financial services available to help achieve the first three aims.

You may think that, while this sounds sensible enough, it is a formula for a deadly boring life – always worrying about how much is in the bank and always being too frightened to buy anything beyond the basic and functional. That is not the idea at all. The point is that poor money management can waste you a hundred pounds or more a year in lost interest, bank charges, credit card charges, missing out on discounts, and so on. This is money down the drain. Spending half an hour a week keeping a check on your money can save you a lot in the course of a year – meaning you have more to spend on things you would either have gone without or perhaps have had to pay dearly for by borrowing.

The suggestions that follow should help achieve the aims listed above and keep your money under control. First, we look at some of the problems that affect almost everyone for some of the time, whether you are single, married or a single parent. For although the amounts of money and the timing may be different, the basic problem is the same whether the income is your salary, your pension, someone else's salary or pension, maintenance payments or social security benefits.

EXAMPLE

Pat Graham earns £500 a month and gets child benefit and one-parent benefit for her two children of £75.20 every four weeks. Over a typical month, her cash situation is as shown overleaf.

You can see that for most of the month Pat seems to have quite a lot of money to play with. But for a few days towards the end she comes very near to having nothing at all. Pat's main problems – all fairly typical – are these:

- Having £500 or more at her disposal for a while each month naturally presents a temptation for Pat to spend some of it on things which are not strictly necessary or could be delayed.

- Having a house to run and two children to support, much of Pat's money goes on essentials – the mortgage, food, clothes and

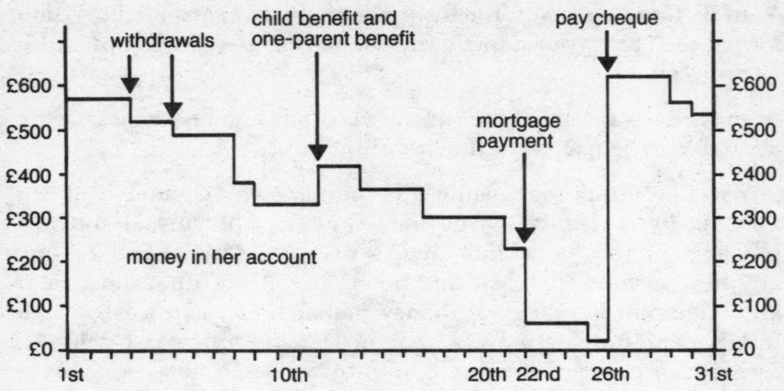

household goods. It is very easy to underestimate the total cost of these.

• Some of the biggest bills come every three months – the electricity, gas and telephone. Pat is lucky in that she gets one each month. If you get two or three in the same month, you have a much greater problem.

• One of Pat's problems is the relative timing of her monthly mortgage instalment and getting her monthly wages. The mortgage is due on the 22nd of each month, whereas she does not usually get paid until about the 26th. This means she has to keep the £160 mortgage money for nearly the whole month, making sure none of it gets spent.

• Pat tries to put a little money each month into her building society savings account. But she finds it very disheartening that just when her savings seem to be reaching a worthwhile amount, there is the coal or a new school uniform to be paid for, or something in the home needs to be repaired.

• If we assume she has a bank current account, Pat is in danger – like millions of other people – of becoming liable for bank charges unless she keeps a very careful watch on exactly how much money is going into and out of her account each day. The reason is that if the amount in your account is less than a certain sum (usually £100, £50 or zero) for just one day, with some banks you pay charges for a *whole three months*. You can see in the diagram that the amount in Pat's account is less than £100 for four days, so if the free-banking limit set by her bank were £100, she would be liable to charges for three months.

The suggestions in the next section would help Pat overcome some of these difficulties. They would also give her a better understanding of what is going on, give her more control over her money and help her realise that she is doing a better job than she might think.

Putting your money plan together

1 Using the most suitable accounts

Banks, building societies and other organisations offer a wide range of accounts which you can use to help manage your day-to-day finances. Some pay you interest, others do not, some allow you to overdraw, others do not. With some you can withdraw money whenever you like, with others there are restrictions. With some you are charged if you do not keep a certain amount in your account, with others you are not. We have grouped the accounts into six types:

- bank current account
- savings account
- savings account with extras
- linked current and savings account
- credit card account
- National Savings ordinary account

There is detailed information on each type for you to refer to in the last section of this chapter, starting on page 30. Here we consider which is likely to be the best account (or combination of accounts) for you.

If you are looking for a home for your own personal money, separate from the main household account, a **building society savings account** is likely to be best. You get interest on every penny in the account, and with some of the **savings accounts with extras** you can now have a chequebook for paying other people and a **cashcard** to get money from cash dispensers. Having your own **credit card** as well will provide more flexibility. If you do not have enough income to pay any tax (and nor does your husband, if you are married), a **National Savings invest-**

ment account (see page 77) would pay you more interest than a building society savings account but, as you have to give a month's notice to withdraw any money, a credit card would be fairly essential in this case to bridge the gaps.

For the account you use to run your household, a linked current and savings account offers an unbeatable combination which will meet most people's needs:

- a bank current account with a chequebook for your spending
- standing orders and direct debits for your regular bills
- a building society savings account with a fairly high rate of interest, for your emergency fund, savings and money you do not need immediately
- no charges, as long as you have some savings
- freedom from worrying about having to transfer money between your current and savings accounts in order to avoid bank charges on the one hand and to avoid missing out on interest on the other. This is because nearly all your money remains in the savings account earning interest until it is needed – when it is transferred automatically to the current account
- access to a credit card, overdraft or personal loan if you want them.

At the time of writing only two such schemes were available (see pages 34–5) and they really are worth finding out about.

If it is much more convenient for you to conduct your business at a post office, a National Girobank current account provides pretty well the same service as any other bank current account. The main snags (which may not affect you) are that you can withdraw money on alternate days only and, unless you already have a cheque guarantee card with another bank, for the first 6 months you do not get a cheque guarantee card and you can withdraw only at two post offices (chosen by you). You will probably also need some kind of savings account for your emergency fund and money you do not need immediately, as National Girobank does not pay any interest. It might be sensible to have a building society account with a cashcard which you can use in a cash dispenser in the town you most often visit.

If you decide on a current account with a High Street bank,

then try to choose the one with the lowest charges (look at the most recent report on bank charges in *Which?*, available at your local library). See if you qualify for 'free' banking (because you are a student or because of your age, for example) and make sure you understand the bank's rules about how charges will be incurred. Find out the dates of the bank's charging periods, and then keep an accurate record of how much is in the account. Ways you can keep down your charges if you do incur them are:

- make purchases with a credit card and settle the bill with a single cheque between 4 and 8 weeks later
- pay several household bills with one cheque by making the cheque out to the bank for the total amount
- make regular payments by direct debit rather than standing order if your bank charges less for them; or have them paid from your savings account rather than the current account
- get cash from dispensers instead of by writing a cheque if your bank charges less for this
- do not pay bills sooner than you need to – a week before the due date is soon enough
- if you can see that you are going to dip below the free-banking limit for a short period, it will normally be cheaper to get some money on your credit card than incur bank charges for a whole three months.

You should also try to make sure you do not have large amounts of money floating around in a current account earning no interest. You should have a savings account as well for your emergency fund and money you do not need immediately.

PAYMENTS DIRECT TO YOUR ACCOUNT

You can have your salary or firm's pension paid direct into a bank current account or deposit account, and your firm may be able to pay it direct to a building society account – though it may take a couple of days longer to arrive. You can have child benefit, state retirement pension, widow's pension or widowed mother's allowance paid direct into almost any of the accounts we mention (but not a National Savings ordinary account, or a deposit account with National Girobank). Fill in the form in leaflet NI.105 (from your social security office) to arrange this. With some of these benefits you can choose whether to receive them every 4 weeks or every 13; choosing 4-weekly payments will make your budgeting easier. (In certain circumstances you have the choice of getting your money weekly by cashing orders at a post office – doing so will help your cash-flow even more.)

If you have both a current account and a savings account, it is often sensible to have your payments made direct to the savings account if this is possible. You then earn interest on the money until you need it, when you can withdraw it or transfer it to your current account.

JOINT ACCOUNTS

Any of the accounts mentioned in this chapter can be for your own use only or a joint account. When you apply for a joint account, you can choose whether you want *either* of you to be able to operate the account (so either of you can sign cheques, for example) or whether you will only be able to do so jointly (in which case you must *both* sign everything). Clearly the first arrangement is much more convenient, but you should not take this on if you do not completely trust the other person. With a joint bank account of this kind, you can each have a chequebook and cheque guarantee card, and it should be easier to avoid bank charges as your joint balance will be higher than the balance on each of two separate accounts. A joint account also avoids problems if one of you were to die, because the other person can simply continue using it (an individual account would be frozen). But you are *each* individually liable for *any* money owed on the account, regardless of who spent it.

2 *Coping with the regular bills*

Most of us have to contend with a mound of pretty well unavoidable expenditure, recurring at different intervals. The most common, with the usual payment intervals, are:

yearly
insurance premiums
car tax and MoT
AA/RAC membership
television licence
service agreements
season ticket
Christmas spending
birthday presents
holiday

half-yearly
water rates
car service
dentist
self-employed tax
and Class 4
National Insurance

quarterly
electricity
gas
telephone
bank charges

monthly
mortgage or rent
rates instalments
credit card payments
loan repayments
HP or rental payments
insurance instalments
self-employed Class
2 National Insurance
newspapers

other periodical payments
coal, oil, bottled gas for heating
clothes
hairdresser
school meals
school fees
help in the home
fares to work

You can spread some of these bills more evenly over the year by paying in monthly instalments. You should always pay rates on your home in monthly instalments because there is no extra charge at all for doing so (see page 113) – so never borrow money to pay your rates, or use a credit card. In Scotland your rates instalments will cover the water rates as well, but in England and Wales there is likely to be an extra charge for paying your water rates by instalments. Most insurance companies allow you to pay insurance premiums in instalments. And you can arrange to pay your estimated bills for the next year for the phone or the electricity by 12 equal monthly instalments from your bank current account. If you overpay or underpay, you settle up at the end of the year. If you have the ready cash or can withdraw savings to pay these bills when they arise, it is best to do so, as the interest rate (the APR – see page 44) you are charged if you pay by instalments will almost certainly be higher than the interest rate you get on your savings. But if you do not have the ready cash, do use the instalment scheme, as it is likely to be cheaper than borrowing the money in any other way.

With some bills, you can spread the cost by paying some of the money in advance. For example, you can buy special stamps at post offices, electricity showrooms and so on, for use as part-payment of your next phone or electricity bill. These are useful if you really cannot trust yourself not to spend the money on something else. If you can, it would be better to put the money in your savings account where it will earn some interest until the bill is due to be paid.

One of Pat Graham's problems in our example (see pages 19–20) is that each month her mortgage payment is due just four days before she gets paid. This means that she has £160 sitting in her account each month which she must be careful not to spend. If you are in this position, there are two things worth considering:

- You could be better off having your salary paid into your savings account where it will earn interest, then transfer it to your current account as you need it. If the savings account allows standing orders, the monthly payment (e.g., the mortgage) can be made directly from it.

- If you are finding it hard to manage, you can ask the mortgage company (or whoever the payment is due to) if you can make each payment a few days later, as soon as you get paid. If you explain the position, they may well agree.

If your bills tend to come in batches, some banks offer a special account to help you even out the cost (usually called a **budget account**). You decide which bills you want to cover and add up the total of what you expect them to be over the next year. You can include major payments, like an annual season ticket or a holiday. You agree the list with your bank, then make a monthly standing order from your current account to the budget account for 1/12 of the expected total. You then pay all these bills with a special budget account chequebook. Sometimes the budget account will be in credit, sometimes it will be overdrawn, but over the year what you have paid in should roughly equal what you have paid out, and you settle the difference with the bank. While the idea of these accounts is very sensible, we do not recommend them because they are not cheap to run. For the small amount of credit involved, the charges can be very high. We suggest you try the cheaper ways of budgeting covered in this chapter.

3 Working out how much you can safely spend

Do you know how much money you have to spend each week *after* all your regular payments and unavoidable bills have been settled? If not, then you will find this is a salutary exercise. First, work out how much money you get in a year (after tax and everything else has been deducted). Do this by multiplying any monthly pay-cheque, pension, or maintenance payment by 12, any weekly one by 52. Include the total amount of child benefit or any other social security benefit or other income you receive. Then, using the checklist on page 25, work out how much all your bills come to over a year (adding up the monthly ones and multiplying by 12, etc.). Subtract this figure from your total income figure and divide by 52. The answer you get is the cash you have left each week.

If you find budgeting difficult, one way to limit your spending is simply to withdraw this amount from your account each week and pay for everything in cash (except the bills you have already allowed for). If you have to write a cheque, you must deduct the amount from next week's cash withdrawal. This system can also be a useful one to operate for a short time to get out of a tight period, such as after a holiday.

EXAMPLE

Income		
pay (12 × 600)		£7,200
child benefit (52 × £7)		£364
		£7,564
Payments		
yearly		
holiday	£300	
Christmas spending	£150	
birthday presents	£100	
season ticket	£320	

Payments – *cont.*

yearly				
car tax and MoT	£130			
television licence	£58			
		=	£1,058	
half-yearly				
water rates	£50			
car service	£50			
dentist	£20			
	£120	× 2 =	£240	
quarterly				
electricity	£60			
gas	£40			
telephone	£70			
	£170	× 4 =	£680	
monthly				
mortgage	£160			
rates	£33			
loan repayments	£30			
insurance instalments	£20			
newspapers	£10			
	£253	× 12 =	£3,036	
Other periodical payments				
coal	£150 a year			
clothes	£300 a year			
hairdresser	£70 a year			
school meals	£150 a year			
		=	£670	
Total payments:				£5,684
which leaves:				£1,880
Cash to spend each week: (£1,880 divided by 52)		=	£36	

4 Keeping track of the money

Whatever the state of your finances, you should find this method a useful way of keeping track of your money. All you need is a spare pocket diary, the cheapest you can find (they're normally half-price after mid-January). A diary with a page or double-page to each week is ideal. Starting from the current week, draw two lines down each page and head the three columns *in, out* and *balance*. You then go through the diary writing in the amounts (in the *in* column) of all regular payments you expect to receive – salary, pension, child benefit, etc. Then, in the *out* column, put in all the standing orders and direct debits that will be made from your account during the rest of the year. Next check when your regular bills need paying – the gas, electricity, telephone, rates instalments, water rates, credit card statements – and write those in. Write in family birthdays, Christmas spending, when you will have to pay for your holiday and when you will need to draw your holiday spending money. In each case write in the amount you will have to pay, making the best guess you can from previous bills and past experience.

Now you will need to know how much you have in your current account (or whatever you use for your day-to-day spending) at the moment. You may be able to work this out from the last statement and your record of in-and-out payments. You can check this when you get your next statement, or ask for an extra statement now. Don't just ask for the balance: you need a statement so that you can see which payments have been cleared through the account. Add to this any amounts paid into your account since, and subtract any payments which you know are on their way out (e.g., cheques you have written). Enter the figure that is left in the *balance* column for today. From now on, whenever you pay money into your account or write a cheque, write the amount in the *in* or *out* column for that day. And whenever there is a figure in the *in* or the *out* column, work out how much money is now in your account and enter the figure in the *balance* column. You will be able to see at a glance how much you have in your account. And you will have an instant reminder of all the other payments which will go in and out of your account automatically, making it easy to see how much money you can safely withdraw this week or this month without the risk of overdrawing or becoming liable for bank charges.

5 If you are already overdrawn

If you are already overdrawn and finding it difficult to get out of the situation, do check through this chapter to see if there are any schemes or ways of rearranging payments which may help you. You are not going to be able to get out of the situation overnight, but your bank manager will probably want to know what you plan to do about it. There may be ways you can raise some cash – e.g., selling unwanted items using the free advertisements in local papers. You could decide to limit your weekly spending to an amount which should clear the overdraft in 3 months or 6 months, say. Because bank charges can be hefty, before the end of the bank's charging period you could draw enough cash on your credit card (if you have one) to clear the overdraft and then pay off the credit card with whatever money you have left at the end of each month – making sure you do have a worthwhile amount left. Or you could ask your bank manager to open an **ordinary loan account** for you (see page 43) and to transfer from this the amount of your overdraft plus a couple of hundred pounds into your current account. You will have to pay off the ordinary loan by monthly payments from your current account.

If these remedies are not sufficient and you still do not seem to be able to manage on the money you have, you will find more help in Chapter 4.

Accounts for your day-to-day finances

We describe below the main types of account which you can pay money into and withdraw from pretty well whenever you like. It is likely that having one or more of these accounts will help you manage your day-to-day finances.

Bank Current account

This is the common chequebook account run by all the major banks (National Girobank, available at post offices, is similar). You can have your wages, pension and most social security benefits paid direct into the account, and you can pay cash or cheques into your account at any of the bank's branches. You get a book of **cheques** and a **cheque guarantee card** for withdrawing cash and paying other people. You can also ask the bank to make regular payments out of your account to other people (called a **standing order**), e.g., for paying the rent, the mortgage or the rates. An alternative way of making regular payments is by **direct debit**, which gives someone else the right to ask your bank to hand over money to them. This sounds risky, but there are safeguards which make direct debit almost as safe as a standing order (you can get a leaflet, *Direct Debiting – an easy way to pay*, from your bank explaining the system and the safeguards). Standing orders and direct debits mean you do not have to remember to make the payments each month – but it is important not to forget that the money is being taken out of your account.

Most banks also issue plastic **cashcards** (e.g. NatWest *Servicetill*, *Barclaybank*, Midland *Autobank*, Lloyds *Cashpoint*). This card is for use in the bank's cash dispensers to withdraw money from your account, to find out the balance in your account, or to order a statement or new chequebook. You are given a secret number which you have to type into the machine before you can use it.

The bank will send you **statements**, usually every month, every 3 months or 6 months, listing all the payments into and out of your account. You should always check that each item is correct as mistakes do happen. Unless your use of the account is very slight, you should ask the bank to send you a statement each month, or you will find checking very hard. The statement also shows the amount of money in your account at the end of each day on which the balance changed.

If a cheque you have written is for more than the amount in your account at the time, a number of things may happen. If the bank can see that there is money coming into your account in a few days (e.g., because your paycheque is due) it may overlook the matter. Alternatively, the bank may write to you pointing out that you do not have enough money to pay it and threatening to return cheques which are not guaranteed or to take away your cheque guarantee card. It may even 'bounce' the cheque – i.e., return it to the bank of the payee marked 'please re-present' – meaning 'please try again in a few days' time when there should be enough money to meet the cheque' – or 'refer to drawer' – meaning the bank will not pay the cheque and the person to whom you gave it must try to get the money out of you in some other way. What line the bank takes depends on the amount by which you overdraw, for how long, and on whether it is an occasional lapse or becoming a bad habit.

If you need to overdraw, it is sensible to ask your branch manager first (you cannot have an overdraft with National Girobank). The manager will want to know why, but is likely to agree if you can show that you will soon have enough money to pay off the overdraft. You will be given a limit, and if you go over this limit the bank may take the same courses of action as if you had overdrawn without asking. However, an overdraft can be an expensive way of borrowing money, as it means paying bank charges as well as interest – which can double the cost. Unless you are already liable for bank charges for the current quarter, a **credit card** (*Access* or *Visa*) is likely to be a cheaper way to borrow money for short periods.

It costs nothing to open or run a current account as long as the amount in the account never falls below a certain limit. With some banks this limit is £100 or £50, with others there are no charges as long as you never go into the red. But once you have dipped below the limit, even for a day, most banks will charge you for every cheque you write, every cash withdrawal, every standing order and direct debit and possibly every credit as well for a whole three months. Your bank should have leaflets available describing its charging system. National Girobank has a different system and is likely to be cheaper than other banks because there are no interest charges and you are only charged for withdrawals on individual days which start off overdrawn; but you are not allowed a prolonged overdraft and are expected to get your account back into credit within a few days. However, many banks make no charges at all to students (except interest when overdrawn) and their definition of student may be quite wide. So if you or your joint account holder can qualify as a student you may save quite a bit of money.

A current account with a bank also gets you a foot in the door for certain other services – though many of these are available to non-customers. They include credit cards, personal loans, mortgages, foreign money, travellers' cheques, investment advice, tax advice and storage of valuables and documents.

Savings account

A savings account – such as a **bank deposit account** or a **building society share account** – is simple by comparison. You can pay cash or cheques into your account at any time, normally at any branch of the organisation running it. You can withdraw cash at your own branch and can usually arrange to withdraw at another branch you name. With some building societies you can withdraw at any branch. You do not get a chequebook for paying other people, but you can ask the bank or building society to give you a cheque made out to someone else (NB: it is important to realise that you cannot 'stop' such a cheque). If you have a deposit account with the same bank as you have a current account, you can ask for money to be transferred between them. With many savings accounts, you can ask the bank or building society to make standing orders or accept direct debits.

Most of the banks and larger building societies will give you a plastic **cashcard** to use in their cash dispensers. Inserting the card and typing in your secret number allows you to see how much money is in your savings account, to withdraw cash from it and to order a statement. Some cards also allow you to pay cash and cheques into your account and even arrange standing orders – the Halifax Building Society's *Cardcash* account, for example.

Of course, you cannot overdraw on one of these accounts. But they cost nothing to run, and you are paid interest on the money in your account each day (except the last seven days with a bank deposit account). There is no basic-rate tax to pay on the interest.

Savings account with extras

A few building societies run accounts with additional features. Some examples at the time of writing were:

- Abbey National's *ChequeSave* account provides a chequebook and cashcard (but no cheque guarantee card) and you can apply for a *Visa* credit card. There are no charges as long as you keep at least £1 in the account.

- Alliance & Leicester Building Society's *Leicestercard* account provides a cashcard for the society's cash dispensers which you can also use to obtain discounts on a range of goods and services. You can make up to 24 transactions a year at post offices. You can also have a **continuous credit account** (see page 43) with a chequebook and cheque guarantee card and can apply for personal loans. You must keep at least £100 in the account.

- Halifax Building Society's *Deposit Cheque* account provides a chequebook but no cheque guarantee card. You can set up standing orders and direct debits, and you can combine it with a *Cardcash* account for more flexibility.
- Leeds Building Society's *Pay & Save* account allows standing orders and you can apply for a *Visa* credit card.
- Nationwide's *FlexAccount* allows standing orders and you can apply for an *Access* credit card and personal loans.
- Nottingham Building Society's *Homelink* scheme allows you to do everything at home using a small keyboard which you plug into your telephone socket and television. You get a savings account with the building society and a current account with the Bank of Scotland. Information about your accounts is shown on your television screen, and you can use the keyboard to pay bills, see how much money is in each account, transfer money between them, apply for loans and even order goods to be delivered to your home. Although you get paid interest on both accounts, the cost of buying or renting the keyboard, using the system and the telephone charges could make it fairly costly to run.

Linked current and savings account

Probably the most suitable arrangement for most people is to have a bank current account into which money is automatically transferred from your savings account whenever the balance falls below a certain level. At the time of writing there are two such schemes which are almost identical. One is the Alliance & Leicester *BankSave Plus* account, which has a current account with the Bank of Scotland. The other is the Midshires *Mastercheque* account which has a current account with the TSB. The advantage of these accounts is that you don't have to watch your bank account like a hawk in order to avoid bank charges. Nor do you have to worry about losing interest by having more than you need in your current account. The reason is that any money you pay *in* goes straight into the building society savings account where it earns a comparatively high rate of interest. Any money that comes *out* is taken from the bank current account. If a withdrawal would mean that the balance in your current account would fall below £100, enough money is automatically transferred from the savings account to top it up to £350. As long as you always have some money in your savings account, you can safely forget about paying bank charges.

You get a chequebook with a cheque guarantee card for paying bills and withdrawing cash, and can ask for a *Visa* credit card. You can have up to 5 standing orders (any number with *Mastercheque*) and any number of direct debits, which are paid out of the bank account. And you can have your salary paid direct into the account. You get statements for both accounts every month.

You can withdraw cash at any branch of the bank or building society. Other banks will cash your cheques for a fee, or you can get cash in the normal ways with the *Visa* credit card.

You should, of course, keep enough in your savings account to cover money going out of the current account. As long as you do, the accounts will cost you nothing. However, you can apply for an overdraft on the current account (*BankSave Plus* charges are likely to be lower than with most other current accounts) or a personal loan or a continuous credit scheme, and of course you can use the *Visa* credit card for delaying payment or borrowing money.

Credit card account

Many people are very wary of credit cards, because of the temptation they present to spend money you cannot repay. But people who are naturally cautious are just the ones who *should* have a credit card because of the flexibility it gives you with your spending. There are two types of card, *Access* and *Visa*. Some banks issue one, some the other (*Barclaycard* and the TSB's *Trustcard* are Visa cards). The cards work in much the same way. You can use them to buy things at any shop, garage, restaurant or other 'outlet' displaying the credit card sign. You simply show your card and sign a slip filled in by the sales staff. Once a month you get a statement listing the purchases you have made and showing the total amount you owe. It also shows the minimum amount you must pay (basically 1/20 of what you owe). It is entirely up to you how much you pay, in between these two figures. If you pay off in full before the payment day (around 3½ weeks later) there is no interest or other charge, so your card has cost nothing to use, you have delayed making payments for between 4 and 8 weeks, and you can pay for all the things you have bought with a single cheque. If you do not pay the statement off in full, the unpaid part will reappear on your next statement along with an interest charge.

You can also use one of these cards to get cash from any bank in the scheme. But cash does not come free. With *Visa*, there is a 1½% charge for each cash advance. With *Access*, there is no such charge but no interest-free period either – interest starts clocking up the day you get the money. However, the cost of borrowing some money for a week or two will be very much less than overdrawing a current account and incurring bank charges, and the cost of borrowing over a longer period is not likely to be much higher than a bank personal loan and will be lower than most HP charges.

Two (or more) people can each have a card on a single account (in which case you will get a single joint statement) or you can apply separately for individual accounts. With each account you get a **credit limit** which is the maximum amount you are allowed to owe. If you exceed it, you will probably be asked not to use the card again until you have paid off enough to get below your credit limit. You can ask to have the credit limit increased if you wish. There is nothing to stop you having both an *Access* and *Visa* card – or even several of each, one from each bank that issues them! However, you would have to be careful that you did not run up debts you could not repay.

Both *Access* and *Visa* are widely acceptable abroad, both for purchases and cash. Other advantages of using a credit card to buy things are given on page 41. The cards cost nothing to obtain – you can get an application form at any bank which issues them, or, with certain savings accounts, you may be invited to apply (see page 33).

Charge cards are different from credit cards. The two best known are *American Express* and *Diners Club*. They do not compare very well with credit cards – they are not free, they are not accepted in so many places, you cannot get cash on the account and you have to pay each statement in full (there is no option to spread the payments). But they do not have a set credit limit so can be useful to people wanting to pay enormous bills.

National Savings ordinary account

This is an account which you can operate at most post offices. You can draw out up to £100 on demand. When you have had the account for 6 months, you can draw up to £250 at a post office of your choice. Larger amounts take a few days. You can have any number of standing orders, and can pay most household bills direct. But there is no chequebook and you cannot overdraw. Interest is added to your account at the end of each year, but the way it is calculated is not very generous and in 1986 the rate is only 3%, unless you have at least £100 in your account for the whole year; if you do, the rate becomes 6% for each complete calendar month that you have £500 or more in the account. Interest is normally tax-free – it only becomes taxable if you get more than £70 in a tax year. But there are a number of building societies offering much higher interest rates on accounts with more services. So a National Savings ordinary account is only worth considering if your local post office is much more conveniently situated for you than the nearest building society branch.

3

Buying and Borrowing

In this chapter we look at the decisions involved in making a major purchase costing perhaps £50 or more – a washing machine, a holiday, a car or whatever. Making these decisions wisely can save you a lot of money and trouble over the years. We also cover the steps to take if things go wrong.

Choosing what to buy

Having decided to make a purchase, you will need to find the best type or model. It is not necessarily the cheapest. The best buy for you will depend on a combination of factors:

- the features that you need
- the price at which you can buy and the different ways in which you can pay
- the quality of the product
- the colour or styling that you require
- what sort of guarantee or after-sales service you get.

To sort out what features are available, look at various models in two or three shops and ask about the differences between them. Shop sales staff often simplify comparisons or don't know about all the features available, so it's a good idea to take leaflets home to read. Also have a look at the most recent report in *Which?*

(available at your local library) or *Good Housekeeping* magazines. Decide which of the features are most important to you – and which you will really use (there must be a lot of people with ten-programme washing machines who only ever use three or four of them). A report in *Which?* may well have information on how well different brands work and how reliable they are, and recommend particular models.

To buy or rent?

Renting is most common with televisions and video recorders, although it is possible to rent most major electrical goods. You usually have to pay 3 or 6 months rental in advance, after which you pay monthly. Many firms offer a reduction if you pay a full year's rent in advance. The cost of all maintenance is included in the rental. But the item never becomes yours.

Years ago, when electrical goods like televisions were both expensive to buy and unreliable, it may have made sense to rent one. But this is no longer the case. Electrical goods have gone up in price much less quickly than most other things, and they are very much more reliable now than they used to be. This means that it is now only worth renting something if you want it for a short period. If you will only want a television for a year, buying a new set is not sensible as you might only be able to sell it for half the price you bought it for; renting (or buying secondhand) would be cheaper. If you intend keeping something for a couple of years or more, buying will almost certainly be cheaper than renting, even if you need to borrow the money to do so.

What if it goes wrong?

If an item goes wrong soon after you buy it, the shop should sort the matter out for you – see page 47 for details. And most manufacturers offer a guarantee that if it goes wrong within a year (sometimes more) they will put it right for you (this normally includes the cost of parts and labour). After that, any repairs will normally be your responsibility. If you want to insure against the possibility of large repair bills, you may be able to take out an extended guarantee or service contract, arranged either by the manufacturer, the shop or an independent company.

An **extended guarantee** normally extends the cover given by the manufacturer's guarantee for a further four years. You pay for this in a single payment when you buy. Some companies only allow you a few days after purchase to apply for the guarantee extension – so don't be caught out. Generally it is better to avoid schemes arranged by independent companies, as several have folded in the last few years. Technically these extensions only cover faults due to poor materials or workmanship when the product was made, so they may not cover parts wearing out – read the small print or ask the company. They do not cover routine servicing, accidental damage, or anything which is not the fault of a part of the item itself. You may have to pay for the repair yourself, then claim the money back. Extended guarantees are generally much cheaper than service contracts and are particularly worth considering on washing machines, dishwashers and possibly colour televisions, which are the most likely appliances to go wrong.

You can take out an **annual service contract** at any time until the appliance is about three years old, and renew it each year until it is about ten years old. It covers parts and labour costs, including replacement of parts wearing out and sometimes a yearly service. But these contracts are not cheap – you are likely to pay much more in premiums than the average person pays in repairs – though you will be protected against the possibility of very high bills. These contracts are more valuable the more you use the appliance.

Ways of paying

You may already have enough money for what you want to buy, perhaps having saved it up over a period of time. If so, well and good, though there are a few points which are worth considering because they could still save you money:

- If you are intending to pay a large amount by cheque, make sure before you trek into town that the shop will accept cheques over £50. Some will not, because banks' cheque cards only guarantee cheques up to £50 and it is against the banks' rules to write out several cheques for one item (though some shops will let you do this).

- If you are paying by cheque from a bank current account, watch that the amount in your account does not fall below the bank's limit for free banking (with most banks this simply means not being overdrawn). If it does, even for a day, most banks will charge you for every cheque, every withdrawal and possibly every deposit for a whole three months (see page 20). If you have withdrawn savings, make sure they have been credited to your cheque account before spending them. Or follow the next tip by paying with *Access* or *Visa*.

• If you have a bank credit card (*Access* or *Visa*) which the shop accepts and you are not being charged interest because you settled the last bill in full, you can delay paying for what you buy for between 4 and 8 weeks at no cost to you. This in turn enables you to give a month's notice to withdraw savings and allow time for a cheque to clear through your bank account.

• There are also two practical advantages in paying the shop with an *Access* or *Visa* card. First, there is no problem buying things over £50 (as long as you have enough unused credit). Second, if something costing over £100 turns out to be faulty and the shop won't put matters right or closes down, you can take the matter up with the credit card company. They are legally bound to honour your rights (see page 48).

• If you have a choice of either withdrawing savings or borrowing to buy something, the basic answer is simple. If the yearly interest rate you are getting on your savings is lower than the interest rate (APR – see page 44) on the credit, withdraw your savings. If it is higher (fairly unlikely), borrow.

• Shops sometimes offer interest-free credit, allowing you to spread the cost over 6 or 12 months at no extra charge. This can be worth taking advantage of, as long as the shop's prices are not much higher than elsewhere. It might mean you can pay for what you want out of your income instead of having to withdraw your savings.

Buying on credit

If you don't already have enough money, there are still lots of ways of buying now and paying later. This goes against the grain with many people, and many more have a healthy concern about not being able to repay debts. Credit is fine as long as you keep it under control – which means being confident you can repay what you owe. The cost of credit varies widely, and it is well worth making sure you get a good deal. It will normally be best to consider the following points in this order:

- Shops occasionally offer interest-free credit on some items – meaning the price is the same whether you pay cash or in instalments. This is well worth taking up, as long as the shop's prices are not much higher than elsewhere.

- If you want to pay off what you owe fairly quickly (in a few months, perhaps), using an *Access* or *Visa* card saves the trouble of arranging a loan and will be relatively inexpensive. You can pay off as much as you like each month (as long as you pay at least 1/20 of what you owe). If you don't have an *Access* or *Visa* card, ask the shop if they run an **option account** (which works in almost exactly the same way).

- Unless you are already overdrawn, avoid bank overdrafts. Although the interest charges are reasonable, you will probably end up paying at least as much again in bank charges, making the whole thing pretty expensive. If you are already overdrawn and paying bank charges, and are likely to be overdrawn for most of the time you'll be repaying this money, then the extra cost is more reasonable. But it would generally be better to ask your bank for an **ordinary loan account** (see below) to repay the whole overdraft and leave you with enough money in your current account to avoid any charges.

- If the amount you need to borrow is £500 or £1,000 or more, and you want a year or more to pay it back, there are a number of options. If you have a job, your firm may provide loans at a lower interest rate than elsewhere (most often for buying season tickets and cars).

- If you have had a **life insurance policy** which involves investment (e.g., an endowment policy) for a few years, you may be able to get a loan at a low or reasonable interest rate from the insurance company. You can borrow the money for any purpose and need only pay interest. You can repay what you originally borrowed at any time – usually out of the money due to you when the policy comes to an end. Write to the insurance company and ask how much they would be prepared to lend on the policy.

• If you have a bank account, ask your manager if you could have an **'ordinary' loan account** – as opposed to a 'personal' loan. The loans banks advertise on the television and in their leaflets are nearly always **'personal' loans**. With these, everything is fixed – the interest rate and the number and amount of the instalments. The interest rate on an ordinary loan is not fixed but has nearly always been lower than on personal loans, and although your bank will normally want you to repay the loan by regular payments made by standing order from your current account, it is a simple matter to amend the arrangement.

• Some banks offer **continuous credit accounts** whereby you agree to pay a regular amount each month and can buy goods up to a multiple of that amount (often 24 or 30 times). For example, if you agree to pay £20 a month into the account, you can buy things up to a credit limit of £480 or £600, depending on the scheme. As you pay off what you owe, so you can borrow more again. You are charged interest on what you owe, at much the same rate as with a credit card. If your account gets into credit, the bank pays you interest (at a much lower rate!).

• The shop may be able to line up credit for you. Shops often show the deposit and instalments on their price tickets, but the credit they are offering may be one of several types. It may be a **personal loan**, under which you are loaned the money, usually by a finance company, to whom you repay it with interest over one or two years. It may be **hire-purchase**, where a finance company actually buys the goods; they don't become your property until you have paid the last instalment.

Many chain stores also offer **continuous credit accounts** under a variety of names. These work in the same way as a continuous credit account with a bank, but with two snags – you can only buy things at one chain of shops and you probably will not be paid any interest if your account gets into credit. When you have paid off what you owe, you would do better to close the account and put your money in a building society where it will earn some interest.

• You will see **finance company loans** advertised fairly widely in newspapers and magazines. If you cannot get credit elsewhere or want a single loan to replace a number of smaller debts, these can be useful as you do not have to be a customer already. But the interest rates they charge vary from quite reasonable to pretty expensive, so be choosy – see below. Some finance companies also offer **second mortgages** to people who own their own homes. As these give the company the right to force the sale of your home to reclaim its money if you cannot afford to keep up the payments, the interest rate may be slightly lower.

Before you go ahead

Interest rates on credit can be anything from 0% to 40% or more. There is no point in paying any more interest than you have to, and you should try not to pay much above 25% in any event. Always look for the APR (Annual Percentage Rate) and ignore any other interest rates you are given. The APR is worked out in a standard way laid down by law to make it easy to compare the costs of different credit arrangements. Don't worry about differences of 2 or 3%, but a difference of 10% or more is certainly significant.

A firm which advertises loans does not have to lend you money, nor does it have to give any reason why it turns you down. You can, however, ask it within 28 days for the name and address of any **credit reference agency** it has approached, and for a fee of £1 you can ask the agency to send you a copy of any file it has on you. If you think any of the information on the file is wrong or misleading, write and ask the agency to correct it. If they refuse or do not reply for 28 days, you can write a correction of up to 200 words and insist they add it to your file. Full details are in the leaflet *No credit?* from your local council's Trading Standards Department.

If you do not have a regular job (full-time or part-time), you may not find it easy to get credit. Credit companies may ask you to put forward a **guarantor** – meaning that that person will be legally liable to make the payments if you do not. This is quite a lot to ask of someone – we would not recommend you to act as a guarantor without giving it very careful consideration. If you are married and do not have a job, you are likely to find you are refused credit even if your husband has a high income and regularly gives you a substantial amount. This is often seen as discriminatory by married women who have to call on their wage-earning husbands to act as guarantors, but the credit companies will say they would treat the opposite case in the same way – a working wife would have to act as guarantor for her non-working husband.

Many loan schemes now offer various kinds of **insurance** which you can take out to cover what you owe. With some schemes, the insurance company will pay off the loan if you die, with others it will also pay the instalments if you are too ill to work (and in some cases if you are made redundant). But most of these schemes are very expensive for the cover you get. Do not be pressurised into accepting insurance you do not want or do not need (with many companies you get it automatically unless you say on the application form that you do *not* want it). Unless the loan is substantial, you may feel you already have enough **life insurance** to cover what you would owe if you were to die (or it may well be cheaper to increase your existing life insurance policy than to take the insurance offered with the loan). If you are ill, your firm may continue to pay your salary for a certain period; or you should have **permanent health insurance** (see page 216) which would cover you. If you became unemployed you might get a substantial redundancy payment, or there might be state benefits you could claim which would cover the loan interest. It is worth bearing in mind that credit companies set up these insurance schemes for their own benefit rather than yours (so that they get their money whatever happens to you) – but it is you who has to pay the cost of the insurance.

Never sign agreements without reading them first and making sure you understand all the implications – a lot of people still get caught out by the small print. You should also make sure you get an exact copy of any agreement you sign. In certain circumstances you can change your mind after you have signed the agreement: if you signed it somewhere other than on the credit company's premises (at home, for example) but had discussed it face-to-face with a representative of the company, and the amount you were borrowing was over £50 and below £15,000, you are entitled to be sent a notice explaining your rights to cancel, giving you 5 days in which to do so.

Problems with credit

If you have taken on a credit agreement which seems extortionately expensive, you may be able to get the interest charges reduced. You will have to give your reasons in court. Get advice from your Citizens Advice Bureau (CAB) first. Details of how to proceed are in the leaflet *Extortionate credit*, available from the Trading Standards Department of your local council, who may also be able to help.

If you want to pay off your loan, write to the credit company and ask how much you would need to pay. If the original loan was between £50 and £15,000, you will not have to pay as much as if you were to keep it going because the credit company must allow a rebate on the total amount of interest remaining.

If you are having difficulty keeping up the payments, don't just stop paying. (With a hire-purchase agreement, if you have paid less than one-third of the total HP price, the company can come and take the goods back if the payments cease.) Write to the credit company and explain your situation, and offer to pay a reduced amount each week or month. They are likely to accept this rather than risk having to take legal action to get their money back. See Chapter 4 for more help in this situation.

Afterwards

Faulty goods

People in the business of selling things must provide you with goods which meet certain standards. This applies to shops, market stallholders, mail order firms, doorstep salesmen, etc. – when we refer below to 'shops', it means any of these sales outlets. It also applies to goods in sales. No one except auctioneers can get out of their responsibility – by putting up notices, for example. Things offered for sale must be:

- of **merchantable quality**, meaning they should be of a reasonable standard and last a reasonable time, taking account of whether they were supposed to be top quality, very cheap, seconds or whatever. A new washing machine that leaks or something which you could expect to last a year but which starts to come apart after a couple of weeks of normal usage is not of merchantable quality.

- **fit for any particular purpose** you have asked for. If you say you want a food mixer which is powerful enough to mix bread dough and the sales assistant assures you that a particular model is, the shop has broken its contract if you get it home and find that it is not. If you only wanted the goods for the purpose for which they were obviously intended (e.g., a shopping bag to carry shopping) you do not need to have made this clear to the seller.

- **as described** Things you buy must conform to the way they were described by the seller, either in conversation or in a mail order catalogue or, if you bought something in a supermarket, on the packet. Pictures and illustrations count as descriptions as well as words.

Even secondhand goods you buy from shops must conform to these requirements: of course, you cannot expect them to be in perfect condition, nor does the shop have to point out every small scratch, but sales staff must answer your questions truthfully and tell you of any major faults you might not notice.

If something you buy does not meet one of the above criteria, go back to the shop (*not* the manufacturer) and point out what you consider unsatisfactory. It is best to take the item with you (unless this is impracticable). Take the receipt if you still have it, though not having it does not lessen your rights at all. If the item was a present, it should be returned by the purchaser, as the recipient does not have any rights in law. If the goods are seriously defective, are still more or less in the condition in which you bought them and you report the defect as soon as you discover it, you can reject them and insist that you have all your money back. If the shop offers a repair, a replacement or a credit note, you don't have to accept it.

If you are not entitled to a complete refund, you can claim cash compensation for the difference in value between a perfect item and the defective one. Again, the shop may offer a repair or replacement, and though you don't have to accept this it may often be better to do so in these circumstances.

If the fault in the product has caused further damage (if, for example, a faulty thermostat in a new washing machine boils your woollens) you can also claim the cost of repairing the damage or replacing anything which is ruined.

If the item is covered by a manufacturer's guarantee, you can alternatively claim under this. Guarantees normally only offer repair or replacement (not a refund) and sometimes they only cover parts, not labour. So it is usually better to approach the shop first.

If you are buying the item on credit, do not stop paying the instalments just because of the fault. However, if the item cost between £100 and £30,000 and you paid for it (in whole or in part) with any kind of credit card or with credit arranged through the shop, and you are not satisfied with the way the shop is dealing with your complaint, you can take it up with the credit company. As long as the amount of the credit was under £15,000, the credit company has the same responsibility to put the matter right as the shop. This can also be useful if the shop has closed down or you have moved home in the meantime.

If you are not sure of your rights in any particular case, or if you are not getting any joy out of a shop, your local CAB should be able to advise you on what you can claim, what proof you will need, and how to take the matter further. There may be a trade association with a Code of Practice who can put pressure on the shop to give way, or there may be an arbitration scheme to use. If the amount you are claiming is less than £500, you may be advised to issue a summons in the County Court – a simple procedure and usually a very effective way of getting money out of a difficult trader (see Chapter 22 for more details).

4

Not Enough to Live On

This chapter describes the social security benefits and other help available to women who don't have enough money to live on. Even if you think you can just about manage, it's worth reading on – you might find you're entitled to some extra help. *Claim all the benefits you're entitled to* – they are not 'charity', they are yours by right.

Most of the benefits mentioned in this chapter are due to increase in July 1986; we give the new rates, which come into effect in the week beginning 28 July 1986. All of the leaflets and forms are available free from social security offices (see under *Health and Social Security* in the phone book).

If you are unemployed

You don't have to register for work in order to claim benefits (unless you are under 18, in which case you must register with the Careers Office or Jobcentre). But it's a good idea to do so, both for help with finding a job and to get information about training schemes. Then go to the unemployment benefit office (*UBO* in the phone book) to 'sign on' and claim benefit. Do this on your first day of unemployment, because benefits can't usually be back-dated.

You will be entitled to **unemployment benefit** if:

- you are available for, and capable of, work, *and*
- you have paid enough National Insurance contributions.

This depends on your contributions record in the tax year *before* the calendar year in which you claim – so if you claim during 1986, it depends on your contributions between April 1984 and April 1985. The UBO will tell you whether or not you qualify. If you do, this benefit is payable regardless of how much other income you have – but only for a year. The full amount is currently £30.80 a week (£38.70 if you're 60 or more). You may be able to get extra money if, for example, your husband is dependent on you. Staff at the UBO will be able to advise you, or ask for leaflet NI.12 which gives more details.

Whether or not you get unemployment benefit, you might be entitled to other benefits – so while you're at the UBO, ask for form B.1 and claim **supplementary benefit**, too. The application form has to be sent to your local social security office; if you have any trouble filling it in, you can get help from a Citizens Advice Bureau (CAB), or there may be a Claimants Union (a self-help group of people who are signing on) in your area.

Most people have to sign on at the UBO before they can claim supplementary benefit. The exceptions are:

- people who are ill or disabled
- women who are due to have a baby within 11 weeks
- single parents with a child under 16
- people over state-retirement age (60 for women).

These people claim on form SB.1 from post offices and social security offices – see below for more details.

Supplementary benefit is means-tested, i.e., whether or not you get it (and if so, at what level) depends on how much other money you have. Any money your children have may also be taken into account. If you are living as a couple (whether or not you're married), *both* of your incomes will be added together to work out whether or not you qualify. And only one of you can claim benefit for both – ask a CAB or Claimants Union group for more information, or see leaflet NI.248.

Your supplementary benefit is worked out as follows:

• **all your savings are added up** (including savings of your husband or partner). The value of the home you live in is ignored, but other savings – such as money in a bank or building society account, premium bonds, etc. – are taken into account. If you have a life insurance policy, the 'surrender value' (what you would get if you cashed it in) may also be taken into account if it's over £1,500.

If your total savings are £3,000 or less (plus £1,500 for the surrender value of a life insurance policy), they won't affect your benefit. If you have *more* than £3,000, however, you won't get supplementary benefit.

Assuming you haven't been excluded by this savings rule, the next step is:

• **your 'requirements' are worked out,** according to figures laid down in Parliament. There are three kinds: normal requirements, additional requirements and some housing requirements (but not rent or rates).

'Normal requirements' are meant to cover everyday living expenses (food, fuel, clothes, etc.) apart from housing. The Government reckons that, at the moment, the following amounts should be enough to cover these expenses:

	£ per week
for a couple	48.40
for a single householder	29.80
for a non-householder aged 18 or over (or 16–17 with a child)	23.85
for a non-householder aged 16–17	18.40
for a child aged 11–15	15.30
for a child under 11	10.20

There are higher 'long-term' requirements for some people – for example, single parents (see page 55) or people aged 60 or over (see page 59).

'Additional requirements' are for people who have special needs – for instance, if they need a special diet for medical reasons, or if their home is difficult to heat. Ask at the social security office, CAB or Claimants Union for more details, or see leaflet SB.19.

'Housing requirements' cover things like the interest on your mortgage. See page 56 if you rent your home, and pages 57–8 if you're buying it, for more about help with housing costs.

All of your requirements, and those of anyone else you're claiming for, are added together. Then the final step is:

- **any income you (and your husband or partner) have is added up.** A few kinds of income may be partly or totally ignored – for example, if you get housing benefit (see pages 56–8) this won't be taken into account.

If your income is less than your requirements, you'll get supplementary benefit to make up the difference. You will also qualify automatically for certain other benefits – for example, free prescriptions, dental treatment, and glasses. And you may be able to get lump-sum grants for clothes, furniture, bedding and so on – see leaflet SB.16.

Unemployment benefit and supplementary benefit paid to those who are unemployed are taxable, but you should get the full (before-tax) amount. The Inland Revenue will probably collect the tax due in a later tax year – when you've found a new job, say. For more information on benefits for unemployed people, see leaflet SB.9.

If you have a job

If you (or your husband or partner) work less than 30 hours a week (or 25 hours if you're disabled), you can claim **supplementary benefit** if your income is less than your requirements (see above). If either of you work more than 30 hours a week but have a child, you can claim **family income supplement** if your earnings are low. Get leaflet FIS.1 from a post office or social security office. If you qualify for family income supplement, you'll also get free prescriptions, glasses, dental treatment and school meals.

Working women may also get help with their housing costs (they *certainly* will if they qualify for supplementary benefit) – see page 56 if you're renting and page 57 if you're buying your home.

If you have just started a job but haven't yet been paid, you can claim supplementary benefit for the first 15 days. Get form A.7 from the social security office and ask your new employer to stamp it.

If you are ill or disabled

If you are off work for more than a few days because of illness, you may get **statutory sick pay** from your firm for up to 28 weeks. The amount you get depends on your normal weekly earnings. If you earn:

- at least £38.00 but less than £55.00 a week, you'll get £31.60 a week
- at least £55.50 but less than £74.50 a week, you'll get £39.20 a week
- £74.50 a week or more, you'll get £46.75 a week.

Some employers will, however, pay you more than this minimum legal amount.

Some people (for example, those earning less than £38.00 a week) don't qualify for statutory sick pay. In this case, your firm should give you form SSP.(1)E, which includes a claim form for **sickness benefit**. You should fill this in and send it to your local social security office.

If you don't get a claim form from your firm – perhaps because you're self-employed, or not working at the moment – claim on form SC.1, available from hospitals, doctors' surgeries and social security offices.

You will get sickness benefit if you have paid enough National Insurance contributions in the previous tax year (i.e., between April 1984 and April 1985 if you claim at any time during 1986). It's not means-tested, so it doesn't matter how much other income you have. The social security office will tell you whether or not you qualify. (However, if your illness is due to an accident at work or an industrial disease, you can get sickness benefit regardless of your contributions record.)

Sickness benefit is currently £29.45 a week (or £37.05 if you're 60 or over). You may be able to claim extra benefit – for example, if your husband is dependent on you. See leaflet NI.16 for more details about statutory sick pay and sickness benefit.

If you are still ill after 28 weeks on statutory sick pay or sickness benefit, you should automatically go on to **invalidity benefit**. The basic amount (called **invalidity pension**) is currently £38.70 a week, and you may get extra depending on your age when the illness began, and whether or not you have any dependants. For more details, see leaflet NI.16A.

If you don't get statutory sick pay, sickness benefit or invalidity benefit (perhaps because you haven't had a job recently), you may qualify for **severe disablement allowance** – but you can't get this until you've been ill for 28 weeks. It's currently £23.25 a week, with extra for dependants (such as husband or children). See leaflet NI.252 for further details.

Regardless of whether you qualify for any of the above benefits, you may get **supplementary benefit** if you don't have enough money to live on. See page 50, above – but note that you claim on form SB.1, available from post offices and social security offices.

If you have a child

During pregnancy, you may be entitled to **maternity grant** and **maternity allowance** – see page 199. If you don't have enough money, you should also claim **supplementary benefit** on form SB.1 (available from post offices and social security offices).

Pregnant women on supplementary benefit can also claim lump-sum payments to buy:

- maternity clothes
- clothes you need for going into hospital
- things you need for the baby – for example, clothes, nappies, bedding, feeding bottles, a pram.

Write to the social security office explaining what you need to buy and asking for a **single payment**.

All pregnant women and mothers of children under one are

entitled to free prescriptions; your children can continue to get these until they reach the age of 16. You and your family may also get other health and educational benefits – see Chapter 14.

Once your child is born, you are entitled to **child benefit** (currently £7.10 a week), regardless of how much other income you have. Claim on forms CH.2 and CH.3. If you don't have enough money to live on, you may be able to claim supplementary benefit or **family income supplement**, depending on your circumstances – see page 49 if you are unemployed, page 52 if you have a job, and below if you're a single mother.

If you are staying at home to look after your child, you must make sure that your pension rights are protected. Check with staff at the social security office or CAB.

If you are a single parent

You are entitled to **one-parent benefit** on top of your **child benefit** – unless you are living with someone as a couple. One-parent benefit is currently £4.60 a week, and you claim on form CH.11.

If you aren't in paid work, or if your job is less than 24 hours a week, you may qualify for **supplementary benefit**. Claim on form SB.1 – and see page 50 for more details. Staff at the social security office may ask whether the father of your child is paying any maintenance; if he's not, they may ask for his name and address. You don't have to tell them – for example, if you don't want any further contact with him. But you must mention any maintenance or other payments you've received from him, as these will affect your benefit.

If you qualify for supplementary benefit, as a single parent you'll go on to the higher (long-term) rate after a year on the ordinary rate – see page 60, below. You will also get help with your housing costs, and certain health and educational benefits.

If your job is between 24 and 30 hours a week, you can claim **family income supplement** (on form FIS.1) to top up your income if your earnings are low – and you may still get supplementary benefit. Over 30 hours a week, you aren't entitled to supplementary benefit, though you may get family income supplement. See Chapter 10 for more information about benefits for single parents, and also DHSS leaflet FR.3, *Help for one-parent* *families*, and the booklet *One-parent families: help with housing* (from your CAB).

If you live in rented accommodation

You may well be able to get help with paying your rent and rates. Even if you have been turned down in the past, you may find you now qualify under the housing benefits scheme.

If you are getting supplementary benefit, you also qualify for **certificated housing benefit**. If you are in council accommodation, your council will pay the full amount of your rent and rates for you. If you are in privately rented accommodation, the council will pay you a **rent allowance** to cover your rent and will pay your rates for you (unless you pay your rent and rates all in one, in which case the council will pay both to you). But the total amount that is paid by the council will be reduced (meaning there will be some cost to you) if:

- you have anyone living in your home who is not a dependant (e.g., a lodger), *or*

- part of your rent covers heating, lighting, or a service which benefits you individually.

If you live in accommodation where meals are provided or in a hostel, you may get a **board and lodging allowance** instead of housing benefits.

What you pay for water rates will either be included in your supplementary benefit or in your housing benefit.

If you are not getting supplementary benefit, you may still qualify for housing benefits – i.e., help with paying part of your rent and rates. In fact, if your rent and rates are high, you can qualify even if you have quite a high income. Ask your local council for the application form and if you have any difficulty filling it in, ask your local CAB for help.

If you used to receive supplementary benefit but are no longer eligible, or if your income is not very much higher than the supplementary benefit level, you may also qualify for **housing benefit supplement** on top of your housing benefit. This brings your rate rebate up to the amount you would have received if you had been on supplementary benefit. It also entitles you to free prescriptions, glasses, dental treatment, school meals and the single payments which people on supplementary benefit can get. To get housing benefit supplement you have to apply to the DHSS for supplementary benefit (even if you know you do not qualify) as well as applying to your council for housing benefit, in order to get the required information passed from one to the other.

SHAC (see page 337) produces guides on housing benefits for council tenants and for private and housing association tenants (each 60p).

If you are buying your home

If you're having trouble meeting your mortgage payments, go and see the building society (or other lender) *straightaway*. They'll be much more sympathetic than if you've allowed heavy arrears to build up. If you have a repayment mortgage, they may agree to extend the term – so you pay it off over a longer period, but with lower monthly payments. Or they may look at any other loans you have, and help you organise your borrowing more cheaply. They may even allow you to pay just the interest on the loan for a time. Don't worry about them repossessing your home – this would be the *very* last resort, after they've explored all the options, and given you plenty of time (and help) to sort out your problems.

If you can claim supplementary benefit (see above), the social security will pay your mortgage interest. You should still talk to the building society, however, to ask if they'll accept interest-only payments for a time. People on supplementary benefit automatically qualify for **certificated housing benefit**, too. For owner-occupiers, this means that your rates will be paid in full (although the Government is considering changing the rules so that you'll have to pay a proportion of your rates yourself). After you've claimed supplementary benefit, the social security staff send a certificate to your local rates office to authorise this rate rebate.

If you do not qualify for supplementary benefit, you may still be able to get **housing benefit** to help pay your rates (but not your mortgage). If your rates are high, you may qualify even if your income is quite substantial. Ask your local council for an application form (they may call it a rate rebate – see page 114 for more information).

If you used to receive supplementary benefit but are no longer eligible, or if your income is not very much higher than the supplementary benefit level, you may also qualify for **housing benefit supplement** on top of your housing benefit. This brings your rate rebate up to the amount you would have received if you had been on supplementary benefit. It also entitles you to free prescriptions, glasses, dental treatment, school meals and the single payments which people on supplementary benefit can get. To get housing benefit supplement you have to apply to the DHSS for supplementary benefit (even if you know you do not qualify) as well as applying to your council for housing benefit, in order to get the required information passed from one to the other.

For more information, see *Home owners: your guide to housing benefits* (60p) and *Rights guide for home owners* (£2.50), both from SHAC (see page 337), or contact the housing department of your local council, your housing advice centre or CAB.

If you are separated or divorced

There are special rules for women who have recently divorced which mean that you can qualify for **unemployment benefit**, **sickness benefit** and **maternity allowance** even though you have not paid the number of NI contributions normally required. Ask your social security office if you think you may qualify, and see DHSS leaflet NI.95, *NI guide for divorced women.*

If you are short of money, you may also be able to get the amount of maintenance you are paid increased or you may be able to get more tax relief. If your maintenance is not being paid regularly, you may be able to get it enforced. See page 176 for further details.

If you are a widow

Details of benefits available to widows are given in Chapter 13. If you were separated from your husband when he died, you may still qualify for these benefits. If you were divorced, however, you won't qualify. But if you are bringing up a child from the marriage, you may get the **child's special allowance** (currently £8.05 a week). See leaflet NI.93 for more details – and if you think you might qualify, claim on form CS.1.

If you are on supplementary benefit or housing benefit supplement (see above), you can claim a lump sum from social security to help with funeral expenses. Write to them *immediately* to say you want a **single payment** for this purpose.

There are special rules which mean that you may be able to get **unemployment benefit**, **sickness benefit** and **maternity allowance** for a short period after your husband dies or after your widow's allowance or widowed mother's allowance comes to an end, even though you have not paid the number of NI contributions normally required. Ask your social security office if you think you may qualify, and see DHSS leaflet NI.51, *Widows: guidance about NI contributions and benefits*.

If you don't have enough money to live on, you may be able to claim other benefits, depending on your circumstances. See the other sections in this chapter.

If you are 60 or over

Chapter 20 describes some of the benefits and pensions available to women aged 60 or more.

If you are claiming sickness benefit or invalidity benefit when you reach the age of 60, you can either defer your retirement and continue to claim one of these benefits – or you can retire and claim a **state pension** instead. Sickness benefit is £37.05 a week for the over-60s, but the full state pension is currently £38.70 a week. However, after 28 weeks on sickness benefit you automatically go on to **invalidity pension** – which is the *same* as the state pension (£38.70). Unlike the state pension, however, it's not taxable.

You'll have to work out whether you'll be better off claiming the (taxable) state pension, or the (not taxable) invalidity pension – staff at your local CAB may be able to help you. But as a rough guide, if you have no other income and don't want to work again, you should probably retire. If you have other income (for example, from an occupational pension), you could be better off if you continue to claim invalidity pension.

Women of 60 or more can get free prescriptions simply by filling in the form on the back of the prescription. You may be able to get free or cheap travel on public transport, and free or cheap entry to exhibitions, swimming pools and so on. Make the most of all these perks!

If you find it hard to make ends meet, you may qualify for **supplementary pension**. This is virtually identical to supplementary benefit (see above), except that your 'normal requirements' are assessed on a (higher) long-term scale:

	£ per week
for a couple	60.65
for a person living alone	37.90
for a non-householder aged 18 or over (or 16–17 but with a child)	30.35
for a non-householder aged 16–17 (without a child)	23.25
any other person aged 11–15	15.30
any child aged under 11	10.20

Claim supplementary pension on form SB.1, available from post offices and social security offices. If you get a supplementary pension, you will automatically qualify for certain health benefits and **certificated housing benefit** (see above). If not, you may still get other help with your housing costs. See page 56 if you are renting your home, and pages 57–8 if you own it.

5

Saving and Investing

In this chapter we have tried to do two main things. To help you decide where to invest, the latter part of the chapter gives details about most of the different investments available, who they are suitable for and the factors to take into account when choosing between them. But if you are thinking of saving or investing you presumably have some money you do not need immediately, and in this case we would recommend you to take a cool look at your financial situation and the arrangements you have made. So first we look at the broader context of your financial life, and explain some of the main facets of investment. These considerations should help you make better long-term decisions and help you get what you want from your money.

Looking to the future

Whatever your personal circumstances, there are three things that can usefully guide your planning:

• **protection** Your best-laid plans could be quickly extinguished if you do not make adequate provision for the unforeseen. It is very important that your home and possessions are insured against loss or damage, that you and your partner will be compensated if the other dies or has a prolonged illness, and that you and your partner have made wills to ensure that your possessions go to the right people on your death.

• **flexibility** A long-term inflexible financial arrangement can be a handicap if your plans take an unexpected change of course. This means, for example, that it is best if you can cash in at least part of your savings and investments fairly promptly without much, if any, loss. It also means owning a home which may not be exotic but for which there should be a reasonable demand if you need to sell it fairly quickly.

• **independence** It is sensible for some of your financial arrangements to be independent of your partner's. This means having some savings or investments of your own and, if possible, some income you can call your own too. Establishing your independence in other ways is equally important. While you are working, it is sensible to contribute to the 'big' payments (especially the mortgage) and not just housekeeping and extras. Building up some pension entitlement of your own is also important – if you are married you will normally have to wait until your husband is 65 before you receive a pension from *his* contributions, and divorce will mean you lose all entitlement to your ex-husband's company pensions. But independence does not mean keeping everything separate: you may feel you have greater rights or independence by having some joint arrangements with your partner. This may be the case with a joint bank account, and it is certainly important that you are joint owner or joint tenant of a home you share with your partner.

Why save?

There are several reasons why you might want to save or invest, for example:

• to put money that you don't need immediately to good use

• to keep some money by in case of emergencies

• for a future event – a wedding, a new baby, retirement – or for a major purchase – a home or a holiday or a new car

• to provide yourself with an income.

If you've money to invest, there are a lot of people out to attract you. Banks and building societies splash enormous interest rates across their windows, life insurance companies send their salesmen to pester you, and the Government wants you to put your money in National Savings and buy shares in the industries it's selling off. But so much choice can make it harder to decide on what is the best investment for you – which will depend on your personal circumstances, what you want out of your investments and how much risk you're prepared to take.

You may hear it said that there's a difference between saving and investing. 'Save' may mean no more than not spending money – like putting it under your mattress – whereas investing it means making your money work for you in the expectation of earning more money. In this chapter we look at the various schemes for doing this – though we use the words *save* and *invest* pretty well interchangeably, as is now common parlance.

Investment explained

With many investments, you are lending your spare cash to someone else. They pay you for the privilege, either by paying you interest from time to time, or by paying you back more than you lent them at the outset. A bank deposit account or building society account is an example of this.

With other investments, you are buying a stake in the fortunes of some enterprise. If you buy company shares, for example, their value will rise and fall: if people think the company is going to do well, more people will want to buy the shares and will be prepared to pay more for them; if it does badly (or if people think it's going to), their value will fall and you won't be able to sell them for as much.

Capital and income

Capital is the money that you invest. With some investments, the value of your capital stays the same, and interest is paid out to you, to give you an **income**.

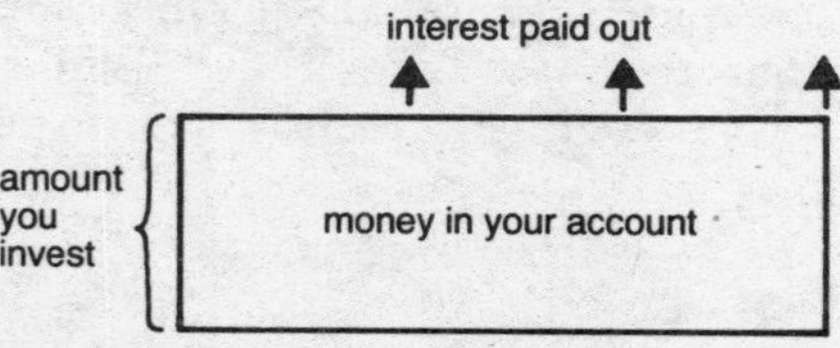

With some other investments, the interest isn't paid out to you but is **reinvested** – i.e., paid into your account (you may be able to choose whether you want the interest paid out or reinvested). At the end of each year (or accounting period), the interest is added to your capital (it becomes **capitalised**), so in the next year you get interest on the interest as well as the capital.

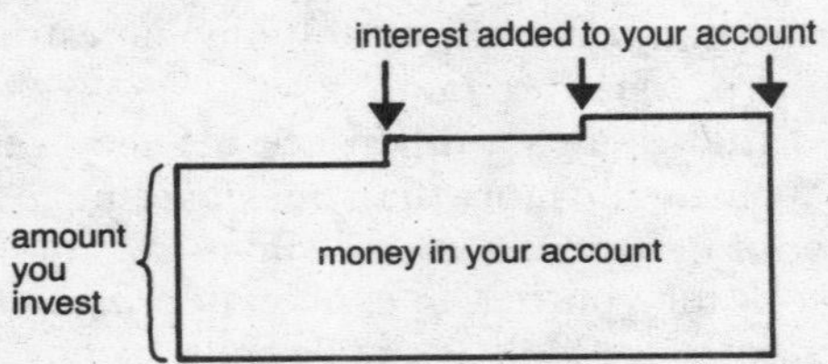

With some investments, you don't get paid any interest, but the value of your capital is guaranteed to increase, so that what you get back is more than what you put in. This is called **capital growth**. With some of these investments, the growth is fixed and guaranteed – as with National Savings Certificates and certain Guaranteed Growth Bonds issued by insurance companies. With Index-Linked National Savings Certificates, there's a different sort of guarantee: the amount you get back in £££ isn't guaranteed, but the value of your capital *is* guaranteed to keep ahead of inflation by a fixed margin.

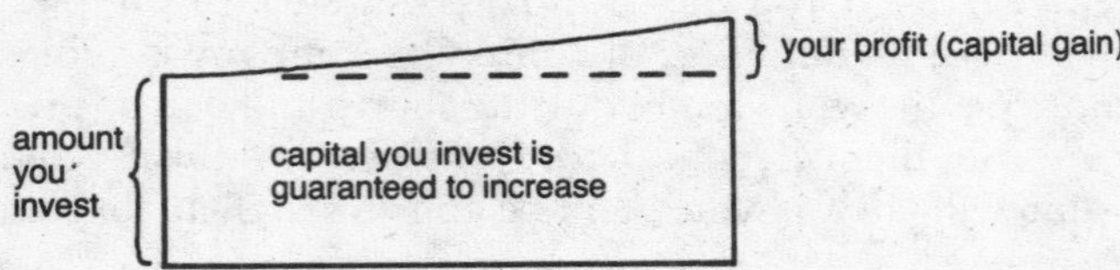

With some investments, the value of your capital can move up or down. This happens with unit trusts and British Government stocks ('gilts'), for example. With company shares and any 'alternative' kind of investment like oil paintings or diamonds, prices can change quite substantially, so these investments are a lot more risky than the three types above. While it's possible to make a killing with these investments, it's quite possible to lose a lot of money too.

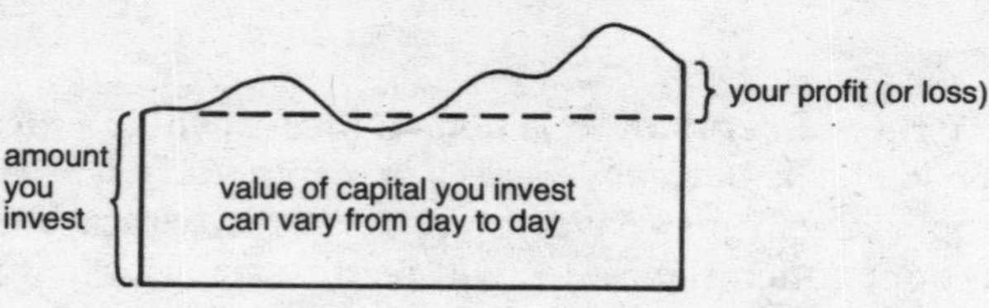

Risk

Whichever form of investment you choose, there's always a risk that you might have done better with a different one – because no one can predict the future. But with any particular investment, the two main types of risk you should consider are:

- How safe is the institution you're dealing with? There's little risk in lending money to the Government or investing in a UK bank, building society or insurance company; even if one of these institutions were to get into difficulties, there are schemes for protecting investors. But investing in a small new company, or in a country which has fewer controls over its financial institutions, is clearly far more risky – and people do lose out heavily.

- Can the capital value of the investment fall as well as rise? If it can, it means that the time you buy and sell is critical – ideally you want to buy when the capital value is in a trough, and sell when it has hit a peak. If you hit it right, you can make a healthy profit. But there's a high risk of getting it all wrong and watching the value of your investment decrease day by day. You can reduce this risk, however, by *spreading* your money between a number of investments – as the chance of them all doing badly is much less than the chance of one of them crashing. But of course you also reduce your chance of doing very well.

No one should put money they can't afford to lose or money they might want back in a hurry into risky investments. This generally means you should have at least a few thousand pounds in safe investments before you start thinking about riskier ones.

Another risk to the success of your investments – one which you can't do much about – is inflation (see page 67).

Return

The **yearly rate of return** you get on an investment is a measure of what you get back for each year, as a percentage of what you put in. If the investment just pays you interest (as with a building society account), then the return will be the same as the interest rate, or very close to it. For example, if a building society pays you interest of 8% each year, your return is simply 8%. In fact, what most building societies would do is add 4% interest every 6 months. This gives a return of slightly more than 8% (actually 8.16%) because in the second half of the year you're getting a little bit of extra interest on the interest that was added to your account halfway through. These differences are too small to bother about, and comparing interest rates is quite adequate.

But how would you compare an investment offering interest at 8% with one where you invest £1,000 and get a lump sum of £1,210 back in two years? You can if you know the yearly rate of return – in this case it's 10%. The reason is that if 10% interest had been added to your £1,000 each year, you would have had:

– at end of year 1: £1,000 + 10% = £1,100
– at end of year 2: £1,100 + 10% = £1,210

Unfortunately, the yearly rate of return is very hard to work out if all you know are the amounts you pay in and get out – you really need a computer. So you're dependent on the company telling you what the yearly return is. If you're told the return on the investment is 10%, you can see that it looks a better deal than the building society paying 8%.

But there are two things to watch. First, are the returns **fixed** or **variable**? Banks and building societies change their interest rates from time to time. They only tell you the current rate, and could be paying 2% less in a year's time. So these returns are variable. On the other hand, with National Savings Certificates and insurance company Guaranteed Growth Bonds, the return is fixed when you invest.

The second thing to watch is: are you going to have to pay tax on the return from the investment? If the taxman were to take 29% of your 10% return in tax you'd be left with a return of only 7.1% – and the 8% from the building society in our example would have been better after all. So it's important to notice whether the returns quoted in advertisements are **gross** (i.e., what you would get if no tax were payable) or **net** (i.e., what you get after the taxman has taken his cut). For more about tax considerations, see page 73.

Keeping up with inflation

Inflation is the phenomenon of rising prices. If prices in general are going up by 5% a year, you need to get 5% return on your money just to keep up. It's only the amount above the inflation rate that is a bonus to you – called the **real return**. Since 1983, inflation has wandered around the 5% mark, and it's been easy to get a real return of another 2% to 4% on top of that.

But there have been periods – like most of the 1970s – when inflation was much higher than the return on investments. For example, if inflation is 15% but you're only getting a 10% return on your investment, you can't buy as much when you withdraw your money as you could when you invested it. It's in times like these that **index-linked investments** come into their own. All issues of Index-Linked National Savings Certificates have guaranteed to keep the value of your savings up with inflation. The third issue pays you up to 3½% on top of inflation, so if inflation is running at 5% you get 8½%, but if inflation were 12%, you'd get a return of 15½%. Index-Linked British Government stock has a more complicated link with inflation, but the same principle applies. It is unlikely that any other risk-free investments can compete with this in times of high inflation.

Choosing an investment

When choosing where to invest, it's worth spending a little time investigating the options. If you always use the same investment, you may be losing out on quite a lot of interest. If you simply pick the highest interest rate, you may find you can't get at your money quickly when you need to. The main things to consider are:

- **Do you want to be able to put money in and take it out whenever you want to?**

If so, a building society, bank or National Savings account would suit you, probably one with a branch near where you live, work or shop. You should certainly have *some* of your savings in one of these accounts.

- **Do you want the discipline of having to save a regular amount every month for a definite period?**

Many building societies and some banks have accounts which will pay you a higher rate of interest if you agree to save regularly.

- **Do you want to be sure of getting your money back with interest? Or are you willing to take a risk in the hope of getting more back, but knowing that you could lose some of your money?**

Investing with a building society, bank or in National Savings is extremely safe. Buying postage stamps or diamonds as an investment is extremely risky. Investments like British Government stock, unit trusts and company shares come in between these two extremes.

- **Do you want the investment to pay you a regular income, or do you want your capital to grow?**

As explained on page 63, some investments are more suited to one or the other. The table on page 75 identifies which investments are particularly suitable for paying out an income.

- **Is inflation on the way up?**

If so, it would be sensible to invest at least part of your money in index-linked investments. Even if inflation doesn't go as high as you thought, it's unlikely that you'll do any worse than with other safe investments.

- **Are you saving up to buy a home?**

If you're saving up the deposit on your first home and hoping to get a mortgage, it's sensible to save with the building society or bank you think most likely to give you one. This is because, if money is short, lenders tend to give priority to people who have been saving with them, as long as they fit the bill. So ask them about their lending policies before deciding where to invest (see page 100 for what to ask). You should also register your savings under the **Homeloan Scheme**. This is a Government scheme under which you can get £600 extra mortgage, free of interest for the first 5 years, plus a small cash payment, if you save for 2 years and meet certain conditions. Ask your bank or building society for details.

- **Is your income (including your husband's, if you are married) too small to pay income tax?**

If so, a National Savings Investment Account, National Savings Deposit Bonds and National Savings Income Bonds are likely to offer you a high return, with no tax deducted and no tax to pay. Compare the returns advertised with the *net* rates quoted by building societies and banks.

• Do you (or your husband, if you are married) pay tax at higher rates on your income?
If so, tax-free investments can be particularly worthwhile, as can investments where a large part of the return you get is capital gain rather than income (e.g., British Government stock with a low interest coupon, and company shares).

How to choose

The table at the end of this chapter gives a brief description of investments under four headings. Use those headings and the pointers above to narrow down your choice, then check the advice and tax considerations in the following sections. Lastly, get details of the investments which are on your shortlist and make your final selection.

Investment advice

• Unless you have a lot of money to invest (more than a few thousand, say), it's sensible to keep your investments simple. Don't go out of your way to get an extra ½% or even 1% interest. Stick to the familiar building society, bank or National Savings investments, where your money is safe and accessible.

• Before you invest in more sophisticated schemes, or tie up your money for any period of time, see that you have some money that you can get at quickly if need be. This might be a few hundred pounds in a building society account.

• It often used to be the case that the longer you invested for, the higher your return. You still hear this said, though it is seldom true now. So don't lock money away in a long-term investment unless you're really sure you won't need it sooner. This also means don't sign up for long-term savings schemes or life insurance/investment policies: if you decide to pull out in the first few years, you'll get back less than you've paid in.

• There's one exception to the last rule, and that concerns **pensions**. If you have some earnings (investment income doesn't count), you are allowed tax relief on money you pay into a pension scheme – a personal one run by an insurance company if you aren't a member of an employer's scheme. This can be worth doing if, like many women today, you want to have your own pension arrangements, independently of your husband. See Chapter 19 for more information.

- If you don't own your own home, you're missing out on what has proved in the past to be a very worthwhile investment. Of course, you don't get your money back until you move – and then you may want to plough back all the profit you've made into buying the next home. But it's often possible to get some of your money back by moving to somewhere smaller, and the value of the last home you own can pass to your children when you die.

- Before putting all your spare cash into an investment, it's sensible to consider whether you and your dependants are sufficiently protected by **life insurance** – see Chapter 15. But don't choose investments just to get some life insurance: the amount of life insurance might be quite inappropriate for your needs, as might the type or length of the investment. Choose your investment purely on the grounds of how well it suits you as an investment.

Be suspicious of advertisements

At the time of writing, a leading insurance company was displaying half-page advertisements in most of the national papers offering:

- up to £25,671 when you save regularly for 'only' 15 years

- the money you get back is 'absolutely free of all tax'

- you get free life insurance, so your dependants will get a payment if you die during the 15 years

- you can choose whether to save £10, £20, £30, £40 or £50 a month. At the end of each year the monthly amount goes up by 50p for each £10 you pay

- if you apply within two weeks, your first monthly payment is only £1 and you get a free electronic calculator

This is fairly typical of the offers you see from insurance companies. It all sounds tempting, and there's nothing wrong with the information in the ad. But consider what isn't made so clear, or isn't mentioned at all:

- The £25,671 is only an *estimate* of the amount you'd get back in 15 years' time. The small print shows that it's what you would get if the current 'bonus rates' (i.e., the increases to the value of your investment) are kept up for the whole 15 years. But it also tells you that the bonus rates are currently at 'record levels'. So you will only get the promised amount if these record levels are maintained for the full 15 years. We don't think you should have too much confidence in that happening.

- That £25,671 estimate represents a yearly rate of return of just over 8%, which is not particularly exciting (unfortunately the electronic calculator you get free isn't sophisticated enough to work this out!). It would be safer to assume you'll get around £20,000 back, which is a return of only 6¼%. And that's only if you're under 44. If you're older the return is less, and if you're over 60 it's under 4¼%.

- In 15 years' time, these amounts will only be worth what they are now if inflation stopped today. If inflation is a modest 5% a year, all the amounts will be worth less than half what they are now (£25,671 will be worth only £12,350). If inflation averaged 7½%, they'd be worth only one-third as much in 15 years' time.

- The reason you don't have to pay any tax on what you get back is because the insurance company has already paid any tax due on the profits it has made from investing your money.

- The only choice you have is over how much you pay each month. You have no choice about how long you invest for, where your money is invested, how much your payments increase by each year, or how much goes into life insurance.

- Unless you can afford to pay £40 or £50 a month, the life insurance cover is too small to be of much use. On £20 a month your dependants would get between £3,450 and £3,900 from the scheme if you died (depending on your age). If you have a family, you should probably have more than ten times that much life insurance. Nor is it worth very much – to buy that much insurance would only cost you between 30p and £2 a month, depending on your age.

So do be wary of advertisements which try to entice you with enormous numbers and free offers. There's usually another side to the story. And do be wary of signing up for a long period; none of us can be sure what our situation will be in a few years' time, let alone 15 years.

Getting investment advice

While there are many people prepared to advise you on where to invest, few of them are completely independent. Most advisers earn their money from the commission they are paid by the savings institutions they recommend. They therefore have a vested interest in recommending certain investments rather than others. For example, investment advisers who are also life insurance brokers may well recommend investments linked to life insurance policies; banks may recommend their own unit trusts. Almost every survey that has been done has shown that different advisers will recommend *different* investments to the *same* person. For most people, the advice in this chapter should be all you need.

If you decide you want to talk over your requirements, your bank manager, solicitor or accountant may well be willing to advise you. Your bank will normally be able to buy company shares or British Government stock for you, but if you want to invest a large amount in these you may well find it useful to have a stockbroker's advice. You could ask your bank to suggest a firm, and to find out what the firm's minimum commission is.

A good measure by which to judge an investment adviser is how much he or she asks about your personal circumstances – your age, state of health, marital status, dependants, home, income, tax position, debts and commitments, pension rights, existing investments, your reasons for investing, how much risk you're prepared to take, your future plans. Advisers should also be able to explain to you why the investments they are recommending are particularly suitable for you. Do make sure you fully understand the implications of what is recommended, and if you're not convinced by what you're told, get a second opinion.

Tax

You don't ever have to pay tax on the capital you own or invest. But the money that you make by investing may be liable to tax. If your investment produces an income (i.e., pays out money at regular intervals) there may be **income tax** to pay on that income. This applies to interest (even if it is reinvested in the account and not paid out), to dividends on company shares and to distributions on unit trusts. If you sell your investment at a profit, there may be **Capital Gains Tax** to pay on the profit you make (see Chapter 23). Whether there's any tax to pay, and how much, depends on the type of investment and on your tax position.

Normally, everyone is allowed to have a certain amount of income which they don't have to pay any tax on; you pay tax on anything you get over this amount. But if you're a married woman, this only applies to money you earn from working and pensions you have earned yourself. Any income you get which comes from your investments is treated as though it is your husband's income. This means that if your husband has enough income to be liable for income tax, any income you get from investments (except tax-free ones) will be liable to tax, however small it is. To add insult to injury, you also have to give details of your investment income to your husband to enter on his Tax Return, though you can avoid this if you ask for **separate assessment** (see page 157).

As far as tax is concerned, investments fall into five main groups:

- Investments that are **tax-free**. However rich or poor you are, there's no tax due on the interest you get or profit you make when you cash in these investments. Examples are National Savings Certificates and National Savings Yearly Plan.

- Investments that are **tax-paid**. Interest from bank and building society accounts, finance company deposits and, from April 1986, local authority investments, is treated as though basic-rate tax has already been paid. So you can keep all of what you are paid. Only if your income (including, if you're married, your husband's) is more than £18,000 or so might you be liable to some higher-rate tax on what you get. But if your income is not high enough for you to be liable to pay tax, you *cannot* reclaim the tax – meaning these investments are not usually very suitable for non-taxpayers.

• Investments where **basic-rate tax** is deducted from each interest payment before you get it – for example, the dividends you get with company shares and unit trusts. These are much like tax-paid investments, except that if your income isn't high enough to pay any tax, you can claim back the tax that's been deducted from the Inland Revenue.

• Investments that are liable to income tax, though **no tax is deducted** from the income you get – like National Savings Investment Account and National Savings Income Bonds. If your income (including your husband's) in the tax year isn't high enough to pay any tax, you can keep all this interest. If your income *is* high enough to pay tax, the taxman will collect it from you.

• If you sell an investment for more than you paid for it, you may be liable for Capital Gains Tax on the profit you make. This can apply to company shares and unit trusts, 'alternative' investments like stamps and paintings. Very broadly, all the gains you make in the tax year are added together and if they come to more than a certain amount (£6,300 in the 1986–87 tax year) there's 29% tax to pay on the excess. Generally a Capital Gains Tax bill is much less than an income tax bill would be on the same amount.

Notice that with some investments (like company shares), there may be both income tax to pay on the income (dividends) paid out to you every six months, *and* Capital Gains Tax to pay on the profit you make when you eventually sell the shares. But this doesn't necessarily make shares a poor investment – other factors are far more important.

There is much more detailed information on the tax system in Chapter 23.

Investing with tax relief

If you are willing to take a risk by investing in shares of certain smaller companies, you can get tax relief on what you invest through the **Business Expansion Scheme**. This means that if you are a basic-rate taxpayer and you invest £1,000, you'll pay £290 less income tax, so the cost of the investment to you is only £710. Only certain companies qualify, and you must buy at least £500 worth of shares in each and keep them for 5 years. Alternatively, you can invest £2,000 or more through a Business Expansion Scheme fund approved by the Inland Revenue. Details of the scheme are in the Inland Revenue leaflet IR.51, *The Business Expansion Scheme*.

A much safer way of getting tax relief on your investment is to put money into a **personal pension plan**. If you have earnings from self-employment or from a job in which you do not belong to a pension scheme, each £100 you invest costs you only £71. For full details see page 285.

Table of investments

Investments are listed in four groups:

- **Ad hoc** – where you can put money in and take it out whenever you want to. You should certainly have *some* of your money in one of these. They are also useful for large amounts for less than a year (e.g., between selling one home and buying another).

- **Fixed notice** – as above but you get a higher rate of interest, in return for which you have to give some warning (usually one or three months) that you want to withdraw. A month's notice may not inconvenience you if you have a credit card which you can use if you need money more urgently than that.

- **Regular savings** – where you agree to make regular monthly payments for at least a year in order to build up your savings.

- **Investing for a year or more** – if you have several hundred (or several thousand) pounds that you want to invest for at least a year.

We have picked out some investments with the following signs:

i means the investment is suitable for producing an income. The institution may be prepared to pay out interest in monthly instalments, or you may be able to cash in units fairly frequently to get an income.

+ means the investment is particularly suitable for people who pay tax at higher rates. It is also a good choice if you are over 64 (or your husband is) and your income is in the band where each extra £1 of taxable income means you lose *age allowance* (see page 312).

– means the investment is particularly suitable for people who do not pay income tax (or married women whose husbands do not pay tax).

These signs do not mean that the investment is unsuitable for other people.

Group 1: Ad hoc

With these accounts, you can simply pay money in and draw it out whenever you want to – though you can't get at money you've paid in by cheque until the cheque has cleared (banks) or for 7–14 days (building societies).

Building Society Share Account
Bank Deposit Account **i**

Check whether you can withdraw at any branch of the society or bank, or whether you are limited to one (unless you make special arrangements). The amount of cash you can withdraw on the spot is likely to be restricted to £250 or £500 (for larger amounts you'll get a cheque or have to give a few days' notice for cash). Interest is added to your account, usually twice a year, based on the average amount you've had invested. You don't have to pay any basic-rate tax on this interest.

Building Society Cheque Account
Like a share account, but you also get a chequebook for paying other people direct – though you must not overdraw. You may be able to have standing orders paid from the account. You generally get less interest than with a share account.

Bank 'High Interest' Cheque Account
Like a bank deposit account, but you also get a chequebook for paying other people large amounts direct, and may be able to have standing orders paid. To get the higher interest rate, there's usually a minimum investment of £2,000 or so, and a minimum amount you can withdraw of £250 or so.

National Savings Ordinary Account
You pay in and withdraw at post offices. You can't normally withdraw more than £100 in cash, though after 6 months you can ask for this limit to be increased to £250. You can also have standing orders and pay certain bills from the account.

In 1986, the interest rate is only 3%, unless you keep at least

£100 in your account for the whole calendar year, when the rate is 6% for each complete calendar month that you have £500 or more in the account. The first £70 of interest you get in a tax year is tax-free, but that doesn't make up for the low interest rate.

Group 2: Fixed notice investments

Building Society Notice Account
Bank Fixed Notice Account **i**

Typically, you'll need £500 to open one of these accounts at a building society, £2,000 at a bank. You can pay in further money as and when you like (there may be a minimum amount each time). To withdraw you must give warning – usually either 1 or 3 months. In return, you get a higher rate of interest than on share or deposit accounts. With some schemes, you can get money out sooner but lose some interest. With others, you always lose some interest when you withdraw – to be avoided if possible.

National Savings Investment Account **i, –**

You can pay money in at post offices at any time (minimum £5). To withdraw, you must give a month's notice. Interest is added to your account at the end of each calendar year. No tax is deducted from the interest, and the rate is usually very good for people who don't pay tax. But if you (or your husband) already pay tax or will have to on this interest, it's likely you could get a higher return from a building society.

National Savings Deposit Bonds **–**

Your initial investment and all subsequent ones must be £100 or a multiple of £100. Each withdrawal must be at least £50, and you must give 3 months' notice. Interest is added to your investment and is taxable, but no tax is deducted from it. If you withdraw within a year you only get half the interest rate. The full interest rate is generally high for non-taxpayers, though only slightly higher than the much less restrictive Investment Account.

National Savings Income Bonds **i, –**

Your initial investment must be at least £2,000, and all subsequent deposits and withdrawals must be in £1,000s. You must give 3 months' notice of withdrawing. Interest is paid out to you monthly and is taxable, but no tax is deducted from it. If you withdraw within a year of investing you only get half the interest rate. The full interest rate is generally high for non-taxpayers, though only slightly higher than the much less restrictive Investment Account, from which you can make monthly withdrawals if an income is important to you.

National Savings Indexed Income Bonds **i**
Much like NS Income Bonds, but your initial investment must be at least £5,000, and the interest rate is initially much lower (8% at the time of writing). But the interest rate is increased each year in line with inflation – so the income you get is index-linked. However, the value of your capital will still be eaten away by inflation.

Group 3: Regular savings

Building society regular savings scheme
Bank regular savings scheme
You agree to make regular monthly payments into the account. You can withdraw all your savings at any time, but there's likely to be a limit on partial withdrawals. You get a higher rate of interest than with a share or deposit account. Interest is added to your account, and you don't have to pay any basic-rate tax on it.

Building Society Save-As-You-Earn Scheme **+**
You save between £1 and £20 a month for 5 years, and get a tax-free return of 8.3% a year. If you leave your savings invested for a further 2 years, the return goes up to 8.6% tax-free.

National Savings Yearly Plan **+**
You make 12 monthly payments (of between £20 and £200) by standing order from your bank account. These earn 6% interest during that year, and buy you a Certificate. The longer you keep the Certificate, the higher the return you get. You get the best return if you keep the Certificate for 4 years – the return was 8.2% when this book went to press – after which you get the **general extension rate** of interest. The interest rates may change, but the ones in force when you apply are fixed for your Certificate. The return is tax-free.

Endowment life insurance policy (with profits) **+**
You make regular monthly payments to an insurance company for an agreed period of 10 years or more. The company guarantees to pay you a set amount at the end of the period, which may be less

than the total you pay in. But as it makes profits on its investments, the company adds 'bonuses' to the amount you're guaranteed. What you get back at the end may have a further bonus added to it and is normally tax-free. You get a small amount of life insurance cover during the term of the policy. If you want to cash in the policy before the end of the term, what you get is largely up to the company; in the first year or two you may get little or nothing back.

Unit-linked regular savings scheme +
You make regular monthly payments to a unit trust company for an agreed period of 10 years or more. After deducting the company's expenses, your payments are used to buy you units in the company's unit trusts. The value of these units will rise and fall over time. You get an income from the units (small at first) from which basic-rate tax has already been deducted. At the end of the period you cash them in, or you may be able to keep them for longer. If you want to cash in early you could be disappointed with what you get back, as your units will have had less time to grow in value and a larger proportion of your investment will have gone in charges. In the first year or two you may get little or nothing back.

Another way of saving regularly is to buy National Savings Certificates (either ordinary or index-linked) at regular intervals (see next group).

Group 4: Investing for a year or more

You could consider any of the schemes in Group 2 above, plus:

Building Society term share i
The minimum you can invest is usually £1,000 or more for a fixed term of between 2 and 5 years. Interest can be paid out to you or reinvested. You may not be able to withdraw until the end of the term.

National savings Certificates (ordinary) +, i
Each Certificate costs £25, and you can invest up to £5,000 (in addition to any other National Savings Certificates you have). Interest is added at the end of the first year and then every three months. The interest rate for the first year is modest, but increases each year for 5 years. Each issue of NSCs has its own interest rate

structure which is fixed for the whole 5-year period. For the 31st issue, the return over the full 5 years is 7.85%. The return is free of tax. Interest cannot be paid out, but you can use these Certificates to provide an income after 12 months by cashing them when and as you need to.

Index-Linked National Savings Certificates (3rd issue) **+, i**

Each Certificate costs £25, and you can invest up to £5,000 (in addition to any other National Savings Certificates you have). After 12 months the value of each Certificate is increased in line with inflation and interest is added, and this subsequently happens each month. The interest rate increases slightly each year for 5 years. The *overall* return you get over the whole period is:

over 1 year	inflation + 2.5%
over 2 years	inflation + 2.6%
over 3 years	inflation + 2.8%
over 4 years	inflation + 3.1%
over 5 years	inflation + 3.5%

So if you have held Certificates for 4 years and inflation has averaged 6% over that time, the return to you is 6% + 3.1% = 9.1%. The return is tax-free. The major advantage of these Certificates is that they stop the value of your savings being eaten away if inflation takes off. If, in our example, inflation had averaged 12% over those four years, your return would have been 12% + 3.1% = 15.1%. Interest cannot be paid out, but you can use these Certificates to provide an income after 12 months by cashing them when and as you need to.

British Government stock (ordinary) **+, i**

These have come to be known as **gilt-edged stock** or **gilts**, because originally the certificate you got when you bought them had a gilt edge. There are now a large number of different stocks, each with its own name (e.g., 'Exchequer 11% 1990'). The name (e.g., 'Exchequer' or 'Treasury') is only for identification. The year (1990 in our example) tells you when the particular stock comes to an end (the 'redemption date'), when the Government will buy back the stock at its face value. In the meantime, the Government will pay people who hold the stock 11% (in our example) of its face value in interest each year, usually in two instalments. This means that if you keep the stock until its redemption date, you know exactly how much you will get back and so, used that way, stocks are a safe investment.

But between now and redemption, the price at which people buy and sell the stock will vary. You may only have to pay £80 for £100 face value of stock, or you may have to pay £115. It all depends on the interest rate paid by the stock, on what people think is going to happen to interest rates in general, and on how close the stock is to redemption. So you will find that the value of your stock varies from day to day. You can therefore buy and sell Government stocks in the hope of making quick profits – a much more risky way to invest in them.

Government stock is a sound investment if you are fairly certain you won't want your money back before the redemption date. There is a charge for buying and selling stock. You can buy many stocks through the National Savings Bonds & Stocks Office (details from post offices), though if you're investing more than about £10,000 it may be cheaper to ask your bank or a stockbroker to buy for you. If you want a reasonable income from the stock, choose one with a high interest rate ('coupon'), but higher-rate taxpayers and people over 64 in the 'age-allowance trap' (see page 312) should go for stocks with a low coupon so that most of the return they get is capital gain. If you sell the stock after 1 July 1986, any gain will be free of Capital Gains Tax. Before then, the gain will be exempt from CGT only if you held the stock for 12 months or more.

British Government stock (index-linked) **+**

Similar to ordinary Government stock, though the interest payments are always small (2% or 2½% a year). However, these are index-linked (i.e., they go up in line with rising prices) and so is the amount the Government will repay at redemption. This means that the value of your investment is largely protected against inflation. At the time of writing, the stocks with the earliest redemption dates had always offered the highest returns. Don't be put off by the complexities of these stocks – investing in them is fairly straightforward and they have not attracted the attention they deserve.

Local authority loans **i**

Often called 'bonds', these are loans you make to a local authority for an agreed number of years. The interest rate is normally fixed at the outset, and interest is paid out to you (after basic-rate tax has been paid).

Local authority stocks and yearling bonds **i**

These are like British Government stock, except that you are liable for Capital Gains Tax on the profit you make when you sell the stock if your total gains in the tax year are large enough.

Finance Company deposits **i**

These usually operate either like a local authority loan (you get a fixed interest rate for a fixed number of years) or like a building society fixed notice account (the interest rate varies and you have to give so many months' notice of withdrawal). Some finance companies have a number of other investment schemes.

Insurance company guaranteed growth bond

You invest a lump sum for a fixed number of years with an insurance company, and get a fixed return which is reinvested (not paid out). The return is normally free of tax for basic-rate taxpayers. The mechanics of these schemes are often quite complicated, and higher-rate taxpayers will need advice on which scheme will give you the best return. If the bond will come to an end after you (or your husband) are 64, avoid ones which are technically life insurance policies producing taxable gains, as they will affect any age allowance you get.

Insurance company guaranteed income bond **i**

Like guaranteed growth bonds, except that the return is paid out to you, usually yearly or half-yearly.

Shares **+, i**

To consider investing in shares, you should have a lot of money you're prepared to take a risk with. Because of the costs of buying and selling shares (a stockbroker has to do this at the Stock Exchange) it is not worth investing much less than £1,000 in each company. But investing in just one company would be far too risky, so you should consider investing in a dozen or more companies in different industries and preferably in more than one country in order to spread the risk. This means you should be prepared to risk at least £12,000 to £15,000 if you are to invest in shares, and you should probably have at least as much again in safe investments. You will also need regular advice from a stockbroker and to take a regular interest in the fate of your investment.

Not for the nervy, but if you want to find out more you could ask your bank to recommend a stockbroker who will buy and sell for small investors.

Unit trusts **+, i**

Unit trusts are a way for small investors to invest in shares with much less risk than investing directly. Because a lot of people are contributing, the trust company can buy large numbers of shares in a lot of different companies, thus reducing costs and spreading the risk. They also manage the investments for you, buying and selling shares to try and get the best return. There's a good chance that you'll get a higher return from a unit trust than most safe investments, but there's no guarantee that you will and even after several years you could have less than you first invested. Nor is there any guarantee that a trust which has done well in the past will continue to do well in the future. There is a huge number to choose from, and you can reduce your risk by spreading your money between several trusts, as the minimum investment for most trusts is only a few hundred pounds. You usually get a dividend payment twice a year (unless the income is reinvested), on which basic-rate tax has already been paid. Any profit you make when you sell the units will be liable to Capital Gains Tax if the total gains you make in the tax year are high enough.

'Alternative' investments **+**

This covers a range of items which people buy in the hope that prices will rise and they will be able to sell them at a profit in the future – coins, stamps, antique silver, precious metals, port, diamonds, old share certificates and Government bonds. Undoubtedly people do make money out of these, but often only because they have extensive knowledge of the articles as well as access to ways of buying and selling that don't involve a chain of intermediaries and commissions. The markets for many of these items have had severe slumps from time to time, leaving a lot of burnt fingers. Of course, there's nothing wrong in using your spare cash to collect things that you like; indeed, it can become an absorbing interest. But don't count on them being a good investment. If you do happen to find many years later that you've got a valuable collection, then that will be an extra bonus.

YOUR HOME

6

Renting a Home

What are the advantages?

The main advantage is that, in most areas at least, renting is cheaper than buying your own home. It also means fewer responsibilities, and makes it much easier to pull up roots and move – if you get a new job, say. So how do you go about finding somewhere to live?

If you're homeless and have a 'priority need' (such as a child to take care of, or a violent husband), your local authority is probably obliged to find you a home. Otherwise, it's up to you to do the searching. Broadly speaking, your options are:

- to rent a bedsit or flat in the private sector.
- to rent a council (local authority) home.
- to rent a housing association home.

Private tenants

It's becoming increasingly difficult to find rented accommodation, particularly in large cities, but look for ads in local newspapers, magazines and shop windows – and ask your friends, family and colleagues if they know of anyone with a room to let. If you register with an accommodation agency, they can only charge you a fee if they find you somewhere to live *and* you actually take it up. If they try to charge you just for 'putting you on their books', refuse – and report them to the local authority. (If you've already handed over a fee, ask for it back. If they say no, you can sue them – contact your local Citizens Advice Bureau (CAB) or advice centre for help.)

If you're desperate for accommodation, you'll probably be tempted to take the first thing you are offered – but always ask for a copy of the tenancy agreement, and check out the following:

• **rent** How much, and how often? Does someone come and collect it, or is it up to you to send off a cheque every month, say? (If the latter, it's easier to get into arrears.)

• **deposit** The landlord can ask you to put down a 'reasonable' deposit against breakages, etc. If it's more than the equivalent of two months' rent, it's probably illegal – and again, you can sue. It's also illegal to charge you 'key money' (a premium just for allowing you to move in).

• **service charges** Are there any extra service charges for maintenance, porterage, and so on? How often can they increase? (If they can be put up each year, you're probably protected against unreasonable increases by the 1980 Housing Act – but check with your local CAB.)

• **gas and electricity bills** How are these to be paid? Unless you have an account direct with the Gas or Electricity Board, there is a maximum price which the landlord can charge you for the 'resale' of gas or electricity. Your local showrooms should have up-to-date information on these maximum prices.

If a meter is broken into, the Board will recover the money from the 'hirer' – normally the landlord, but check in the agreement.

• **inventory** Ask for a list of any furniture, crockery, etc., provided – and make sure it's accurate.

• **repairs** Make sure you're not responsible for doing repairs to the building – they can be extremely expensive.

• **subtenants** Check whether you are allowed to sublet the property to someone else (in case you want to get a flatmate in the future).

• **joint tenants** If you are renting with someone else, find out whether you are joint tenants. If so, you could be held responsible for the other person's rent arrears.

• **name and address of the landlord** You'll need these details in the event of problems arising on which you want to enforce your legal rights.

Private tenants' rights

Most tenants are covered by the provisions of the **Rent Acts**, which give them a certain amount of protection. For one exception, see *Licensees*, on page 90. Another exception is if you've got a **holiday let** – but this must be a *genuine* holiday let, and not just a disreputable landlord trying to evade his legal responsibilities. Make sure he knows that the bedsit or flat is your main residence – then a court is unlikely to find that it's a holiday let.

Provided you're covered by the Rent Acts, you have a right to a **fixed** (or **registered**) **rent** – which is a fair rent decided by an independent Rent Officer or Rent Tribunal. Once it's been decided, it can't normally be increased for at least two years. To find out whether the rent has already been registered, contact the Rent Officer (see the phone book). If not, and you think the rent is too high, consider applying for registration – but check the registered rents for similar properties first, otherwise the Rent Officer may decide that an *increase* would be fair!

Apart from rents, the other main concern of tenants is **eviction**. Broadly speaking, you have less protection under the Rent Acts if:

• your landlord is resident in the same building (if he uses part of it as a home – even if it's not his only home), *or*

• he provides certain services – such as cleaning, laundry or meals. These services must be *substantial* – for example, a cup of tea wouldn't count as a meal.

If either of these applies, the general rule is that the landlord can evict you simply by getting a court order – even if you've been a model tenant. The most you can hope for is that the court order won't be made for three months, to give you time to find somewhere else to live.

However, if neither of those things applies, the general rule is that you can only be evicted in certain specified circumstances – if you have very bad rent arrears, for example, or if you've broken the terms of the tenancy agreement.

There are exceptions to both of these general rules, so always get legal advice if faced with an eviction order.

Licensees

A licensee is a person who simply has permission to occupy a property, but is not a tenant. She has no right to a fixed rent, and can be speedily evicted. Some landlords have tried to introduce **licences** rather than tenancies because then the Rent Acts don't normally apply. If in doubt, get legal advice as to whether your agreement is in fact a licence.

Council tenants

Your chance of getting a council flat or house varies considerably from area to area: in some places you can wait for literally *years*, but elsewhere the lists are much shorter.

Some local authorities allocate properties on the basis of a simple waiting-list only ('first come, first served'), but it's more common for this to be combined with a **points system**, which takes account of factors such as overcrowding in your present home, lack of facilities (for example, no bathroom), and your age and health.

If you want a council home, first find out what your local authority's allocation policy is, and which factors are taken into account in any points system. You'll then be able to make the most of your application by directing it accordingly. Go to a local housing advice centre or your town hall for more information.

Council tenants' rights

The law is much more straightforward for council tenants: broadly, you have considerable protection against eviction, but little or no protection from rent increases.

The council needs a court order to evict you, and this will only be granted in certain narrowly-defined circumstances: if you have very bad rent arrears, for example. However, your rent can be increased at any time and by any amount. You have no right to a fixed rent, and the only proviso is that the rent must be at a 'reasonable' level.

If you are offered a council home, you will have to accept it on the council's terms. In some places you'll have to sign a formal tenancy agreement; elsewhere you'll just get a rent book. You should find out what the full terms are, though: the council will be responsible for keeping the property in a reasonable state of repair, but you may be responsible for a few minor repairs yourself.

You can take in lodgers without getting permission, but if you want to sublet the property, you'll have to get approval first.

Tenants' associations

There may already be a tenants' association in your area; if so, join it, as it will probably campaign for tenants' rights, and for improvements to the area. If not, consider setting one up yourself– again, a housing advice centre or the council itself will be able to give you more information.

The 'right to buy'

Council tenants have the right to buy their flat or house after they've been living there for 3 years. You'll have to pay the market price less a discount, which varies according to your length of occupation:

- 33% after three years, *plus*
- 1% for every extra year, *to a maximum of*
- 50% (i.e., after 20 years).

However, the discount can't be more than £25,000.

The price will initially be fixed by the council, but you can appeal against this valuation to the **District Valuer**. You must appeal within 3 months.

If you resell the property within 5 years of buying it, you'll have to repay part of the discount to the council:

resale before	*discount repayable*
1 year	100%
2 years	80%
3 years	60%
4 years	40%
5 years	20%

You also have the right to a mortgage from the council. If you are under 60, you will be able to borrow 2½ times your yearly income; if you are aged 60 to 64 you can borrow twice your income; and if you are 65 or over, you can borrow one times your income.

For more information on buying a council home, contact your local authority.

Housing associations

The idea behind these is that a group of people can get together and register as a housing association with a view to building new homes or renovating old ones. They can get grants from the Housing Corporation to finance the building costs – and then let out the homes at **fair rents**. Often they liaise directly with local authorities, and they may agree to make some properties available to people on the council's waiting-list.

Housing association tenants will pay a fair rent, as registered by the Rent Officer – and they can only be evicted in specified circumstances, such as if they are badly behind with the rent.

To find out more about housing associations, go to a housing advice centre – or look in Yellow Pages and contact them direct.

Help with paying your rent

If you are finding it hard to pay your rent out of your income, you may qualify for a rent allowance or rent rebate. You may also be able to get help with paying your rates. Many people who do not qualify for other social security benefits are entitled to these **housing benefits**. See page 56 for details.

7

Buying and Selling a Home

Why buy? The main advantages are:

- your money is buying you a tangible asset – which you can sell and turn into cash if necessary.
- as house prices rise, so does the value of your investment.
- the Government pays part of your mortgage interest by giving you tax relief (see page 99).

If you rent, your money goes straight into the landlord's pocket, and at the end of the day you've got nothing to show for it. There's no tax relief on rent, either – though it's usually cheaper than paying off a mortgage.

If you can afford it, however, buying your own home can be a very wise investment – so the first thing to look at is how much it will cost.

House prices

These vary considerably from area to area: in London, for example, a house can cost at least twice as much as a similar property in the north of England or in Wales. There are also variations *within* an area, depending on the type of property, its condition, the immediate neighbourhood, and so on. The first step is to decide what type of home and area you are interested in, and then either buy a local newspaper and check out the property columns, or else contact a few local estate agents and ask them to send you some particulars.

Whether or not you can afford the home of your dreams depends on how much you have in savings (to put down as a deposit), and what size mortgage you can take out. There might also be some profits from selling your present home – though don't forget to take account of fees to estate agents and solicitors.

Getting a mortgage

How much you can borrow

This depends on two factors: your income, and the value of the property you want to buy. Most building societies and banks will lend you 2½ to 3 times your yearly income – so if you earn £8,000, you could expect to borrow £20,000 to £24,000. If you want to buy jointly with someone else, you can probably borrow 2½ to 3 times the main income, plus one times the lower income – and note that these days lenders are quite happy to give loans to unmarried couples.

Normally, however, you will also be restricted to a percentage (say, 80%) of the value of the property – so if it's valued at £25,000, you may be able to borrow only £20,000. You'll have to pay the remaining £5,000 yourself, as a deposit. Yet in the last few years there has been a trend towards granting higher percentage loans – you may even be able to get a 100% mortgage – but in this case you will probably have to take out a **mortgage guarantee policy**. This is an insurance policy which covers the top 20% cent or so of the loan, and you usually pay for it with a single premium at the start of the mortgage.

Choosing a lender

Building societies are the main source of mortgage finance, followed by the banks – and if you work for one of these (or for an insurance company), your first port of call should be your employer, as you may qualify for a cheap mortgage. In fact, *whoever* you work for, it's worth asking whether they'll offer you a cheap loan to buy your own home. If not, it's a matter of shopping around for the best deal.

If there's a shortage of mortgage-funding, you'll probably have to accept whatever you can get, but when finance is readily available there should be quite a lot of choice. You need to consider:

- the **interest rate** on the mortgage loan. Both banks and building societies now have to quote the 'annual percentage rate' (APR – see page 44), so it's a lot easier for you to make comparisons
- the **size** of the loan – how much the lender is prepared to let you borrow
- the **period** of the loan – perhaps 20 or 25 years
- **how long** you have to wait to hear whether or not your mortgage application has been accepted (important if you want to buy in a hurry) – and whether you have to pay an arrangement fee
- how much choice you have over which company **insures** your home (some building societies charge you extra if you don't use a company they recommend)
- the **type** of mortgage you are offered – see below.

What to do if you can't get a mortgage

If a bank or a building society is unhappy about lending on the property, ask yourself whether it's really wise to take it on. It may have serious structural defects, which could cost a lot to put right. If they are unhappy about lending to *you*, it's probably because they think you'll have a struggle to meet the repayments. Sit down and go through your finances carefully: as a very rough rule of thumb, the monthly payments shouldn't be more than your before-tax *weekly* income. Make sure, though, that you've told the lender about any overtime payments, bonuses, etc., that you get regularly. If the answer is still no, you would do best to wait until you get a rise, or until you can put down a bigger deposit – because the alternatives to building societies and banks are likely to be even more expensive.

However, if you can't get a mortgage simply because there's a shortage of funds at the time, try the following:

- **insurance companies** may be able to help by arranging a mortgage for you. You will nearly always have to buy one of their endowment policies (see below) – and you may have to pay a higher-than-normal interest rate.

• **finance houses** Again, they may insist on an endowment mortgage – and, again, interest rates are likely to be high.

• **mortgage brokers** may be able to arrange a repayment mortgage for you – at a price. If they arrange an endowment mortgage, though, you shouldn't be charged, because they'll get commission from the insurance company.

• **asking around** Your estate agent, solicitor, or even the builder may have contacts with a building society.

With all of these, think very carefully about taking on a mortgage that is more expensive than normal, because it's difficult to switch to a cheaper one in later years.

Homeloan scheme

Under this scheme, first-time buyers may qualify for a tax-free grant of £110, and a £600 loan which is interest-free for the first 5 years. To qualify you must have registered *and* saved with a bank, building society, or other institution in the scheme for at least 2 years.

To get the maximum £110 grant, you must have at least £1,000 in your savings account for the year before you apply (if your balance is lower than this, you may get a reduced amount). To qualify for the loan, you must have at least £600 in your account when you apply. For more details, contact the Department of the Environment, Room N11/21, 2 Marsham Street, London SW1P 3EB.

The different types of mortgage

There are two main kinds of mortgage: repayment and endowment.

A **repayment mortgage** is a loan to be paid off in monthly instalments, often over a period of 20 or 25 years. Part of each instalment is interest on the amount you still owe, and part goes towards paying off the loan itself. With a *level* repayment mortgage, the instalments are the same every month (unless interest rates change); with an *increasing* repayment mortgage, the instalments are cheaper in the early years, and then rise later on. Remember, though, that inflation is likely to erode the real cost of the repayments over the years.

An **endowment mortgage** is a loan linked to an insurance policy. Both the loan and the policy last for the same set period – again, often 20 or 25 years. Every month you pay interest on the full amount of the loan, but you don't pay off any of the loan itself. You also pay a premium on the insurance policy, which provides life cover *and* a sum of money at the end of the set period – see page 215 for more details. At the end of the period the policy 'matures', and you get a sum of money which should be enough to pay off the loan in full *and*, usually, leave some over for you.

There are three types of endowment mortgages:

- **non-profit** These only pay off the loan, and don't leave any money over for you.
- **with-profits** These should leave you with a large cash sum, but are very expensive.
- **low-cost** These should leave you with a smaller cash sum, but are much cheaper – if you want an endowment mortgage, this is the type to choose.

You can also get **low-start low-cost** endowment mortgages, where the payments are lower to begin with, and then increase over the years.

PROS AND CONS

Repayment mortgage	*Endowment mortgage*
If the interest rate when you take out the mortgage is less than around 10%, the monthly cost may be slightly higher than for a low-cost endowment mortgage. But if interest rates rise, the monthly cost will not go up so much as with an endowment mortgage	The monthly cost goes up and down more, as interest rates change – it is lower when rates are low, but higher when they are high. Endowment mortgages cost more than repayment ones when the interest rate is above 10% or so
If you have problems meeting the repayments (e.g., because	If you have problems meeting the repayments, there is little

Repayment mortgage	*Endowment mortgage*
the interest rate goes up or your circumstances change) the lender may agree to extend the term of the loan or let you pay interest only for a while (this is useful because if you get supplementary benefit the interest will be paid by the DHSS)	that can be done. Supplementary benefit will cover the interest payments but you will have to continue paying the insurance policy premiums. The only way out is to ask the lender if you can convert to a repayment mortgage. In the early years this would mean poor value from the endowment policy
Life insurance cover is not built-in, but you can arrange it at a small extra cost	You get built-in life insurance
There's more flexibility if you want to move and take out a new mortgage or increase your mortgage	Less flexibility in these circumstances
You don't get a cash sum at the end of the mortgage	Except with a non-profit policy, you are likely to get a cash sum at the end of mortgage

WHICH IS BEST?

A repayment mortgage is likely to be cheaper although, of course, there's no cash sum at the end. Don't be dazzled by promises of huge pay-outs on endowment mortgages, though – for a start, there's no *guarantee* that you'll get a large sum, and even if you do, it's likely to be worth a lot less in 25 years' time, because of the effects of inflation. Unless you're fairly well off, and pay tax at higher rates, a repayment mortgage is likely to be best for you.

Other types of mortgage

- **pension mortgages** for company directors and the self-employed, or people who are employed but not in a company pension scheme. You pay interest on the full amount of the loan for the whole period, plus contributions to a personal pension plan. At the end of the period the plan provides enough money for you to pay off the loan *and* retire and get a pension.

These mortgages are worth considering if you need a pension anyway, and can work out relatively inexpensive for higher-rate taxpayers. They're not very flexible, however (for example, if interest rates rise, you have to increase your payments). And you should make sure the remaining pension will be sufficient for your needs. Consult an accountant if you're thinking about taking one out.

- **unit-linked** endowment policies and pension plans to link to your mortgage. Your premiums buy units in an investment fund, plus some life insurance. At the end of the mortgage the units are cashed in and the money used to repay the loan. However, the units can fall as well as rise in value – so there's no guarantee of how much money you'll get.

- **index-linked** mortgages. These are supposed to be good for first-time buyers who may be short of money – because the interest rate is very low to begin with. With most schemes, though, the interest is linked to the rate of inflation, so your payments may rise very steeply.

Tax relief

You get tax relief on the interest you pay on a mortgage for your 'principal home' (your only or main home) – up to a limit. The first £30,000 of loans qualifies for tax relief (and that includes any other loans you may have for buying or improving your principal home). If you have a £28,000 mortgage and a £4,000 bank loan for home improvements, say, you won't get tax relief on the £2,000 excess.

If you are married and living with your husband, your joint limit for tax relief is still £30,000, not £60,000. If you're buying a property with anyone other than your husband, however, you can get relief on up to £30,000 *each*.

Most people get their tax relief by making lower interest payments to the lender, and the Government makes up the difference. For example, if the interest rate is 10%, you are only charged 7.1% and the Government pays the remaining 2.9%. This system is called **MIRAS (Mortgage Interest Relief At Source)**. A few borrowers aren't yet in the MIRAS system, so they have to pay the full amount of interest to the lender, and then get all their tax relief through **PAYE (Pay-As-You-Earn)** or a lower tax bill.

The government subsidy is equivalent to giving you tax relief at the basic rate of tax (29%), but you get the subsidy even if your income is not high enough to pay any tax. If you are a higher-rate taxpayer (or would be, if it were not for the mortgage), you get the extra relief through the PAYE system or by getting a lower tax bill.

Buying your home – step-by-step

Step 1: **plan ahead** If you think you might want a mortgage in the future, start saving with a building society (or open a bank account) right away. Whenever there's a shortage of funds, lenders look more favourably at their existing customers – also, the money you save will be needed as a deposit and for all the fees you'll have to pay. If you're a first-time buyer, don't forget to register your savings with the Government's **Homeloan Scheme** – see page 96. You might also consider increasing your chances of a mortgage by saving with more than one society or bank.

Step 2: **talk to your lender** Tell the building society or bank manager that you are planning to buy a home, and ask them how much you can borrow – based both on your income and the sort of property you are after. Find out whether there are any restrictions or waiting-lists, what costs you'll have to pay, what sort of mortgage they'd recommend, and what the interest rate is.

Step 3: **house-hunting** Register with estate agents and property shops, scour the local newspapers, and search the area yourself. As soon as you find a property which seems promising, make an appointment to view it – but be prepared to be disappointed. Sometimes you'll be hard-pressed to believe that those particulars referred to *that* house (the 'third bedroom' is really a broom cupboard, the 'period detail' is just a bit of old woodworm, and so on).

Make a list of all the things you want to check on (location, condition, room sizes, etc.) – and take pen, paper and measuring rule with you. View as many properties as you can: eventually you'll find the one you want.

Step 4: **make an offer** Do this as soon as you've made up your mind, either direct to the seller or through their estate agent. Make your offer 'subject to contract and to survey', which means that you're covered if you decide not to go ahead; and don't be afraid of offering less than the asking price, as many sellers will be prepared to drop.

If your offer is accepted, the estate agent will ask you for an 'initial deposit'; don't pay more than £100 or so, and get a receipt, again saying that the payment is subject to contract and survey. Then if anything goes wrong, it must be returned to you in full.

Step 5: **arrange a mortgage** Go back to your lender and ask for a mortgage application form. He may fill it in with you there and then, so take with you details of the property and of your finances (including a payslip as proof of your earnings).

If your application is accepted, you'll have to pay for the lender to carry out a valuation of the property; the fee normally depends on the purchase price, but will probably be between £35 and £100. The valuation is to assess whether the condition and value of the property is adequate security for the loan you want.

You'll also have to pay for the lender's solicitor to prepare the mortgage contract for you – but not until later (see Step 6).

Step 6: **conveyancing** This is the legal work involved in transferring the ownership of the property to you. It's possible to do the conveyancing yourself: it can take a lot of time, but also save you a lot of money. The Consumers' Association publishes a guide for do-it-yourself conveyancers; see page 342 for the address. However, if there's anything at all complicated about the property – if it's a leasehold flat, for example, or if it's not wholly occupied by the seller – it's best to use a solicitor or a firm of conveyancers.

If you've used a solicitor in the past, you could start by asking to be put in touch with a member of the firm who is experienced in conveyancing. Alternatively, ask your friends, family, bank or building society manager, estate agent, etc., for a solicitor they can recommend – or the local library or Citizens Advice Bureau (CAB) should have a list of firms in your area. If possible, arrange for the same solicitor to do both your conveyancing *and* the preparation of your contract with the lender, as this can save you money.

You can get a list of conveyancers from the National Association of Conveyancers (2–4 Chichester Rents, Chancery Lane, London WC2A 1EJ). This is usually cheaper than using a firm of solicitors, but some of the saving will be cancelled out by the higher fee to the lender's solicitor (for preparing your mortgage contract).

Whichever you choose, try to find out in advance how much the fee is likely to be – it depends on many factors, but will probably be in the region of ½ to 1% of the value of the property.

If you are married, you should certainly make sure that your home (and your mortgage) are not in your husband's name alone. However much or little you have put into buying the property, joint names give you greater security. If you are buying a home jointly with someone who is not your husband, you should make sure it is in joint names if you are contributing to the cost. In England and Wales, there are two ways in which you can own a property jointly: as **joint tenants**, and as **tenants-in-common** – see page 147 for what difference it makes and tell your solicitor which you want.

Step 7: **a survey?** The valuation which the lender arranges is *not* a full structural survey, so if you want to make sure that the property has no serious defects, you'll have to pay extra for a survey. (The lender may even insist on this.) Again, ask around for a recommended surveyor – or your solicitor or conveyancer may be able to advise you.

Give the surveyor as much information about the house as you can – particularly details about any defects you noticed. And, again, find out what the fee is likely to be; it usually depends on how long it takes to look at the property and write the report, so you can cut the cost if you'll accept a verbal (rather than written) report.

Step 8: **stamp duty – and how to avoid it** You don't have to pay stamp duty on homes costing £30,000 or less – but above this figure, the duty is payable at a rate of 1% of the purchase price of the property. Consequently, if you can get the seller to reduce the price to £30,000 (perhaps by charging separately for any carpets, etc., that they're leaving), you can save yourself £300 or more.

Step 9: **exchange of contracts** This happens after the solicitor or conveyancer has sorted out all the legal aspects, any surveyor's report has been accepted, and the mortgage has been agreed. At this point you'll have to pay a deposit (normally 10% of the price of the property). You may need a **bridging loan** from a bank or finance house for this; you can pay it off once the mortgage comes through. You get tax relief on the interest on a bridging loan up to £30,000 (as long as it is a loan and not an overdraft).

You should take out **house buildings insurance** (see page 125 for more details) on the property from the date contracts are exchanged, as you would still have to buy it for the agreed price even if it burned down beforehand.

Step 10: **moving in** A few weeks after you exchange contracts, 'completion' usually takes place. This is when you pay for your new home in full, and are free to move in. If possible, arrange your own removal – hiring a van and asking friends or family to help is usually a lot cheaper than using a professional firm. If you have to use a firm, however, get quotes from several, as prices can vary enormously.

Make sure your goods are insured while they're being moved. If your current house contents policy does not cover removals you can:

- extend it
- take out a separate 'goods-in-transit' policy
- arrange insurance through the removals firm.

Don't base your decision on which to choose solely on cost – you should find out exactly what you're covered for, and how much of any claim you would have to pay.

Scottish procedures

These are the main differences if you're buying a property in Scotland:

- Solicitors, as well as estate agents, can buy and sell property for clients.
- There is very little leasehold property – most flats and houses are owned on **feus**, which is not the same as freehold. The main distinguishing feature of a 'feu' is that the original developer of the land can impose conditions on its future use – although it's possible to apply to the Lands Tribunal (1 Grosvenor Crescent, Edinburgh EH12 5ER) to alter the feuing conditions.
- if you want a survey, you usually have to arrange this *before* you make an offer.

• your offer is usually made through your solicitor in a formal letter. This is a very detailed document which even includes the date you want to move in!

• if your offer is accepted in writing, the contract is then legally binding.

Selling your home

The first thing to decide is whether to use an estate agent or to sell your home yourself (in Scotland, a solicitor will also act as an estate agent, if required; you should in any case contact a solicitor immediately – see below). An estate agent will do some of the work for you and may bring your home to the notice of a larger number of people, but their charges are generally very high. A good compromise is to try to sell your home yourself first, and then consider using an agent if you do not seem to be having any luck.

Selling the home yourself

The main things you will have to do in the initial stages are:

• **Decide on the asking price** If you live on an estate of similar homes, this will not be difficult; if your home is more unusual, it may be harder to value. You can ask a surveyor for a professional valuation (costing perhaps £25) or, if you have not yet decided whether to use an estate agent, you can ask one or two to call to assess the value of your home. Agents have to tell you beforehand if they intend to charge you for this.

• **Decide what is included in the sale** and make a definite list. You must include permanent fixtures, and you may decide to include things like fitted carpets, curtains and light fittings in the price. But it is often better to offer these for sale separately. Make a separate list of things you are selling separately, and fix prices for those, too.

• **Consider getting a cheap survey done** Some firms of surveyors offer a fixed-price survey of all the main structural aspects of your home, after which they give you a brief written report. This may cost the best part of £100 but will be a lot cheaper than using an estate agent to sell your home, and if the report is favourable it will impress potential buyers. If the report points out things that need doing, either get them done or find out what they will cost and be prepared to offer a 'reduction' to potential buyers.

- **Write an accurate description of your home**, get it typed and some copies run off. This will not only look more professional, but will save potential buyers the bother of measuring up rooms and, very important, will give them something to look at at home. You must be truthful, though you can leave out the less attractive aspects of your home. Include a photograph and plan if you think these would be helpful.

- **Advertise your home** Again, it may be sensible to start with a small advertisement in the local press, and work up to small ads in national newspapers and large advertisements in local papers. Do not forget your humble local store or post office – an advertisement there, complete with a colour photograph, may only cost a few pence a week. It may be a good idea to make a 'For Sale' board and put it up outside. If you want people to make appointments, put your phone number on it and write *viewing by appointment only*, though you will always get some people who just turn up.

Using an estate agent

Estate agents will tell you what price they think you should ask for your home, measure it up, write a description and duplicate it, send particulars to people who ask for them (though they may only send out lists of addresses and prices), put up a 'For Sale' board, display a photograph of your home in their offices, advertise it in local papers, tell enquirers something about it (though often nothing more than is written in the particulars) and arrange for people to come and look at your home. Do not assume that the agents will necessarily do any more than this, and if you want them to do anything extra (e.g., handle all the negotiations) make it clear when engaging them.

Most agents charge a percentage of the price you finally sell your home for, usually between 1½ and 2½% plus VAT. On a £50,000 house this would mean a bill of between £862 and £1,437. Some agents now charge a fixed fee. In addition to these fees the agent may charge extra for taking photographs, putting up a 'For Sale' board, advertising in newspapers, showing people round your home, general expenses, handling negotiations and anything which they do not consider to be part of the normal service. However, agents must tell you about all their charges in advance – if they do not, you do not have to pay them. Newspaper advertising is very expensive, and you should give the agents a limit they are not to exceed without your permission.

Be very careful about the conditions under which you are engaging the agent. There are two things you must be clear about:

- Whether the estate agent wants a **sole agency**. If he does, this means you cannot put your home in the hands of a second agent without the permission of the first. If you did do this and the second agent sells your home, you could be legally obliged to pay commission to *both* agents. If an agent asks for a sole agency, it may be worth agreeing to it for a limited period only, as he may then have a greater incentive to sell your home. If you do not want to give the agent a sole agency, he may demand a higher percentage fee.

- The conditions under which the commission becomes payable. With the best agents, you only have to pay their fee if they introduce the person who ends up buying your home. But some agents use standard letters or contracts through which they get their commission simply by introducing someone who is *ready, willing and able to purchase*, whether or not they end up buying your home. Some are worse still, claiming **sole selling rights** – under which the commission becomes payable if *anyone at all* comes along who is ready, able and willing to buy your home, even if the agent has done nothing at all and even if the person does not buy it. Agents must explain conditions like this to you before you engage them, and if they do not they will have to get a court order to make you pay up. You should avoid such conditions completely if you can – though again, you may have to pay a higher percentage fee.

Having agreed a fee and what your agents will do for it, do not be frightened to make them work for their money. If you have any problems with an estate agent, contact your CAB or Trading Standards Department (see also page 335).

The remaining stages

Once your home is on the market, the main things you will need to do are:

- **Stay at home as much as possible** to answer the telephone and show people round who arrive unexpectedly. Keep the house as tidy as possible, and do not leave anything valuable lying about – people often ask to have a look round on their own after you have shown them round. Before anyone comes, work out what the running costs are – of your central heating, for example. You must answer questions truthfully; if you do not know the answer, say so. But do not believe everything potential buyers tell you – there may be no obligation on them to be truthful.

- **Assess potential buyers** in terms of how easily they could go ahead with the purchase of your home. Do they have a home to sell and, if so, how saleable is it? Have they already got a buyer lined up and, if so, is a long chain involved? Have they got a provisional mortgage offer, and can they afford a big enough mortgage? How soon would they want to move, and how important is it to them that they move by that date?

- **Decide whether to accept any offer you get.** You do not need to say yes or no immediately – you can consider it for a few days. If you have two very keen potential buyers, it may be sensible to go for the one who looks less likely to have problems rather than the one who offers more money. Be wary of offering people first refusal if the purchase falls through – an even better buyer might turn up later.

- **Having accepted an offer,** get it in writing, and if the offer letter does not make clear what is to be included in the sale, put this in your letter of reply and keep two copies (one for your solicitor). Get your buyer's full name and address, and his solicitor's. Ask the buyer for a deposit of perhaps £100 or £250. This will show that they are genuinely interested, though if they back out you will have to repay the deposit in full. Continue to show your home until you exchange contracts if you want to, though you must tell people that you have accepted an offer.

- **Agree provisional dates with the buyer** for exchange of contracts and for completion – when the ownership will be finally transferred. But if you are buying another home, do not exchange contracts on it before you have exchanged contracts on the home you are selling – if you were landed with two homes you could not sell, the cost could ruin you.

• **Give all the details to your solicitors,** and ask them to draw up a draft contract. Ask them what their charges will be.

• **If you have a mortgage,** inform the building society or other lender of the completion date, and ask them to tell you how much money will be needed on that day to redeem the mortgage. Do not delay doing this, as there may be charges if you do not give sufficient notice. In addition to the legal costs, some banks and building societies make a redemption charge of up to 3 months' interest in certain circumstances (it can usually be avoided by applying for another mortgage from the same institution).

• **If you have an endowment mortgage,** and are buying another home, you will have to decide what sort of mortgage you want and what to do with the endowment policy. If the new lender will accept the policy as security, then it is best to keep it going (you get a poor return if you cash it in early). But if the new mortgage is bigger than the old one, you do not have to take out more endowment policies; you can get a repayment loan for the extra.

• **Expect the buyer to have your home surveyed and valued.** Depending on how thorough the survey is, this may take up a whole day and involve lifting carpets or arranging access to the roofspace. If the potential buyer reduces his offer as a result of the survey or for any other reason, there is not much you can do about it.

• **Do not be frightened to keep asking your buyers** about the sale of their own home, their mortgage application, the survey results and so on.

• **If you are buying another home,** it is best if you can arrange the completion of both sale and purchase on the same day, or just one day apart. You will have to move pretty well everything out of your old home the day before completion, as your buyers may arrive early in the morning expecting to move in. If the completion of your sale is even a day later than the completion of your purchase, you will need to ask your bank for a bridging loan to bridge the gap. Make sure the bank opens a separate **loan account** for this, not an overdraft, so that you can get tax relief on the interest (allowable on up to £30,000 for up to a year, in addition to the tax relief you already get on the mortgage on your old home). Do try to avoid your sale being more than a couple of weeks after your purchase – the interest charges quickly mount up.

• **Exchange contracts** with your buyer. This means you are legally obliged to sell to the buyer at the agreed price on the agreed date, and he is legally obliged to buy.

• **Arrange your move** Inform the local council, water, gas, electricity and telephone services of the date you will be moving so that they can read meters and apportion bills. Arrange to take over the telephone and mains supplies in your new home. Check what insurance cover the removal firm has and arrange for extra coverage if necessary. Make arrangements for handing over the keys.

Scottish procedures

In Scotland you will need to inform your solicitor at the outset; this is because the contract to sell and buy is legally binding as soon as you accept an offer in writing. In fact your solicitor can perform much the same role as an estate agent, or you can sell your home yourself. Any survey will be done before an offer is made. You should not agree to sell the home to anyone without first consulting your solicitor, and you should say that all formal written offers are to be put to him.

Afterwards

If you receive a Tax Return from the Inland Revenue, you should enter details of the sale in the section headed *Chargeable assets disposed of*, even though there will not normally be any Capital Gains Tax to pay (see page 138 for the occasions when tax may arise).

8

Running a Home

In this chapter we look at aspects of running a home which concern you whether you rent your home or own it. Points which apply only to tenants or owners are covered in Chapters 6 and 9 respectively.

Home filing

A home filing system does not need to be grand, and need not cost any money at all. It just needs to be organised so that you can find things easily at a later date. It's quite likely that you won't ever need most of the papers you keep but, as one of Murphy's Laws is bound to state, you can be certain that if you throw something away you'll need it next week.

The checklist below suggests a way of organising your papers. All you need for each group is a large used envelope clearly marked, and a cardboard box to keep the envelopes in. To stop your files getting ever fatter, have a yearly clearout. The list also suggests how long to keep things for.

Life insurance policies are valuable documents and it might be worth asking your bank to keep these for you. The same applies to the deeds of your home if you own it and don't have a mortgage (if you've got a mortgage the lender will have the deeds).

In addition to your file of papers, it's also a good idea to keep a list of important numbers (passport numbers, account numbers, insurance policy numbers and so on) and a list of any documents or valuables away from the home (e.g., with your solicitor or bank). Keep this list *away* from the rest of your files so that, if anything happens to your documents (if they are stolen or damaged by fire, say) it will be easier for you to inform people who need to know and to obtain replacements.

The files you're likely to need

Most documents need to be kept as long as they're current (e.g., keep documents about your *current* car, your most recent statements, etc.) unless a longer period is indicated.

Important documents (keep for ever): birth certificates, marriage certificate, divorce papers. Also current wills, passports, National Health cards, driving licence, TV licence, dog licence. Educational certificates (providing evidence of qualifications and experience, references and testimonials).

Home: papers relating to purchase; copy of lease; rental agreement, inventory and record of payments; receipts and certificates for work done, e.g., building work, damp or wood treatment (keep for 7 years after home sold unless given to purchaser); surveyor's report; applications for planning permission; home contents insurance and buildings insurance (policies, endorsements, schedules, renewal confirmation, descriptive leaflet, agreement to pay by instalments, claims correspondence).

Mortgage: copy of agreement, mortgage conditions, valuer's report, copy of endowment policy or mortgage protection policy, mortgage statements, documents concerning further advance, home buildings insurance (if paid through lender).

Life insurance, health insurance, accident insurance: policies, descriptive literature, renewal certificates, correspondence.

Investments: details of building society and bank investments and deposit accounts, passbooks, statements, National Savings Certificates, Premium Bonds, unit trust holdings, share certificates and contract notes, tax vouchers and tax credits, Government Stock certificates, correspondence with stockbroker or investment adviser.

Pensions: details of schemes you have belonged to and the pensions, life insurance benefits and widow's benefits you are entitled to from each. Details of any contributions refunded.

Papers relating to your National Insurance record and contributions to state pension schemes. Policies for any personal pension plans.

Benefits: copies of forms and leaflets for any benefits you claim – e.g., unemployment benefit, supplementary benefit, family income supplement, rate rebate.

Work: contract of employment and conditions of service for current job. Details of any loans from employer (e.g., car, typewriter, money for season ticket). Papers relating to any appraisal of your work, disciplinary action or industrial tribunal. Details of current pension scheme and entitlement. Trade union membership card and benefit details. Payslips for this year and last year. P.60 forms for the last 7 years. Leaving agreements from previous jobs.

Tax: copies of Tax Returns, correspondence, records of expenses claimed and other relevant papers for the last 7 tax years. List of major things you have given away over the last 7 years (for Inheritance Tax purposes).

Car: receipt for payment and warranty; vehicle registration document; current MoT certificate; insurance policy with endorsements and certificate; correspondence on accidents and insurance claims (keep for 3 years); bills for servicing and repairs.

Receipts for things you've bought, guarantees and instruction books (useful if you want to sell things).

Bills: gas, electricity, coal, oil and telephone bills (keep for 1 year); current year's rates and water rates bills and instalment records (but a record of rates payments should really be kept for 20 years); budget accounts: original agreement and current year's statements and correspondence.

Bank account statements and cheque stubs (keep for 1 year); recent correspondence, original agreement, overdraft and loan agreements, leaflets on charges and use of cashcard.

Credit card statements (keep for 2 years); receipt slips and credit slips (keep until checked against statements); leaflets describing facilities, charges, where you can get cash, etc.

Loans, HP and rental agreements: copies of agreements, statements, correspondence.

Children: immunisation records (keep for ever); savings details and passbooks; school reports, details of choice of schools, school organisation and policies, choice of subjects studied; grant applications and details.

Rates

Rates are a tax collected by local authorities from people who occupy homes, offices, shops, factories and so on. The money pays for about a third of local authority services (schools, council houses, roads, police, fire service, libraries, etc). Councils get the rest of their money from central Government funds – raised mainly from other taxes like income tax and VAT.

The amount you have to pay depends on the **rateable value** of your home and the **rate-in-the-pound** in your area. The rate-in-the-pound is set each year by local councils in order to collect the money they need, after taking into account the amount they will receive from the Government. The rateable value of your home will depend very much on how large it is and where it is. The value is set by the Inland Revenue when a home is built, but is revised when there is a Revaluation Year (1973 was the last in England and Wales, 1978 in Scotland). If you improve your home the rateable value may be increased, though repairs and minor improvements won't affect it, nor, in England or Wales, will installing central heating. If you think your rateable value is too high you can appeal against it (see page 115).

Your rates bill is one you should *not* refuse to pay, however good your reasons, as it's a simple matter for your council to get a warrant to send the bailiffs round and sell your furniture to pay the bill.

Paying rates by instalments

The rates bill you get each April gives you three ways to pay. You can pay the full amount in April, or half in April and half in October, or in monthly instalments, usually starting on 1st May. Unless your council gives a small discount for paying promptly, the cost is the same whichever way you pay. It's well worth paying in instalments, as you're effectively getting interest-free credit. Because of this, *never* pay rates with a credit card or any other sort of borrowed money.

Water rates

Like local authority rates, water and sewerage charges are normally based on your rateable value (unless you have a water meter, in which case the water part of your bill is based on the meter reading). In England and Wales you are sent a bill by your water authority, of which you have to pay half in April and half in October (though some authorities let you pay in instalments, usually at an extra charge). In Scotland, water rates are combined with general rates, so you can pay the whole lot in instalments at no extra cost.

If the rateable value of your home is very high and your water consumption is quite low (for example, if you live alone in a very spacious house) it may be worth your while having a water meter installed, as this could reduce your future bills. In most other cases it's unlikely to be worth changing over.

Many water authorities now charge extra if you want to use a hose or sprinkler in the garden. You could be fined if you're found using a hose without a special permit.

Rate rebates

After your mortgage or rent, your rates are likely to be your largest monthly payment. So a rate rebate (now part of **housing benefits**) is one of the most valuable benefits you can get from the state. If you are entitled to a rebate, the council will reduce your monthly instalments or, if you have already paid your rates, you'll get a refund. If you continue to qualify in future years, your rates bill will be reduced. If you get supplementary benefit the rules are different – see pages 56–7.

The amount of rebate you get depends on your income, the composition of your household and the amount of your rates. The income limit may be quite high. For example, in 1985–86 a single parent with two children and a rates bill of £500 a year is entitled to a rebate if she earns less than £8,350 a year.

If you think you may qualify, get the leaflet *Who pays less rent and rates?* and an application form from your council offices or Citizens Advice Bureau (CAB). The rules are complicated and it's hard to work out exactly if you qualify, so apply anyway – the council will tell you if you don't. Rebates can't normally be backdated, so don't delay. You'll have to give details of your income (including earnings, pensions, investment income, social security benefits and maintenance), and of the people who live with you. If you have any problems completing the form, ask at your CAB for help.

If you're getting a rebate and your circumstances change in any way which could affect your entitlement you should let your council know. After some months your rebate will end and you will need to apply for a continuation – you should do this within one month.

Getting your rateable value reduced

If you can get your rateable value reduced, your rates bill will be reduced, too. The saving is unlikely to be great, however – £10 to £30 a year – though you could be lucky and get a much larger reduction.

In England or Wales, to get your rateable value reduced you'll have to provide evidence *either* that something has happened since the rateable value was set to make your home worth less to the people living in it; *or* that the rateable value is high in comparison with other similar homes in the area. In Scotland, you can only apply soon after your home's rateable value has been set, unless your surroundings have subsequently changed or another home's rateable value has been reduced for a reason that also applies to yours. If you think you may have a case, call in and discuss it with your local **Valuation Officer** (**Assessor** in Scotland) – listed in the phone book under *Inland Revenue – Valuation Office*. Ask for a proposal form on which to apply, fill this in and return it.

If you hear nothing within three months, your proposal has been accepted. But it's more likely the Valuation Officer will make an objection. This means that you and he will eventually have to present your case in a **Local Valuation Court** – in fact, a fairly informal procedure. The Valuation Officer is likely to contact you shortly before the hearing to discuss the matter, and he may offer you a reduction. If you accept, the court hearing will be cancelled.

Getting a lower valuation won't cost you anything, but can take a long time and mean quite a lot of work for a small reward. If you are prepared for this, the Consumers' Association publishes a *Rates Kit* with detailed information and guidance (address on page 342).

Rate relief for disabled people

If someone in your household is disabled, and your home has extra space or special features to help you cope, you can apply for a reduction in your rates. For example, a disabled person may need an extra room, central heating, a lift or escalator, a downstairs or specially adapted bathroom or toilet, space to allow a wheelchair, or a garage or carport. It doesn't matter whether you had these features added to your home, or if you moved to the home because it had the special features. Nor does the disabled person need to be registered as disabled with the local authority to qualify for reduced rates.

If you think you may do so, ask your local council for the leaflet *Rate relief for disabled persons* and an application form. If your claim is successful, the rateable value of your home will be reduced by the value of the special features for the disabled person. If you've already paid your rates for the year, you'll get a refund, while in future years your rates bill will automatically be reduced. The relief can be backdated to the beginning of April if you've been eligible for that long.

Insuring the contents of your home

The insurance we're talking about here covers all the things in your home, garage or outbuildings – e.g., your furniture, carpets, clothes, books, jewellery – against being destroyed or damaged by fire, storm or flood, removed or damaged by burglars or intruders, and against damage from certain other causes. This type of insurance is essential whether you own or rent your home, as the risk of losing all or most of your belongings is too high for almost anyone to accept. It does *not* cover replacing things which have worn out or the repair of things which have broken down; for these you'll need a **service agreement** (see page 40).

There are around eighty insurance companies offering **home contents insurance**, and many offer several different levels of cover at different prices. Some companies only deal through insurance brokers (who often have a shop in the High Street) while others will deal direct with you (from their area office) or through their own agents (who work from home). You may find your bank or building society will offer to arrange this insurance for you. If you belong to a trade union or professional association, it may have an arrangement for you to get a discount with a certain company (a few big unions have their own insurance companies). But charges for home contents insurance vary enormously, especially if you live in a major city, and these special arrangements may not provide the best cover for you at the cheapest price. It's definitely worth looking at the latest report in *Which?* at your local library to compare charges. You might find an equally good company which offers wider cover than you get now for less than half the price.

Most companies publish leaflets describing what their policies offer, and it's worth obtaining these for the companies you are interested in. But it's not always easy to make comparisons as different companies may use different terms for the same thing, and there may be a number of small differences between policies which aren't mentioned in these brochures. Each company has its own system for dividing the country into areas, and you may find that something one company includes in its policy costs extra with another company. So use the following sections to help you decide on the cover you need.

What items are covered

Home contents insurance covers almost everything that you and the members of your family normally keep in your home, garage, outbuildings, garden shed and so on. It includes most things you rent but not things that are permanently fixed in the home and which you'd expect to leave behind if you missed, like fitted kitchen units (these are covered by a **home buildings policy** – see page 125). Nor does it cover cars, trailers, caravans, boats, aircraft, pets or other animals, documents, certificates or manuscripts. And money, vouchers, tickets, stamps, travellers' cheques, postal orders and so on are only covered up to a certain amount, usually between £50 and £250.

Valuable items

Most companies count items which have a lot of value tied up in a small space (like jewellery or anything made with gemstones or precious metal, furs, works of art, collections and collectors' pieces) as **high-risk** items. They will get the same cover as everything else in your home, but only up to certain limits. For example, your policy may say that the company won't pay out more than 1/20 of the amount for which you are insured to replace one of these, and that it won't pay out more than 1/3 of the total amount you're insured for to replace them all. If you want more cover than this for your valuables you must inform the company and be prepared to pay an extra premium.

In what circumstances can you claim?

This depends on *what caused* the loss or damage. Most home contents policies list all the causes of damage they cover. The usual ones are:

- theft, and damage by thieves (though if you let or sublet part of your home or have a lodger you may only get this cover if there are signs of a break-in)
- fire, explosion, lightning and earthquake
- storm and flood
- water or oil escaping from central heating systems or plumbed-in washing machines (NB: the repairs to the system are *not* normally covered, only the damage caused by the water or oil)
- riots, disturbances and vandalism (not covered in Northern Ireland)
- being hit by a vehicle, aircraft, train, animal, falling aerial or tree (unless it's being cut down at the time)
- subsidence, heave and landslip.

In addition, three items in the home – televisions, mirrors and glass in furniture – are usually covered for *accidental* damage or breakage, i.e., any damage which isn't deliberate apart from breakdown. With some policies this also extends to hi-fi equipment, videos and home computers.

All-risks policies work the other way round – they list all the causes of loss and damage which they *don't* cover; your belongings are covered for loss or damage caused by anything else.

Taking things out of your home

You only get your policy's full cover while your belongings are in your own home. For loss or damage occurring in another building, the most you can claim is usually limited to 15% of the amount you're insured for and you are only covered against theft in the event of a break-in. If your belongings are in a furniture depository, exhibition room, saleroom or outside the UK, they are not covered for theft, storm or flood. There's not usually any cover for items which are out of doors (e.g., in your garden) or being moved from place to place (e.g., in a car), though a few policies cover your belongings while you are moving home.

This means that you should consider taking out additional insurance for such things as cameras, watches, jewellery, money, travellers' cheques, tickets, stamps, vouchers, furs, musical instruments, sports equipment and bicycles. Most home contents insurance policies offer special **all-risks extensions** for the above, covering accidental loss or damage anywhere in the UK, and abroad for specified periods. But 'all-risks' isn't as comprehensive as it sounds; gradual deterioration is never covered, and there may be other exceptions, like theft from an unattended car.

What you get back if you claim

If something is damaged in a way that is covered by your policy and it can be repaired, the insurance company should pay you the cost of getting it repaired. If something is stolen or is damaged beyond repair, what the company pays depends on what type of policy you have:

- With a **new-for-old policy** you get the cost of buying a new item of equivalent quality to the old one, even if yours was quite old and even if the price has gone up since you bought it.
- With an **indemnity policy** (which is cheaper) the company pays you the approximate cost of buying a replacement of similar quality *and* age – see the next section for how this is worked out.
- Some policies offer a mixture of the two – you get new-for-old cover for items of a certain type (e.g., electrical goods) or up to a certain age (e.g., 5 years) and indemnity cover on the rest.

Clothes and linen usually get indemnity cover, whichever type of policy you have. And with some policies (usually cheaper ones), you have to pay part of certain claims (£15, say) – called an **excess**. If the claim is for less than the excess, you get nothing at all.

If you are unable to live in your home as a result of damage which is covered by the policy, you can also claim the cost of having to live somewhere else, usually up to one-tenth of the amount you're insured for. If you rent the home, you can claim instead the rent you pay while you can't live in it.

Working out the indemnity value

The amount the company pays for replacing something (except an antique) which gets indemnity cover is worked out as follows:

- Find out the current price of a replacement of similar quality.
- Multiply by the age of the item in years.
- Divide by the number of years the item could have been expected to last from new.

This gives what the company calls the **deduction for wear and tear**. Subtract this from the current shop price to find the indemnity value.

Insuring for the correct amount

It's important that the amount you're insured for is roughly correct. If it's too high, you are throwing money away. But more often it's too low, which means the insurance company is likely to scale down any claim it pays. For example, if you've insured your contents for £7,500 when they should be insured for £10,000, the company may only pay three-quarters of any claim you make.

The amount you should insure for is the total amount it would cost you to replace the lot. The way this is calculated differs with different types of policy. With most new-for-old policies, it's the current shop price of everything in your home (except things which aren't covered like pets and trailers), less a deduction for wear-and-tear of clothes and linen. With other policies, you'll need to make a deduction for wear-and-tear for all the things (except antiques) that get indemnity cover (see above for how to work this out).

It's not a good idea to just guess at the total shop price of everything in your home as you'll almost certainly underestimate. If you have a fair idea of current prices, go from room to room writing down the prices of all the major items, then add up the totals. Make a list of any you are not sure about and price these when you are next at the shops. Then add on a substantial allowance for all the minor things – rugs, cushions, books, papers, bags, brushes, cutlery, pots, pans, food, tools, and so on. The total you get may well surprise you.

If you decide on a new-for-old policy, you should add on a few per cent to allow for the fact that the shop prices of many things will go up during the year for which you are insuring. This is particularly important when inflation is high. However, many of these policies are now **index-linked**, which means that the amount you're insured for goes up each month in line with an index, though your premium doesn't go up until you renew the policy. If you decide on an index-linked policy, you don't need to add anything yourself for price rises.

Where you live

The home you live in can affect the cover you get and how much it costs:

- If your home has not got brick or stone walls with a slate or tile roof, you may find insurance costs you more – particularly if you live in a half-timbered house or a thatched cottage.

- If you live in a flat with a shared access, your theft cover may be restricted.

- The cost of your insurance can vary greatly according to the area you live in, as the risk of burglary is much greater in inner cities, for example, than country districts. But nearly every company has its own way of dividing up the country. If you live in Norfolk, say, you're likely to find that you're in the lowest price band for almost every company, so the difference in cost between companies won't be great. But if you live in a large city like London, Birmingham, Manchester, Liverpool or Glasgow, you may be in the highest price band for one company but the next-to-lowest for another. This can make the difference in cost between different companies very substantial – over £100 a year. So if you live in a large town it really is worth getting quotes from a number of companies. At the time of writing, companies which could be very cheap for people in high-risk areas included Congregational (tel. 0274 41351), Economic (tel. 0795 24321), Methodist (tel. 061-833 9696), Municipal General (tel. 01-222 8177) and Wesleyan & General (tel. 021-236 7894).

Leaving your home empty

If you're going away and leaving your home unoccupied, check what restrictions your policy imposes. Often you get no cover for theft, malicious damage or escaping water or oil if you leave it empty for more than 30 days. And you may find your company insists you take precautions like turning off the gas or water.

Extras

All policies provide very useful cover for your legal liability to other people in almost any situation. For example, if you cause a road accident as a pedestrian or cyclist, the policy will pay any damages and costs you're legally liable for. It will also cover your liability as occupier of the property (e.g., if your dog savages someone calling at your home) and as employer of domestic staff (e.g., if your cleaner or gardener is injured by something in your home). This cover comes at no extra cost.

Some policies provide a certain amount of cover for the food in a deep-freeze, if it should be spoilt because the freezer breaks down or because of a power cut (unless caused by industrial action). With most other companies you can buy this cover for a few pounds a year.

Some policies add **accidental damage cover** to the normal risks covered. These policies cover damage you cause by accidentally breaking, dropping, scratching, burning or otherwise spoiling anything in your home, except in most cases glassware and china. So you could claim if you spilt paint all over an antique table or your dog ate the carpet. This extra cover adds about a third as much again to the cost of a new-for-old policy, though the cheapest of these policies costs less than the most expensive standard policies.

A few very expensive policies give you **all-risks cover** on everything in your home. So they cover not only accidental damage but also accidental loss both at home and away. This cover is unnecessary for most people; it's nearly always cheaper to insure the things you want to take out of your home on an **all-risks extension** to a standard policy (see above).

Employing people at home

You may need help at home – looking after children or a relative, help with the housework or garden – for a number of reasons, such as being out at work or being unable to do much physical work. As well as advertising locally (local shops are usually cheaper than newspapers), it is also worth asking at your local Jobcentre – they may well have someone on their books who could fit the bill. If you are wanting living-in help you could also advertise more widely – such as in a magazine like *The Lady*.

Generally, if you want someone to work only a few hours a week for a small wage, the arrangement between you can be very informal and no authorities need be involved. But above certain limits a more formal relationship must be established.

If you are wanting someone to work more than 16 hours a week, they will acquire certain rights under the employment laws. For example, with each pay packet you must give them an itemised payslip showing the amount of deductions from their wages. After 4 weeks they have the right to be given a minimum period of notice, and within 13 weeks you must give them a written contract of employment. After 2 years of working for at least 16 hours a week (or 5 years of working for 8 hours a week) the employee becomes entitled to maternity pay and maternity leave, the right to claim unfair dismissal, and to a redundancy payment. (People over pension age do not get all these rights.) Information about your rights at work is set out in the booklet *Individual rights of employees* and in other Department of Employment leaflets which you can obtain free at any Jobcentre.

If you pay your employee more than the National Insurance **Lower Earnings Limit** for the tax year (it is £38 a week in the 1986–87 tax year), you will have to deduct National Insurance contributions from your employee's pay, and pay employer's National Insurance contributions yourself. (It is not worth paying someone just a little more than the Lower Earnings Limit because they will actually end up with less money in their pocket than if you paid them wages just below the limit.) You may also have to deduct income tax under the PAYE system. As soon as you have appointed someone (or as soon as you have agreed to increase an existing employee's wages above this level) you should tell your local DHSS office and also your tax office. They will want to know the employee's name, address, National Insurance number, the date they start work and their rate of pay. They may also ask for information about the person's previous employer. You will be sent deduction cards on which you have to record how much you have paid the person each week or month, and how much tax and National Insurance you have deducted. Sets of tables are provided for working these out, and payment must be made to the Collector of Taxes every three months. If your employee is off work through illness for more than three days you will have to pay statutory sick pay for up to 28 weeks, but you can deduct what you pay from the National Insurance contributions and tax you send to the tax collector. Each April you have to send in the completed deduction cards and an employer's declaration. You will be sent leaflets explaining all these procedures. If you want to see what is involved in advance, ask at your social security office for NP.15, *Employer's guide to National Insurance contributions* and NI.227, *Employer's guide to statutory sick pay* and at your tax office for P.7, *Employer's guide to PAYE.*

9

Owning a Home

In this chapter we cover matters that concern anyone who owns their own home or is buying it with a mortgage. Aspects of running a home that apply to both owners and tenants are covered in Chapter 8.

Insuring your home

Your home is almost certainly your most valuable possession, so insuring it against possible loss or damage is extremely important. Of course, the chance of your home being totally destroyed is fairly low. But the chances of broken windows, decorations ruined by a small fire, damage caused by burst pipes, fences blown over by a gale, roof repairs needed after a storm or cracks in your walls due to subsidence are all much more likely. The bills for repairs of this kind can be very high, so adequate insurance is essential. (You should also, of course, make sure that your possessions in the home are adequately insured – see page 116.)

If you have a mortgage, it is likely that the mortgage company (e.g., the building society or bank) insisted that you insured your home when you bought it. This is because they want to make sure that their stake in your property is protected. The mortgage company may have suggested a particular insurance company (though building societies are now supposed to offer you a choice of at least three companies) and may have arranged the insurance for you. But there may well be other insurance companies which offer wider cover at a lower cost, and it could be worth changing. However, some building societies (not banks) will make a charge of anything up to £25 if you want to insure with a company they do not regularly deal with – and this could take away the benefit of changing.

We list below the main things which your policy should cover. Whether you are choosing a policy for the first time or assessing your current policy, use this as a checklist for comparison. The only place you will find a detailed comparison of all the different policies available, with recommendations, is in *Which?* magazine (available at your local library). This is well worth consulting to find a policy that is good value for money, and to make sure you avoid any companies with a poor rating.

The amount you pay for **buildings insurance** depends on two things – the amount your home is insured for and the insurance company's rate for each £1,000. The rate is generally around £1.60, so if your home is insured for £50,000 you will pay around 50 × £1.60 = £80 for a year's insurance. If you can find a satisfactory company offering all the cover you require for £1.30 for each £1,000, you would save around £15 a year. The amount you are insured for should be the total cost of rebuilding the house from scratch. This may have been estimated by your mortgage company's surveyor when you bought the home. As building costs are going up all the time, the amount you are insured for should also be increased from time to time. Many policies are now **index-linked**, which means the amount you are insured for (and your premium) goes up automatically each year in line with rebuilding costs.

In some circumstances, you may find you have to pay more than the normal rates for your insurance. This is most likely if:

- the roof of your home is not slates, tiles, concrete or asphalt – e.g., if it is thatched

- the walls of your home are not built of brick, stone or concrete – e.g., if they are timber (but most modern timber-frame homes don't cost any more to insure)

- your home is very large

- you use part of your home for your business

- the insurance company considers you a higher-than-normal risk because of your occupation – e.g., if you are a professional entertainer, a market trader or a journalist.

Checking what the policy covers

It is not just the structure of your home that is covered by house buildings insurance. It also covers things permanently fixed in your home which you would normally leave behind when you move – like kitchen units, baths, basins and fitted furniture (but not fitted carpets). And it covers all the permanent fixtures in your garden – outbuildings, sheds, garages, greenhouses, garden walls, fences, gates, drives, paths, patios and even swimming pools. But you must include the rebuilding cost of all these in the amount you insure for, and you must maintain everything in good condition, as policies do not cover any damage which arises from gradual deterioration. And companies are unlikely to accept that it was a storm that brought your chimney down if the cement holding it together was already crumbling.

Whether or not damage to your home is covered by your insurance depends on what *caused* it. Policies normally list all the causes of damage that they cover. Your policy should cover damage caused by any of the following:

- fire, lightning, explosion or earthquake ('fire' is usually taken to mean flames, so damage caused by smoke on its own may not be covered unless the policy specifically says so)

- storm, flood and possibly frost

- subsidence, heave or landslip of the ground under your home (but not natural settlement or coastal erosion, and you are not normally covered during structural alterations or repairs to your home)

- impact by vehicles, animals, trains, aircraft and things falling from them

- impact by falling trees and branches (unless you are cutting them back or down at the time) and television aerials

- water or heating oil leaking from plumbing and heating systems, radiators, washing machines, etc.

• theft, attempted theft, damage done by thieves and malicious damage

• riots, strikes and political disturbances (except in Northern Ireland).

Not all these things may matter to you. For example, it will not matter if your policy does not include impact by trains if you live several miles from the nearest railway line.

A few things in your home are covered for accidental damage. These are the glass in windows, doors and greenhouses, sanitary fittings (baths, basins, lavatories, etc.), and underground pipes and cables. So if your children kick a ball through the window or you put your spade through your water main, you can claim for the cost of the repairs.

There are some extras included in most policies:

• If your home is too seriously damaged to live in by one of the causes listed in the policy, the insurance company will pay the cost of you living somewhere else while it is being repaired, up to a maximum of 10% or 20% of the amount you are insured for. This is quite valuable cover – make sure you have it.

• Architect's, surveyor's and legal fees incurred in rebuilding or repairing the home.

• Your legal liability as owner of the property and as owner of *previous* homes you have owned (you can be liable for injury or damage if it is due to faulty work carried out while you lived there).

Damage due to poor construction, materials or workmanship is not covered by insurance. But if your home is less than ten years old and was built by a builder registered with the National House-Building Council, you can claim under their protection scheme.

Types of policy

Most policies are the **new-for-old** type, meaning that if your ten-year-old kitchen units, say, are badly damaged by fire, the company will pay for replacing them with new ones. Some cheaper policies are of the **indemnity** type. With these, the company may not pay out the full cost of repairs, because it will allow for the condition things were in before the damage occurred. This is unlikely to make any difference if a wall needs rebuilding, say, but it means you would not get the full cost paid of replacing things like fitted furniture which was not new at the time of the damage. So it is wise to go for a new-for-old policy.

Some policies (normally more expensive ones) include **accidental damage** cover. This would cover things like replacing a fireplace cracked by dropping a heavy ashtray, redecoration after spilling a drink or paint over the wallpaper, repairing the ceiling after putting your foot through it while working in the loft. **All-risks** policies are similar but are worded differently – they cover you for anything at all *except* the things listed in the policy.

With most policies you are insured for the full amount for the whole time so if your home happened to be burned down twice in a year the company would pay up twice. But a few policies say that the total the company will pay in a year will not be more than the amount you are insured for. If your policy says this, we recommend that you change – it should not cost you any more.

Many insurance companies offer a combined policy covering both the buildings and the contents of your home. It is up to you whether you insure both with the same company – you are seldom offered any discount for doing so. Some building societies offer combined policies where the amount of cover you get for your *contents* is a fixed proportion (perhaps half) of the cover you get for the buildings. Before accepting one of these policies, you should check that the contents cover is sufficient and that it is not going to cost you more than having a separate policy for the contents.

Many policies say that the company will deduct an **excess** of around £15 from certain claims. This keeps down their costs, as it prevents a large number of very small claims. You can often pay a bit extra to have these excesses removed. All policies have much larger excesses on claims for damage caused by subsidence – usually around £500. Subsidence damage can be very expensive to repair, often running into tens of thousands of pounds, so it is likely that the insurance company will hold a thorough investigation before it decides to pay up.

Checking the amount you are insured for

It is important to check that the amount you are insured for is roughly correct. If it is too low, the insurance company may refuse to pay any claim you make in full. If it is too high, you are paying more than you need to.

The amount to insure for should be the total it would cost to rebuild your home (including plumbing, wiring, fitted furniture and other fixtures) as well as the garage, outbuildings, swimming pool, fences, gates and so on. Do not be surprised if this figure is higher than the whole property is worth – the value of your home is irrelevant. There are four ways you can solve this problem:

- If your home is insured by your building society for the amount the society's valuer suggested when you bought it, and it has been increased each year (e.g., by index-linking) to take account of increases in rebuilding costs, the insurance company should treat you as fully insured even if the figure turns out to be too low. But it may be sensible to check yourself that the figure is roughly correct.

- If your home is less than a hundred years old and is of conventional construction, you can work out the rebuilding cost using a free leaflet, available from Leaflets (H), ABI, Aldermary House, Queen Street, London EC4N 1TU.

- In other cases, you can get round the problem by insuring with TSB (ask at your local branch) or the Northern Star insurance company (tel. 0452 24444). Both offer policies where, instead of you having to say what the rebuilding cost is, the premium you pay is simply based on the size of your home. There is no set limit on the amount you can claim, and there is no danger of the amount the company pays out being reduced because you are under-insured. However, a smaller home may cost more to insure with one of these policies than with a conventional one.

- The final option is to ask a professional to tell you what it would cost to rebuild your home. A surveyor can do this for you, but might charge £100 or more. It would probably be a lot cheaper to ask a local builder – preferably a small firm which builds individual houses, not estates.

Improving your home

There are two main reasons for improving or extending your home:

- to provide additional space or facilities for you and your family

- to add to the value of the home when you come to sell it.

Unfortunately, the second reason on its own is seldom sufficient justification for spending money, though it depends on the current condition of your home and on the area it is in. If your home is below the standard of most of those around it and would fetch less money because of this, you can probably bring its value up to that of the surrounding properties by improving it to a comparable standard. But if your home is already rather smart for the neighbourhood, there is likely to be a limit on how much you can increase its value, however much you spend. If your home is individual, its value will be less determined by others around it.

One of the most valuable improvements is central heating, as it will often increase the value of your home by as much as it costs to instal (though this may not be the case with electric storage radiators). If most of the homes in your area have a garage and yours does not, it is likely to be worth less, but the difference may be less than the cost of building a garage. An extension to the house can be very expensive to have built, and may add only half its cost to the value of the home. Smaller alterations which are much cheaper coupled with redecoration can improve the appearance of your home considerably, and make it more saleable as well as increasing its value. But you are unlikely to get more than half your money back on some of the most widely sold products, like replacement windows and cavity-wall insulation. Expensive luxuries like swimming pools are risky too – the potential running costs may put off a lot of potential purchasers, so may add nothing at all to the value. Of course, any improvement becomes more worthwhile if you reduce the cost by doing a lot of the work yourself – unless you could be earning money at a higher rate by spending your time doing something else.

If the alterations or extensions are fairly major, you will need an architect or builder to help you draw up detailed plans. Discussing your ideas with an architect may be helpful too – they may be able to suggest alternative solutions to the problems you are trying to solve. But architects are not cheap, and there is no reason why you should not draw up your own plans. However, they must be detailed enough to show exactly how the building work will be done, so you will probably have to do quite a bit of research at your library to make sure that what you are proposing conforms to the

Building Regulations. Although the regulations themselves are fairly technical, there are a number of guides and information sheets explaining the requirements more simply. It will almost certainly be worthwhile calling at the building control department of your local authority to discuss your plans with the inspectors there and to get their views on what you are proposing before you submit your plans formally. They will also be able to give you the application forms and instructions for submitting them.

You may also need to apply for **planning permission** if you intend to change the use of any part of your home (e.g., from a garage to a playroom) or extend it more than the permitted amount. Again, you will find the planning officers at your local authority the best people to tell you which aspects of your plans will require permission and how to apply. They will be able to give you a free leaflet, *Planning permission: a guide for householders*. You may also need to contact the highway authority if your plans affect the pavement outside your home or access to the road, and possibly one of the service authorities – gas, electricity, water or drainage. If you live in a conservation area or your home is a listed building, you will need additional consent – the planning department will be able to advise you.

Improvement grants

You may be able to get a grant from your local authority towards the cost of the improvements you want to carry out to your main home or one you let out for other people to live in (but not a holiday home). Grants are intended mainly to help with the cost of bringing older housing up to modern standards. In most cases the grant will provide half the total cost of the improvements, but in certain cases it can be higher, up to a maximum of 90%. As long as you comply with all the conditions, grants do not have to be repaid.

There are four types of grant available. **Intermediate grants** are mandatory – if your home qualifies, the council has to give you the grant. The other grants are at the discretion of your local council – who may simply not have enough money to give you a grant, however worthy your claim:

- **intermediate grants** These are for putting in standard amenities which you do not have already – an inside toilet, bath or shower, sink, washbasin, hot and cold water system. The grant can also cover the cost of repairs and replacements associated with the work. You do not need to instal all these at once. Unless the alterations are to help a disabled person, your home must have been built (or converted into flats) before 1961.

- **improvement grants** These are intended for bringing your whole home up to a good standard, or for converting a house into flats. You may find that, in order to get a grant, you have to do more than you had originally intended because the council may insist that the whole home is brought pretty well up to the standard of a new one. Unless the alterations are to help a disabled person, the home must have been built (or converted into flats) before 1961 and the rateable value must be below a certain limit.

- **repairs grants** These are for homes built before 1919 needing major repairs – like re-roofing or repairs to foundations. They are not given for minor repairs. The rateable value must be below a certain limit.

- **special grants** These are for homes which you let out to more than one household where the tenants share facilities. The grants cover putting in basic amenities (as with Intermediate grants) and means of escape from fire. Special grants are not available in Scotland or Northern Ireland.

Higher-than-normal grants can be paid for a home in particularly bad condition, in a Housing Action Area or general improvement area or occupied by a disabled person. And in Housing Action Areas there are no limits on the rateable value.

Further information is given in the free booklet *Home-improvement grants*, available from council offices, Citizens Advice Bureaux (CABx) and libraries. Your council can supply the application forms and explain what information you need to supply – normally detailed plans and estimates. The fact that a grant has been given before does not prevent you from applying again – though you may get less. It is very important that you do not start any work at all until the grant is approved in writing. You must, of course, also get any necessary planning and building permission. The council will not normally hand over any money until the work is completed to their satisfaction, but may be prepared to pay in stages as the work progresses.

Grants are also available for insulating your loft. These are easy to obtain – ask at your local council or CAB for details.

Raising the money

If you are buying your home with a mortgage, one of the best ways to pay for home improvements is to ask the mortgage company if you can increase the loan (called a **further advance**). This is because the interest rate on mortgages is lower than with most other kinds of loans, and the repayments are lower because they are spread over a longer period. However, there can be a number of costs involved, which could make this way of borrowing more expensive – especially for small amounts. Do ask about the costs in advance. There may be an arrangement fee, a valuation fee and legal fees and the company may charge a higher-than-normal interest rate on the advance. A few will charge a higher rate on the whole loan – so ask in advance what the new repayments will be and compare the extra with the cost of borrowing elsewhere.

If you have a life insurance policy which involves investment (e.g., an endowment policy), you may be able to get a loan from the insurance company. Write to the company and ask how much they would be prepared to lend on the policy. Interest rates are usually quite reasonable, and the monthly cost is kept low because you need only pay interest; the loan is repaid from the policy proceeds when it comes to an end.

There are other alternatives, though they will usually cost more. The most common are a **home improvement loan** or **personal loan** from a bank or a finance company. These may involve granting a second mortgage on your home to the lender. See pages 41–45 for more details.

Whichever way you borrow (except with credit cards and bank overdrafts), you get **tax relief** on the interest you pay on money you borrow to pay for permanent improvements and major repairs like re-roofing (but not minor repairs). But you only get this subsidy if you currently owe less than £30,000 on your mortgage. If the additional loan takes you over the £30,000 limit, you do not get tax relief on the excess. A list of the sort of improvements which will qualify for tax relief is given in Appendix 1 of Inland Revenue leaflet IR.11 (free from tax offices). If you are not sure whether the improvements you want to make will qualify, you can ask your tax office in advance.

Afterwards

Your improved or extended home is likely to cost more to rebuild than it did previously, so you will probably need to write to your insurance company asking them to increase the amount you are insured for. This will, of course, mean higher premiums. Improvements may also mean higher rates to pay.

Letting your home

Before you let out your home or a part of it, you should get permission from the mortgage company if you have a mortgage. You must decide whether you want to let for a fixed period or indefinitely, and whether you want the tenant to be responsible for paying the rates and for carrying out any decoration or maintenance. It would be as well to ask a solicitor about this, particularly if you are going to be away from the home. You can find tenants by advertising in local papers or using an accommodation agency or estate agent. You can ask an estate agent to collect the rent and keep an eye on the property, though do ask them what they will charge – usually a percentage of the rent.

You should always have a written agreement between you and the tenant setting out the rights and obligations of each. The laws governing rented property are not only extremely complex but also different in different parts of the UK, and you would be well advised to ask a solicitor to draw up the agreement. You could otherwise find that your tenants had legal rights which you never intended them to have. In England and Wales you may, however, find the following *Housing Booklets* useful (free from your local council or CAB): *Letting your home or retirement home; Letting rooms in your home; Assured tenancies; Regulated tenancies; Shorthold tenancies; Controlled tenancies; The Rent Acts and you; Service charges in flats; Notice to Quit.*

If the accommodation is furnished, you should draw up an inventory of all the contents and get the tenant to agree it; this helps to avoid any dispute later.

Rent that you receive counts as income and may affect the amount of some social security benefits that you get. You may also be liable for tax on what you get, and may have to pay **Capital Gains Tax** (see page 138) on the home when you eventually sell it –

though under the current rules the amount is likely to be comparatively small.

Income tax on rent

If you (or your husband) get a Tax Return, you have to enter details of any rents that you receive; if you do not, you should write to your tax office at the end of the tax year (i.e., in April) and tell them. You should also tell them about any mortgage or other loan which was used for buying or improving the property, and about the expenses you have incurred (see below). A month or so later you will receive an assessment showing how much tax is payable for the year, and telling you to pay up within 30 days (if you are married, the assessment will probably be addressed to your husband even if it is your home and your income, unless you have asked for **separate assessment** – see page 157). The year's tax will be based on the rental income you received during the tax year, less the loan interest and less the expenditure (details below).

After the first year, you will normally get a Tax Assessment towards the end of each calendar year, asking you to pay a whole year's tax during January (or within 30 days). This is the tax for the period from the last 6 April to the next 5 April. Because this period has not ended, the tax office do not know exactly how much income you will have received or what your expenses will be. They therefore base the assessment on the same amount as in the previous year and adjust it (by sending you a rebate or asking for more) after the end of the tax year. You can, however, ask your Tax Inspector to reduce the assessment if you know that your rental income will be less this year than last, or if your expenses have been higher and it will cause you hardship to pay more tax than will eventually be due.

There are two cases in which your income from letting will be treated differently. If you run a guest house or hotel, or if the accommodation counts as **furnished holiday lettings**, all your income from letting the property will count as income from self-employment. In these cases the rules on page 264 will apply. The income will count as earnings, so if you are married you can claim **Wife's Earned Income Allowance** against them. Accommodation counts as furnished holiday lettings if:

- it is available for letting to the general public for at least 140 days in the year, and is actually let for at least 70 of those days, *and*

- for 7 months of the year, it is not normally let to the same person for more than 31 consecutive days.

In most other cases income from letting counts as investment income. This is not particularly significant unless you are married, in which case it means that you cannot deduct your Wife's Earned Income Allowance from it. There are two exceptions to this. If the accommodation you let is furnished and you provide services (e.g., meals, cleaning, laundry) for the tenants and you charge separately for the services, what you are paid for providing the services can count as earnings. The other exception is that if it is your husband who lets the accommodation but you carry out services for the tenants, your husband can pay you a reasonable amount for doing so; your husband can then count what he pays you as an allowable expense, and the money you get counts as your earnings, so the Wife's Earned Income Allowance can be set against it. If this means that you can claim the full allowance of £2,335 in 1986–87, you will save up to £677.15 in tax.

Expenses

You are taxed on the amount of rent left after most of the expenses involved in maintaining the home and letting it out have been paid. So you can deduct from the rent that you get:

- the cost of normal repairs and redecoration, but not extensions or improvements
- rates, water rates and ground rent
- the cost of providing services (e.g., heating) which you are not paid for separately
- wages of people you employ to provide services (but you cannot claim for your own time)
- the cost of collecting rent
- insurance premiums, and cost of valuation for insurance
- expenses as a landlord (e.g., stationery, telephone, advertising)
- professional fees (e.g., solicitor's, accountant's, estate agent's).

You can also deduct the amount of interest you pay in the year on any loan you used to buy or improve the property. If the income counts as investment income, you cannot count interest paid on an overdraft or credit card and the property must have been available for letting for at least 52 weeks (unless building or repair work was going on, or you, your separated or divorced husband or a dependent relative were living in it) and it must actually have been let for 26 of those weeks.

With accommodation you let furnished, you can also deduct any bills you pay for heating, lighting or telephone, any costs involved in preparing an inventory, and for any fixtures, fittings or furniture you replace. In the last case you can alternatively claim a yearly allowance for replacements of 10% of the rent (less rates, if you pay them). More details of tax on rental income are given in Inland Revenue leaflet IR.27, while tax relief on interest payments is covered in IR.11 (both free from tax offices).

Your home and Capital Gains Tax (CGT)

Many people worry about the possibility of Capital Gains Tax when they sell their home, but in many cases their fears are unfounded.

If you have only used your home for you and your family to live in, it is exempt from Capital Gains Tax. Taking in lodgers who share your living space and have some meals with you does not make you liable for any tax. The only times CGT may arise are:

- If you spent money on part of your home in order to increase its value, and then sold that part off. For example, you may have converted part into a separate flat or built another house at the end of your garden and then sold it.

- If your garden is bigger than one acre *and* is bigger than the home warrants. Or if you sell the home and keep part of the garden and do not build a new home on it to live in yourself.

- If you make a habit of buying homes, doing them up and selling them again for quick profits.

- If you have more than one home. Only two homes that you own can have *any* exemption from CGT at any one time. One is the home you have nominated as your main one (see page 367 for how to do this – it is important). The other is a home you own which is occupied by a dependent relative of yours (or your husband's). A married couple also get exemption for only one home they nominate and one home occupied by a dependent relative. If you (or your husband) own any other homes at any time, CGT will be worked out in the usual way on the gain attributable to the period of time that the home was not your main one for CGT purposes. But the first year and last two years of ownership are always exempt.

If you have used your home for purposes other than for you and your family to live in, you could be liable for some Capital Gains Tax. The three most common cases are if you have used part of the home for business, if you have let out part of it, or if you have lived away from it (possibly letting the whole home). In each case, part of the 'gain' you make when you sell could be liable to CGT. The 'gain' is basically the figure you sell for *less* the total of the following:

- what you paid for the home
- the costs involved in buying and selling
- money you spent on improvements, extensions and conversions
- allowances for inflation since 1982 (which may be roughly one-sixth of the selling price).

Business use

Capital Gains Tax can arise if you use part of your home *exclusively* for your business. But if you use that part also for domestic purposes, CGT will not normally arise (for more information, see page 279).

There is no CGT on the gain on the part of the home you use for living in. For example, if you use one-third of your home exclusively for your business, then only one-third of the gain will be taxable.

Even if you are liable to CGT, if you use the money you get from selling the property to buy another property in which you run a similar business, you can carry over the gains you have made by claiming **roll-over relief**. If you continue doing this until you are at least 60 you then qualify for a special **retirement relief**, and can have up to £100,000 of gains arising from the business free of tax. This also applies to a hotel, guest house or furnished holiday lettings (see page 136) that you sell, but not to other let property.

Letting part of your home

If you let out part of your own home, there is no Capital Gains Tax on the gain attributable to the part you live in. Tax will only be charged on the gain on the part you have let for the period you let it (the same as with business use). But if you have occupied the let part at some time yourself, there will normally be no tax on the first £20,000 of the gain on the part you let.

The effect of these rules is that only a small amount of tax may be payable on quite a large gain. For example, if you had bought a home for £15,000 and sold it in mid-1985 for £120,000 and your buying and selling costs were £5,000, you would have made a raw gain of £100,000. Even if you had let out half the home for three-quarters of the time you owned it, the Capital Gains Tax payable would only be around £1,200 (assuming you had no other taxable gains in the tax year).

If you live away from the home

The gain you make when you sell the home may be liable to Capital Gains Tax. But in certain circumstances you can live away from your home and even let the home without incurring any CGT liability:

- while you are living in a home which goes with your job or is provided under the terms of your business (as long as you have nominated your own home as your main one for CGT purposes – see page 367)
- if your job requires you to work elsewhere (up to four years in the UK, unlimited abroad), as long as you live in the home before you go and, if possible, after you return
- during the first year you own the home (as long as you live in it straight afterwards), and during the last two years you own it
- any period you were away before 6 April 1965

- any other periods away, up to 3 years in total, as long as you lived in the home before the first one and after the last one.

For more about Capital Gains Tax and how it is worked out, see page 364. There is more information about how Capital Gains Tax can affect your own home in Inland Revenue leaflet CGT.4 (free from tax offices).

THOSE YOU LIVE WITH

10

Living Together

This chapter explains your financial position if you are living with a man but not married. Some of it may be relevant to lesbian couples, but on the whole the law deals with people who are living together 'as husband and wife'.

Your legal position

If you are living with someone, the main differences between your legal position and that of a married woman relate to:

- your rights over the family home
- your right to maintenance for yourself and any children
- your right to state benefits
- your tax position.

These differences are explained more fully below, together with tips on how to make the most of your financial position.

Your home

If the home is **rented**, your legal position depends on whether or not you are a **tenant**, and has nothing to do with your marital status. If a man leaves his wife, she has a right to stay in the home (at least until the decree absolute is granted) – even if the man was the sole tenant. If you are living together, however, and then your partner leaves, you have a right to stay in the home only if *you* are a tenant. See Chapter 6 for more on tenancies. It therefore becomes crucial whose name is on the rent book, lease or tenancy agreement. Broadly speaking:

• **if it's your name only,** you are responsible for paying all of the rent, and if you wish you can evict your partner (after giving him notice). If *you* want to leave, you can do so without giving notice to your partner – and he is unlikely to have any right to stay in the home after you've gone.

• **if it's your partner's name only,** he is responsible for paying all of the rent. He can give you notice to leave, and if you refuse, he can apply to the courts to evict you. If *he* leaves, you are unlikely to have the right to stay in the home. If he dies, however, you may be in a stronger position. If you have lived together for six months or more, you should claim the tenancy as a 'member of the tenant's family', because the courts have held that a common-law wife can count as a member of the family in these circumstances.

• **if it's both your names,** you are both equally liable for the rent, and neither of you can force the other to leave. If one wants to leave and the other to stay, provided the tenancy isn't for a fixed period only, either tenant can give the landlord notice that they are leaving. The remaining person can stay on and become the sole tenant – although he or she will then be responsible for the whole of the rent. If the tenancy *is* for a fixed period, however, the situation is more complicated and you should get advice from a housing advice centre or Citizens Advice Bureau (CAB). Regardless of the type of tenancy, if your partner dies, you can stay in the home as the sole tenant.

If the home is **owned**, your legal position depends on who owns the property. A wife may be able to claim a share in the property even if it is owned solely by her husband; for couples who are living together, the situation is broadly speaking as follows:

• **If you bought the home together in joint names,** you are both equally liable for the mortgage payments and the rates. If you split up, the home can be sold and the proceeds shared between you. The legal documents drawn up when you bought the house may set out how the proceeds are to be shared, but if not (and you can't agree with your partner), the courts will decide. If only your partner wants to leave, he'll have to get a court order before the house can be sold.

If your partner dies, your position depends on whether you are a **joint tenant** or a **tenant-in-common** – this may be set out in the legal documents from the house purchase; if not, the courts will decide. If you are a joint tenant, you'll automatically acquire your partner's share of the house on his death. If you are a tenant-in-common, your partner can leave his share of the house to whomever he wants. If he dies without making a will, it will be passed on according to the laws of **intestacy** (see page 329).

• **If your partner bought the house in his name only,** he is responsible for the mortgage and the rates. However, he can add your name to the legal documents if he agrees that you, too, should have a stake in the ownership of the property. If he does this, your position will be as outlined above. Alternatively, he can give you a stake in the ownership by creating a **trust** for you. This is a legal agreement which gives you a right to share in the proceeds if the house is sold. However, you may not have any rights over *when* the house is sold: your partner could decide to put it on the market, and although you could sue him for your share of the proceeds, you would meanwhile have lost your home. If you think this is happening, get legal advice quickly. If your partner dies, your position is exactly the same as if the house was in both your names, and depends on whether you are a joint tenant or a tenant-in-common – see above. If you are thinking of creating a trust, get legal advice about how to do it and what your rights will be under it.

If there is no written trust, you might still have an **implied trust**, which gives you certain rights. There might be an implied trust if, for example:

• you contributed towards the deposit on the property

• you contributed towards the mortgage payments

• you paid for, or worked on, major repairs or improvements to the property.

If there is an implied trust, your position is broadly the same as if there was a written trust (for example, you have a right to share the proceeds if the house is sold; the courts will decide on the size of your share).

If you have neither a written nor an implied trust, you may have a **tenancy** or a **licence**, and your rights will be as set out in Chapter 6. If your partner dies, you will probably have no right to stay in the home.

- **If you bought the house in your name only,** your position is as above, but in reverse. For more on home ownership, see Chapter 7.

Maintenance

A married couple have a duty to maintain one another. If the marriage ends, either may still be able to claim maintenance from the other partner. If you are not married, however, your partner has no duty to maintain you, and if the relationship ends you have no right to claim maintenance for yourself.

You may, however, be able to claim maintenance for your children from their father, both during the relationship *and* if it ends. You may be able to draw up a legally binding agreement to this effect, but you should get advice from a solicitor on whether such an agreement would be enforceable in court. Alternatively, you can apply to the Magistrates Court for an **affiliation order**, and so get maintenance for the child.

The order can cover:

- the expenses of the birth
- weekly maintenance payments
- a lump sum of up to £500.

It will generally run until the child's sixteenth birthday, although it can be extended further – and the amount to be paid depends on things like the income of both parents and the age of the child.

To get an affiliation order you have to be *either* a single woman (i.e., unmarried, divorced or widowed), *or* a married woman living apart from her husband and with no right to be maintained by him. You must normally apply within 3 years of the child's birth. However, if you can show that the father contributed to the child's upkeep (for example, by paying for clothes) during those first 3 years, you may be able to apply later.

The man can get tax relief on the payments he makes under a court order. These can be paid either to you or direct to the child – the latter arrangement usually has tax advantages (see page 171). The payments are taken into account when working out your entitlement to supplementary benefit – see below.

State benefits

There are two main types of state benefits:

- **contributory benefits,** which are based on your National Insurance contributions. If you've paid enough contributions, you are entitled to these benefits regardless of your income.
- **supplementary benefits,** which don't depend on your National Insurance contributions, but which will only be paid if your income is below a certain level. (Maintenance payments made under a court order will be taken into account when working out how much income you have – even if they are paid direct to your child.)

Contributory benefits (e.g., sickness benefit, unemployment benefit, state retirement pension)

There are two important differences between your position if you are living with someone, and the position of a married woman. Firstly, a married woman may be able to claim contributory benefits for herself *and* for her husband (provided his income is below a certain level). If you are living with a man, however, you cannot normally claim benefit for him – regardless of how low his income is. The only exception is that you may be able to claim certain benefits for an 'adult dependant who looks after your children' – more details from social security offices.

Secondly, a married woman is entitled to receive certain benefits – notably retirement pension and widow's benefits – because of her *husband's* National Insurance contributions. If you are unmarried, you can't claim any of these benefits on your partner's contributions. Even if you've been married and widowed, your widow's benefits will be suspended if you begin living with another man as 'husband and wife'. Because you can only get a state pension on your own contributions, it's very important that you start planning for this as early as possible – see page 271.

Supplementary benefit

The DHSS treats an unmarried couple who are 'living together as husband and wife' in exactly the same way as a married couple when working out entitlement to supplementary benefit. To decide whether or not you're living together as husband and wife, the **cohabitation rule** is used. For example, if you share the same household and you've had children together, or you're publicly known as the man's wife (if you use his name, say), the DHSS is almost certain to decide you are cohabiting. In this case you will be treated as if you were married, and both of your incomes will be taken into account when working out your entitlement to supplementary benefit.

However, if your partner has another household elsewhere, or if you have only an occasional relationship, you should argue that you are *not* living as husband and wife, and that only your income should be assessed.

For more on state benefits for people on low incomes, see Chapter 4.

Your tax position

Unlike the DHSS, the Inland Revenue treats you as two single, separate people. You are each responsible for paying the tax on your own income, whereas a husband is usually responsible for the tax on both his and his wife's income.

If you are living together, you and your partner each get the **single person's allowance** (£2,335 in the 1986–87 tax year) – which means that you can each have an income of up to £2,335 before having to pay any tax. You don't have to claim this allowance; the Inland Revenue gives it to you automatically.

If you were married and had some earnings, you'd be entitled to the **wife's earned income allowance** of up to £2,335. However, your husband would get the **married man's allowance**, which is currently £1,320 *higher* than the single person's allowance (i.e., £3,655 in the 1986–87 tax year). This means that a married couple can have £1,320 more in allowances than two single people living together – and so less tax to pay.

That's the bad news – now for the good news. If you have a child living with you for at least part of the tax year, you may be able to claim an extra allowance – which means that more of your income can be free of tax. Single parents with a **qualifying child** can claim the **additional personal allowance** (of £1,320 in the 1986–87 tax year) – which brings your allowances up to the level of those for a married man. (If you were married, you couldn't claim the additional personal allowance.)

A qualifying child is one who is under 16 at the start of the tax year (6 April), *or* who is in full-time education, *or* who is in full-time training (lasting at least two years) for a trade, profession or vocation. The child must be either:

- your own child, step-child or legally adopted child, *or*
- any other child who is under 18 at the start of the tax year and who is maintained at your expense.

If you have one child, either you or your partner can claim the additional personal allowance or you can split it between you. If you have two children, you can *both* claim the allowance – which means that you'll have £1,320 *more* in allowances than a married couple. However, if you have three children, you can't claim the allowance three times – each partner can only claim it once, however many children there are.

You claim the allowance when you fill in your Tax Return; if you haven't had one, ask the Inland Revenue (see the phone book) to send you one. For more details on allowances for single parents, see leaflet IR.29, free from Inland Revenue offices.

Using your allowances

If either you or your partner doesn't have much income, you may not be using all of your allowances. If, for example, you are entitled to the single person's allowance (£2,335) but don't have any income, you aren't using this allowance at all. In this case your partner can make **covenant payments** of £2,335 to you. (A covenant is a legally binding agreement under which one person promises to make a series of payments to another – for more details see page 151).

You wouldn't have to pay any tax on the payments, because you can have income of up to £2,335 free of tax – and your partner might have *less* tax to pay than before. This is because he can get tax relief on covenant payments he makes (provided certain conditions are met – see page 206). So you would have a lower tax bill *between you* than before. A married couple can't use covenants to save tax in this way.

If you have a child, another way of saving tax could be through an affiliation order (see page 148). If you don't have enough income to make the most of your allowances, your partner could pay you maintenance for the child under a court order. Provided he doesn't pay you more than the amount of your unused allowances, you wouldn't have any tax to pay – and he could get tax relief on the payments, and so a lower tax bill.

If you don't have any unused allowances, he could make the payments direct to the child – because children also get the single person's allowance, which means that they, too, can have income of £2,335 free of tax in the 1986–87 tax year. The payments would count as the child's income (against which he or she could set the single person's allowance) – and your partner could still get the tax relief. For more details, see Chapter 12.

Tax and your home

If you are buying your home, you can get **tax relief** on the mortgage interest, within certain limits (see Chapter 7). You and your partner can *each* get tax relief on the interest on up to £30,000 of mortgage loans – i.e., on up to £60,000 altogether; a married couple can get tax relief on only £30,000 between them.

If your partner dies

Except in Scotland, if your partner dies without making a will, his property will go to his family, not to you – although you may be able to make a claim in the courts for a share of the inheritance. If a married man dies without making a will, his property passes automatically to his wife (within certain limits – see page 329).

If your partner makes a will which doesn't provide sufficiently for you (or for the children) you may be able to claim a larger share of the inheritance through the courts.

If you live in Scotland, see page 330.

Sharing expenses

Your home

If you are buying a home, even if it's not in your name, try to contribute towards the mortgage payments. This could mean that you have an implied trust (see page 147) – and so give you the right to claim a share in the home. If you are buying in your name only and don't want to let your partner claim a share, make all the payments yourself. (He may still, however, have an implied trust if he contributes in some other way – perhaps by doing major repairs.)

If you are buying the home in joint names, the legal documents from the house purchase may set out the size of your share. If not (and there is any dispute), the courts will decide, taking account of factors such as how much you contributed towards the mortgage. The larger your contribution, therefore, the larger share you may have in the home.

If you are renting a home as joint tenants, it normally makes no difference who pays the rent (though you are both equally liable for all of it). If the home is rented in your partner's name only, you may have slightly more rights if you, in turn, pay rent to him – or if you have an agreement that you can live there in return for paying the housekeeping bills, say. If you are the **sole tenant** and have no wish for your partner to be anything more than a guest, don't take any rent from him, or enter into any agreements with him.

Joint bank accounts

If you have a joint bank account to which you both contribute, you will both own the joint amount. If you buy things from the joint account which are obviously for you (for example, clothes), they will probably count as yours, and you alone will own them. The position is the same, but in reverse, for things your partner buys which are obviously for him. If you buy things which are for both of you (e.g., furniture), they will probably count as jointly owned.

If you have a joint account to which only one partner contributes, it will be difficult for the other partner to claim ownership of anything the money is spent on. However, in the case of a husband or wife, the money counts as the wife's as well as the husband's, even if only he contributed to the account.

If you have your own bank account, anything which you buy with the money will count as yours (even if it's furniture for the home) – unless it's a gift to your partner.

Housekeeping and bills

If your partner gives you a housekeeping allowance, anything that you buy with it will probably count as *his*; if you were married, you would normally be able to claim a share in things bought with your husband's allowance.

With bills such as gas or electricity, the person who signs the forms from the gas or electricity board is responsible for payment. If the plan is for these bills to be paid out of the housekeeping allowance which your partner gives you, make sure *he* signs the forms.

The above rules mean that a single woman with little income of her own can be in a more vulnerable position than a wife. However, if you have more income than your partner, there are certain advantages to staying single – for example, you have no obligation to support your partner. For more details on the pros and cons of marriage, see the next chapter.

You could consider drawing up a **contract** with your partner – i.e., an agreement which sets out your obligations to each other, and which could cover financial arrangements, responsibilities for children, and so on. However, it's not clear whether such an agreement would be enforceable in court. To find out more, read *The Cohabitation Handbook* (Pluto Press £5.50), which contains lots more useful information for cohabiting women.

11

Marriage

The previous chapter described your financial position if you are living with someone but not married; here we explain your finances if you've taken the plunge. First, however, for those who are still undecided, there's a summary of the main differences for single and married women.

Married v. Single

	Married	*Single*
Your home	You both have a right to live in your home. If your husband leaves, you have a right to stay (at least until the divorce comes through) – see Ch. 12	You have fewer rights over the family home – see Ch. 10
Maintenance	You and your husband have an obligation to maintain each other during the marriage, and possibly afterwards, too – see Ch. 12	Neither you nor your partner has an obligation to maintain one another, during the relationship or afterwards

	Married	*Single*
	Your husband has an obligation to maintain the children during the marriage and afterwards – see Ch. 12	The father only has a duty to maintain the children if you take out an affiliation order – see page 148
State benefits	You can claim a state retirement pension in your own right, but if you haven't paid enough National Insurance contributions, you may well be able to claim a pension on your *husband*'s contributions	You can only claim a state retirement pension on your own contributions, not on those of your partner
	If your husband dies, you can claim widow's benefit (provided he paid enough NICs)	You can't claim widow's benefit if your partner dies
Tax	You are normally taxed with your husband as a single unit; he gets the (higher) married man's allowance. See below for more details	You are taxed as a single person, separately from your partner; he can't get the married man's allowance. See page 150
Inheritance	If your husband dies without making a will, you automatically inherit his property (within limits – see page 329)	If your partner dies without making a will, his property will go to his family; you may be able to claim a share through the courts. Different rules apply in Scotland (see page 330)

Married	*Single*
If he makes a will that doesn't provide sufficiently for you (or the children), the courts can alter the will	If he makes a will that doesn't provide sufficiently for you (or the children), the courts can alter the will

Your tax position

You and your husband are normally taxed as a single unit, and only he is sent a Tax Return (on which he has to enter details of *your* income, too). He is legally responsible for paying the whole of the joint tax bill – although if you have a job, your earnings are likely to be taxed under **PAYE (Pay-As-You-Earn)**. The position is different in the tax year in which you marry (see page 159), or if you're separated or divorced (see Chapter 12). More information is given in Inland Revenue leaflet IR.30.

You can, however, choose to be **separately assessed**, which won't affect your joint tax bill, but which means it will be split differently, with the aim of making each of you responsible for paying the tax on your own income. If you choose separate assessment, you'll both have to fill in your own Tax Returns – for more details, see leaflet IR.32, free from Inland Revenue offices.

Your allowances

A married woman is entitled to the **wife's earned income allowance** if she has any earned income – for example, from a job, or from a pension based on her own contributions (not her husband's). The allowance will be the amount of your earned income, up to a maximum of £2,335 in the 1986–87 tax year. This is the same as for a single woman, and means that you can have earned income of up to £2,335 before you have to pay any tax. However, if you only have income from **investments** you aren't entitled to the wife's earned income allowance.

Your husband gets the **married man's allowance** (of £3,655 in the 1986–87 tax year) – which is higher than the allowance for a single man. Therefore a married couple can normally get more allowances than two single people – which often means a lower tax bill.

There are two main reasons why this isn't always the case:

• because you can't use the wife's earned income allowance to reduce the tax on any investment income you have (a single woman can use her single person's allowance for this purpose). Your investment income is always taxed as if it were your *husband's*.

• because your income and that of your husband is added together and tax charged on the joint amount (after deducting allowances and tax reliefs). In the 1986–87 tax year, the first £17,200 of joint income is taxed at the basic rate only (currently 29%) – but anything over £17,200 is taxed at higher rates. Two single people can *each* have the first £17,200 of their income taxed at the basic rate only. So if you are a fairly wealthy couple, you could find that your income, when added together, is taxed at higher rates than before you married. In this case, consider having your earnings taxed separately: the **wife's earned income election**.

Separate taxation of your earnings

If you choose to have your earnings taxed separately (the wife's earned income election), you and your husband each get the full £17,200 basic-rate tax band – but in return, he'll lose some allowances. Note that you can't choose to have your investment income taxed separately – this always counts as your husband's.

You'll be taxed on your earned income as if you were a single woman with the **single person's allowance** (£2,335 in the 1986–87 tax year). Your husband will be taxed on all his income *and* your investment income as if he were a single man – again, with allowances of £2,335. This means that your combined allowances are lower than before – but you could save on higher-rate tax.

Broadly speaking, if your joint income in 1986–87 is at least £26,520, and the less well-off partner has at least £6,986, you could save more in higher-rate tax than you'll lose in allowances. If your joint income is higher than £26,520, the minimum income for the less well-off partner reduces on a sliding scale – but you'll *never* be better off having your earnings taxed separately if one of you has income of less than £4,890.

This is only a rough guide, and you'll need to do your sums properly – the *Which? Tax-Saving Guide* (available at your local library) helps you work out whether separate taxation is right for you. And for more details, see leaflet IR.13, free from Inland Revenue Offices.

Tax in the year you marry

In the tax year that you marry, the Inland Revenue treats you as if you were still single. But if your wedding was on 6 April (the first day of the tax year), the normal rules for a married woman will apply, and you'll be taxed with your husband as a single unit (see above).

If you married after 6 April, for that first year only you'll be responsible for paying your own tax on your own income – and you may get your own Tax Return to fill in. You'll get the single person's allowance (£2,335 in the 1986–87 tax year) to set against all your income, whether from earnings or investments. You may also be entitled to other allowances; for example, if you already have a child, you may get the **additional personal allowance**. See Chapter 10 for more details on tax and the single woman.

If you both had mortgage loans which qualified for tax relief before you married, and you intend to sell one of the homes, you can:

- continue to get tax relief for up to 12 months on the home you're selling, *and*
- continue to get tax relief as before on the home you're living in.

Alternatively, if you intend to sell *both* homes and buy a new one, you can:

- continue to get tax relief on both old homes for up to 12 months, *and*
- jointly get tax relief on up to £30,000 of loans on the new home.

Other tax points

- If one (or both) of you can get the additional personal allowance (see Chapter 10) you could be as well off (or better off) staying single. A married woman can't get this allowance, and your husband can only get it if you're totally incapacitated for the whole of the tax year.
- If you and your husband could both earn the same amount but only one of you can work (because the other is looking after the children, say), you'll be better off if *you* are the one who goes out to work. This is because your husband can transfer his unused

married man's allowance to you – so you'd get that *and* the wife's earned income allowance to reduce the tax on your earnings. If you stay at home, however, you can't transfer your unused Wife's Earned Income Allowance to your husband.

- A married couple can get **tax relief** on the interest they pay on up to £30,000 of mortgage loans; an unmarried couple can get tax relief on up to £30,000 *each* – i.e., £60,000 in total.

Joint accounts

If you are both earning and have separate accounts, don't organise your finances so that your husband pays the 'big' bills (for example, the mortgage) and you pay for the housekeeping. Your contribution could be as large – but if you ever separated, it would be a lot harder for you to prove it. So, are joint accounts a better idea? If you both contribute to the account, the money counts as jointly owned. If only your husband contributes, you still may be able to claim a share in the ownership. If your husband dies, you'll be able to continue drawing on the account without waiting for probate. And a joint account can mean only one set of bank charges, of course.

On the other hand, it's harder to keep track of your finances – the gas bill may arrive just after your husband has depleted the account, and you could find yourselves suddenly in the red. If this becomes a real problem you could consider arranging with the bank that *both* of your signatures have to appear on every cheque, though this is less convenient.

See page 21 for more advice on which kind of account to have.

12

Separation and Divorce

Undoubtedly, the period in which you're splitting up will be one of the most difficult periods of your life. You can expect several months of what will seem insuperable problems – emotional, financial, over the children, over your possessions, over where you live, and so on. As soon as it is clear (or you have decided) that you are going to separate, it is sensible to think about your future life, plan it in detail, and feel that this is what you are working towards. The second part of this chapter deals with the permanent arrangements you will need to make, but it's very important that you think about these from the outset.

We don't cover much of the legal side of divorce here – there are a number of books available on this, some of which explain how to conduct your own divorce without a solicitor. In fact, you're not likely to find that the legal side causes problems; it's far more likely that your main problems will be about money and possessions (which we do cover in this chapter) and over your children.

Immediate concerns

Living arrangements

As long as you are married, both you and your husband have a right to live in your home, whether it is privately owned or rented, and whether it is in his name, your name or your joint names. But you may find it impossible to continue living under the same roof, and we look here at your rights in the various situations.

If your husband leaves or is prepared to leave, you will need to make sure that the mortgage payments (or rent) and the rates continue to be paid. If your husband is going to continue paying the mortgage, ask the mortgage company to tell you straightaway if any payments are missed. If money is going to be tight for paying these, see page 57 for how to approach the mortgage company, and apply to your local council for a **rate rebate** (see page 114).

If you want your husband to leave the home, you can apply for an **Ouster Order** in the County Court or High Court (under the Matrimonial Homes Act). This prevents your husband entering the home and sometimes from coming within a certain distance of it. In deciding whether to grant this injunction, the Court will want to be convinced that you cannot reasonably be expected to live with your husband, and will consider your own and your husband's conduct, your own and your children's needs and your financial resources. It may not be easy to get such an order if the home is in your husband's name and he has not been violent.

If your husband has threatened violence towards you or your children, you can apply to the Magistrates Court for a **Personal Protection Order**. If he has actually been violent, you can either apply to the local Magistrates Court for an **Exclusion Order**, or apply to the County Court for a **Non-Molestation Order** or Ouster Order under the Domestic Violence and Matrimonial Proceedings Act. You will probably have to prove violence to get one of these, so if you or your children are assaulted always go to your doctor or hospital so that there is evidence, even if you do not need special treatment.

If you have been forced to leave your home, you can ask the court to make an order insisting that you are allowed to return and live there.

There's much more information on getting these orders and what happens afterwards in a book called *Women's Rights* (see page 340). You'll almost certainly need a solicitor's help in getting an injunction, though procedures are simpler in the Magistrates Court than the County or High Court. It's also likely to cost £250 or so, though you can get Legal Aid if you qualify (see page 339). These orders aren't a final solution, generally lasting for only 3 months, nor an easy one: getting an injunction may be distressing for you and may antagonise your husband further.

IF YOUR HOME IS PRIVATELY OWNED

If the home is in your husband's name alone, he has a right to sell it or get another mortgage on it without consulting you. You can prevent this happening by having the ownership transferred into your joint names, but this will take time and need his cooperation. A much faster (and cheaper) way is to **register a charge** on the home. You can ask a solicitor to do this for you (Legal Aid is available) but it is quite easy to do yourself. A Citizens Advice Bureau (CAB) should be able to tell you exactly what to do. Your husband won't be told about your application, though once the charge is registered, he can find out if he asks. He cannot then sell the home or use it as security for a loan without your consent.

Don't assume that splitting up will mean you have to sell your home. If it is you who remains in the home, there are a number of ways of reducing the cost of doing so (see Chapter 4).

IF YOU LEAVE HOME

You don't give up any of your rights to your home by leaving it, but doing so may make it harder for you to win the home back. If you can't stay with friends or relatives, ask your local council to find you accommodation. Councils have a duty to find or provide accommodation for any woman and her children who are homeless because of violence or the threat of it – so you will need evidence. The accommodation you get may be very poor, and you may be told to apply for injunctions so that you can return home. Alternatively, you could go to a Women's Aid refuge, for advice as well as accommodation. You can get the address from your local CAB, social services office or police.

If you have to leave your home and you have children, try to take them with you if you want them to live with you in the long term. If you leave them for more than a few days, this could reduce your chance of getting custody of them.

Money problems

JOINT ACCOUNTS

A joint bank or building society account from which either of you can draw money independently can be dangerous when you're splitting up. You couldn't stop your husband withdrawing all the money, or going on a spending spree which left a large overdraft. What's more, a bank can hold *either* of you responsible for money owing on the account, regardless of who spent it, and it even has the right to transfer money from *your* deposit or investment account to pay off debts *your husband* has run up on your joint current account. So it's best to tell the bank or building society what's happening, close the joint account, agree on how much of the money in it you are each going to get, and open individual accounts if you need them. At the very least you should write immediately to the bank or building society telling them only to accept cheques or withdrawals signed by both of you (though this will mean you both lose any cheque guarantee cards you have). You'll also need to sort out who is going to pay the bills that have been paid by standing order or direct debit.

There's a similar danger with credit cards (like *Access* and *Visa*): if one of you has a card on the other person's account, it's best if they hand it over or destroy it.

SHORT OF MONEY

If you don't have enough money to support yourself and any children living with you, you can ask the court to make a temporary order for your husband to make you regular payments (maintenance) and/or a lump sum. If you are getting divorced or legally separated, you can ask the Divorce Court to make such an order (see page 170). If you're not currently suing for divorce and your husband has failed to provide reasonable maintenance for you or one of your children, you can apply for maintenance to the County Court. But you are unlikely to get Legal Aid if you apply to the County Court, and it may be better to apply to the Magistrates Court. In this case, unless you are asking for a consent order (see below), you will have to prove that your husband has either:

- deserted you, *or*
- failed to provide reasonable maintenance for you or one of your children, *or*
- behaved in such a way that you cannot reasonably be expected to live with him.

You will be asked to provide details of all your income and expenditure and what you own. The court can order your husband to pay you and your children a certain amount each week, fortnight or month, and can also order him to make a lump-sum payment of up to £500 for each of you.

Even if your husband has agreed to pay you or your children maintenance voluntarily and is doing so, it is still worth getting a court order. This is known as a **consent order**, and you won't need to prove any of the three things above. You both benefit from the existence of an order, because your husband will get tax relief on the payments he makes (see page 171), and you will get any tax rebates or reduction sooner (see below) and you will have the security that the payments are enforceable if your husband becomes reluctant to make them.

Whichever application you make, you will find a solicitor's help very useful. He or she will also be able to show you how to apply for Legal Aid (see page 338).

CLAIM ANY BENEFITS YOU'RE ENTITLED TO

You may find that because of your reduced income you qualify for a number of social security benefits, particularly if you have dependent children. These benefits include **family income supplement**, **supplementary benefit**, **housing benefits** (rent and rate rebates) and certain free health benefits. You may be entitled to **unemployment benefit**, even if you are married and aren't currently claiming it. If you are living apart from your husband and receive **child benefit**, you are also entitled to **one-parent benefit** of £4.60 a week. Your children may qualify for free school meals and uniforms and educational maintenance allowances: see leaflet FB.3, *Help for one-parent families* from your social security office. More details of these benefits are given in Chapter 4. If you have any difficulties claiming them, ask your CAB for help.

ARE YOU DUE FOR A TAX REBATE?

A woman gets very favourable treatment in the tax year in which she separates from her husband. This means that if you have some income which is taxable (e.g., earnings, maintenance payments, income from investments) you will pay less tax on it than you would have done otherwise. You may be entitled to a rebate of tax you have already paid this tax year (i.e., since the last 6 April). You should therefore write to your tax office (or your husband's if you haven't got your own, or your nearest one if you don't know which your husband's is) telling them the date on which you separated. They will start treating you as separated when there is either a separation deed, or a decree of judicial separation, or if maintenance is payable under a court order. Even if none of these exists, you'll be treated as separated when you've been separated for a year, backdated to the date you split up. If you are working, you should get a new, higher PAYE code which means your employer will deduct less tax from your earnings. When the new code is first used, you may get a rebate as well (though if the rebate is less than the tax due on that payday you'll still have some tax deducted).

In the year of separation, you get the following tax allowances (the amounts given here are those proposed for the 1986–87 tax year):

- **Up to the date of separation,** you get the **wife's earned income allowance**. This means you pay no tax on £2,335 of what you earn between 6 April and the date of separation. Your husband is liable for any tax on your investment income in this period.

- **From the date of separation** to the next 5 April, your income is treated as a quite separate pool from your husband's. You get the **single person's allowance** which means you pay no tax on £2,335 of your income (from earnings or investments) in this period. If you have one or more of your children (or anyone else who was under 18 on the previous 5 April and who you maintain at your own expense) living with you for at least part of the tax year, you also get **additional personal allowance**. This means you can have £3,655 of income in this part of the year before you pay any tax. (If the child was 16 or 17 on the previous 5 April, they must be in full-time education or in full-time vocational training lasting at least two years.) You also get any other allowances you qualify for (see page 362).

- **In each of the following tax years,** you get single person's allowance and, if you qualify, additional personal allowance and any other allowances you're entitled to.

The formalities and costs involved in splitting up

If you're **separating** and you and your husband agree over the children, your home, your possessions and any maintenance payments, and you trust each other to stick to what you agree, there's no need to go through any official procedures. If you wish, you can ask a solicitor to draw up a written agreement between you (called a **separation deed**). Technically this will be legally enforceable, but it will be much easier to enforce if you register it with a Magistrates Court. The court will examine the financial arrangements and those concerning children and will want to be sure that they are satisfactory before approving them. The court will then make a court order so that either of you can in the future apply to a Magistrates Court for the agreement to be enforced.

You can get a separation formalised with a **decree of judicial separation**. This will be heard in the Divorce County Court, and the judge can make the same orders about custody of children, division of property and maintenance as with a divorce. The differences from divorce are that a judicial separation is available in the first year of marriage, the marriage is not actually ended, and you don't have to prove that your marriage has broken down irretrievably (though you still have to prove one of the five grounds for divorce given below).

Divorce involves the legal ending of the marriage. You can now get divorced after one year of marriage. Technically, the person suing for divorce (the **petitioner**) has to prove that the marriage has broken down irretrievably for one of five reasons:

- the partner has committed adultery and the petitioner finds it intolerable to live with them
- the partner has behaved in such a way that the petitioner cannot reasonably be expected to live with them
- the petitioner has been deserted by their partner for 2 years or more
- the couple have lived apart for 2 years or more, and the partner agrees to a divorce
- the couple have lived apart for 5 years.

If the divorce is undefended (as 98% are), 'proving' that the marriage has broken down is unlikely to be difficult. You probably won't have to appear in court (except possibly to swear that your written statement is true) and the divorce will be decided on the basis of your written statement. If you and your husband agree on all the arrangements about children and money, you may not need a solicitor. However, if any part of the settlement is contested, the hearing will be transferred from the County Court to the High

Court and you will have to appear and give evidence. You will need a solicitor in this case.

Finding a solicitor

Don't just choose a solicitor at random. Ask any friends who are divorced if they would recommend their solicitor. You can also ask your CAB for a list of local solicitors who are prepared to deal with divorce (this is important) and they may be able to recommend some; or you can ask the Solicitors' Family Law Association (154 Fleet Street, London EC4A 2HX) for a list of their members in your area. You may feel it is important for you to have a woman solicitor. If your income is such that you qualify for advice under the **Green Form Scheme** or for **Legal Aid** (see page 339), make sure the solicitor operates these. To make your final choice, it may be worth asking for an appointment under the scheme where you get a half-hour consultation for a flat fee of £5 (see page 338).

The cost of splitting up

The legal costs involved in a formal separation or undefended divorce are likely to be something between £150 and £500 for each of you. If you're getting divorced and any part of the arrangements is contested, the legal costs may well run into thousands. Even if you are getting Legal Aid, there are two reasons for not feeling free to run up a large legal bill:

- if you oblige your husband to run up enormous bills to defend himself from your solicitor, there will be less in the pot for both of you at the end of the day
- if any money or property (for example, your home) which has been contested is awarded to you in the settlement, the Legal Aid fund can reclaim from you what it has paid your solicitor, apart from the first £2,500. So if money had been at issue and you were awarded a lump sum of £4,000, you would probably have to hand £1,500 over to the fund. If your home had been at issue but you were allowed to keep it, you may have to repay all your Legal Aid when you eventually come to sell it, even if it's years later. Ask your solicitor how the Legal Aid charge will affect your particular case.

Making permanent arrangements

Your home and possessions

While you are married, you each individually own the things that you bought, inherited or were given. But when you split up, either of you can lay claim to the other's home, car, investments or possessions, or a share of them. It's best if you can agree with your husband who is going to have what, and ask the court to approve what you've arranged. If you don't agree, the court can decide for you, using the general guidelines given to it in law.

IF YOUR HOME IS RENTED

If the court decides that you are to stay in the home, it will transfer the tenancy to you. Don't try to do this yourself, as only the court has the power to insist on a transfer. If the lease says the landlord must consent to a transfer, it is sensible to ask for this in writing first, though the landlord cannot refuse unreasonably.

IF THE HOME IS PRIVATELY OWNED

Whether your home is in joint names or one name alone is not usually very important in deciding who is going to live in it, or how its value will be shared between you. The facts of your particular case are more important. For example, if you have been married for twelve years, are now getting custody of your three children and do not work, you will have much more claim on the home even if it is in your husband's name than if you have been married two years, have a good job, have no children and live in a home bought outright by your husband, even if it is in joint names.

Where there are children, the court must put their interests first and will try to ensure that whoever has care and control of them has a roof over their heads, at least until the children have finished their full-time education. But the other partner will want to get something for their share in the home. There are three ways of arranging this, each with an associated snag:

- You and the children stay in the home and it becomes your sole property. You buy your husband's share in the home either by increasing the mortgage and paying him a lump sum, or by agreeing to get little or no maintenance for yourself (though your children can still get maintenance). The snag with this arrangement is that it can leave you very tight for money, with either a larger mortgage to pay or insufficient maintenance.

• You stay in the home with the children until the youngest one finishes in full-time education (or until you remarry). Your husband pays all or part of the mortgage payments in the meantime, then the home is sold, the mortgage is paid off and you share what's left. This is a better arrangement for you, but means your husband gets nothing for a long time. He is also likely to be liable to pay some Capital Gains Tax on what he eventually gets when the home is sold (though under the current rules the amount is likely to be small). See below for the best way for the husband to make the mortgage payments.

• You sell the home now, pay off the mortgage and split what's left. Whether or not this is a good option depends on how much will be left to each of you and on your individual incomes. The vital question is: will the amount remaining to you plus any new mortgage you can raise on your own be enough to buy you a new home? Remember that the most you're likely to be able to borrow on your own is around 2½ times your income.

Maintenance payments

In many cases there will be a need for one person to support the other (and any children) for a set period if not indefinitely. The advice we give here applies if you are applying for **interim maintenance** from a Magistrates Court when you separate, or **maintenance pending suit**, but it's most important when you are making permanent arrangements, normally after a decree nisi has been granted. In this section we assume that it is your husband who will be paying the maintenance, though much the same applies if it's you who is paying.

If your husband can't afford to pay any maintenance at present, it is still well worth while getting a court order for a nominal amount of maintenance to be paid – even 5p a year will do. Then if circumstances change, it is a fairly simple matter for you to apply for an increase in the amount (see page 176).

If the Divorce Court makes maintenance orders to you or to children in your custody, you can ask to have the orders registered with your local Magistrates Court. This only costs £2 and means your husband will have to make the payments to the court who pass them on to you. Then, if payments don't arrive, you can ask the court to enforce them (see page 176). There is also the advantage that if you want to ask for your payments to be increased, you do this through the local Magistrates Court rather than the Divorce Court.

Unless the court order says something different, maintenance payments to you end if you remarry or one of you dies; payments to your children end when the child is 17 (16 in Scotland) or when the paying parent dies. Bear this in mind when considering to whom payments should be made. In recent years there has been a tendency for husbands and wives to settle with one-off payments (e.g., a lump sum or transferring ownership of a home) and for the only maintenance payments to go to the children. Doing things this way can reduce resentment and have tax advantages (see below).

Maintenance payments which are legally enforceable (e.g., under a court order or separation deed) get special treatment under the tax system. Your husband gets **tax relief** on the payments he makes. For you (or your children) the payments count as **taxable income** – in other words you will have to pay tax on what you get if you are liable to pay income tax at all. However, this is nothing like as disadvantageous to you as it sounds at first. In fact, it is very likely that you and your husband will be paying a lot less in tax between you than you did when you were married.

To start with, each of your children, however young, gets a personal tax allowance (of £2,335 in the 1986–87 tax year). This means that each child can each receive up to £2,335 in maintenance under a court order without any tax being due. It is usually advantageous for payments to each child to be no more than either £48 a week or £208 a month. If they are more than this there is a slight complication: your husband has to deduct 29% tax from the amount he is obliged to pay, and your child has to reclaim this from the Inland Revenue. NB: it's very important that the maintenance payments are made under a court order stipulating that they are to be paid *to* the child, not *for* the child. Otherwise the payments will count as *your* income and could be taxable. But it doesn't matter if the money is actually paid to you on the child's behalf. (If you remarry, your husband can claim a reduction of maintenance paid to the children.)

This arrangement means you will get a reasonable amount of maintenance for each of your children tax-free. If you will be continuing to live in your own home and it is to become your sole property, the next priority is to claim as large a share of it as you can, so reducing the amount you will have to pay your husband to buy out his share. If you increase your mortgage or get another kind of loan in order to raise this money, make sure that the divorce or separation agreement says that the money is being used for buying out your husband's share. You will then qualify for tax relief on the interest you pay on the loan or extra mortgage. If the home was in your name alone, the precise wording is critical and you will need your solicitor's advice.

If your husband is prepared, or is ordered, to pay maintenance to you, the next priority, if you own your home, is for the mortgage payments to be covered. It is quite possible for your husband to pay these direct to the mortgage company, but it's much more sensible for him to pay maintenance to you equal to the amount of the mortgage payment, and for you to pay the lender. There are several reasons for this, the two most important being:

- If the home is now your property, your ex-husband won't get any tax relief on your mortgage payments, whereas he will get tax relief on maintenance payments. If he is still the owner or part-owner he would get tax relief on the mortgage interest, but would be limited in the amount he could borrow to buy himself a home and get tax relief.

- If you pay the mortgage, you can get tax relief on the interest you pay on loans of up to £30,000, even if you don't pay tax (in fact this 'relief' is now a subsidy paid by the Government direct to the mortgage company).

If the maintenance payable to you is more than £48 a week or £208 a month, or if the payments are enforceable but there is no court order, your ex-husband *must* deduct 29% tax from what he pays. For example, if the court order is for £300 a month (the *gross* amount) he will only send you £213. If your income in the tax year (including the gross amount of payments) is high enough to be liable to tax, you will have received the correct amount and there will be no further tax to pay. If, however, you are not liable to tax, you should claim back the tax he has deducted from the taxman. At the end of the tax year, ask your ex-husband to get a form R.185 from his tax office, complete it and send it to you. You should ask your tax office for form R.40, complete it and return both forms.

You will then be sent any rebate you're due. If you want to receive repayment of tax more frequently than once a year (e.g., monthly), ask your tax office to arrange this – you may be asked to complete form R.249.

If the maintenance payable to you is under a court order and is not more than £48 a week or £208 a month, the full amount will be paid. If your income (including the amount of the payments) is not high enough for you to be liable to tax, you keep the full amount. But if it is high enough for you to pay tax, you will be asked to pay whatever tax is due.

The £48 and £208 limits given above are changed from time to time, so you should check on the current figures.

If maintenance is going to be your only (or almost only) income, then there's no point in your ex-husband paying you an amount which is only slightly above the supplementary benefit level. You'd both be better off if he paid you nothing (or only a nominal amount) and you got supplementary benefit. This is because you'd have a much more reliable source of income as well as the 'perks' that go with SB – free prescriptions and dental treatment, free school meals, special needs payments, and so on (see pages 50–5 for more on SB). If you have some other income in addition to maintenance, the sums are more complicated – ask your solicitor or CAB for advice.

Maintenance payments can be made voluntarily instead of under a court order or separation deed. The only circumstances in which voluntary payments may have a small financial advantage over enforceable payments are:

- if you are separated (not divorced) from your husband, *and* he is your only means of support (other than very small amounts of income from elsewhere), *and* he won't have any children living with him, *and* he will be paying you less than £1,320 a year; *or*

- if your top rate of income tax is higher than your husband's (e.g., you're a higher-rate taxpayer and he's a basic-rate taxpayer, or you pay tax and he doesn't), *and* you have no unused tax allowances.

Pensions

If your husband has worked for a longer period than you have, it is likely that he will have built up rather more in pension rights than you. If you had remained married, you would have shared his pension entitlement – both from the state and from the firm's pension schemes he had belonged to and any personal pension policies he had. And if your husband had died before you, you would probably have been entitled to lump sums and widow's pensions from these schemes. What happens to these rights if you separate or divorce?

Separation does not affect your right to a **wife's state pension** based on your husband's contributions: you get this once he is 65 and drawing his own pension. This pension is paid directly to you and you should claim it if it is higher than the **state basic pension** you are entitled to (when you are 60) on your own National Insurance contributions. Even if you have by then lost track of your husband, the DHSS can trace his National Insurance record from his NI number, and tell you how much pension you would be entitled to on his contributions. He does not need to know this is happening.

But all other pension entitlement earned by your husband will be paid to him, not to you. If you are separated from your husband, you won't be there to share his pensions and will have to rely on your own pension entitlement and on him paying you maintenance out of the pensions he gets. If he were to die before you, it will be up to the rules or the trustees of the pension scheme as to whether any of the widow's benefits will be paid to you; you will, however, still be entitled to widow's benefits from the state (see page 189).

On **divorce**, you are formally likely to lose all your entitlement to benefit from your ex-husband's company or personal pension scheme. If he dies before you, whether or not you can benefit depends on the rules of the scheme and may be at the trustees' discretion.

A married woman can get a wife's state pension based on her husband's National Insurance contributions if this is higher than the amount she would get on her own contributions.

But if you are divorced, the only contributions of your ex-husband's that can be counted towards your pension are those he paid before the date of the divorce; from that date to age 60 it is only your own contributions which count. However, if you divorce and remarry before you are 60, you lose all entitlement to a state basic pension based on your ex-husband's National Insurance contributions. You can, however, get a wife's state pension (of about ⅗ of the amount your new husband gets) when your new husband retires and starts drawing his pension (he must be at least 65), if this is higher than the basic pension you are entitled to on your own contributions. You are in fact in the same position as any other married woman – see page 295.

You can also lose out on state pensions after your ex-husband dies. As his widow, you would have received widow's benefits plus half his graduated pension and possibly some of his state additional pension. If you are divorced when he dies you cannot claim these.

The combined loss of these pension rights and widow's benefits is substantial. Although it would be possible to buy insurance policies to make up the deficiency, in most cases this would be prohibitively expensive. Often the only way of getting you some compensation for this loss is for you to have a larger share in the equity of your home.

Life insurance

When you split up you should review the life insurance cover you both have. Make sure you understand who the benefits of each policy will go to (you can ask your solicitor for help on this) and consider whether you want to change anything. In some cases you can't change the policy, though you can simply stop paying and take out another policy. If you have any policies which include investment (e.g., endowment policies), remember that these are a very expensive form of life insurance and if your budgets are tight it may be sensible to make them paid-up or cash them in (see page 214) and take out **term insurance** instead. This insurance is much cheaper because it only pays out if the insured person dies within a set period you select.

Maintenance payments you or your children get from your ex-husband would stop if he were to die. You would therefore be well advised to make sure there is life insurance cover on your husband's life which would pay you a lump sum or an income if this were to happen.

If you have custody of your children, your husband may also want to have insurance cover on your life. This is because if you were to die, he might well have to employ someone to help look after the children.

Your will

It's very important when you separate to review your will as soon as possible; if you haven't made a will you should certainly do so. Do discuss this with your solicitor – and if you're not using a solicitor for your divorce you should consult one on this. The rules are complicated and are different in different parts of the United Kingdom, so you do need professional advice (see page 328). A solicitor isn't likely to charge much more than £25 or so for drawing up your will – and you may qualify for assistance under the **Green Form Scheme** (see page 339).

Managing afterwards

If you find yourself having to manage on a very tight budget, you should find the advice in Chapters 2 and 4 useful. If you have children, see also Chapter 14, and if you start to live with someone else, Chapter 10. Below we look at points which affect you when you're divorced or permanently separated.

Changing the amount of maintenance

You can apply to the court at any time for a **variation order** to increase the amount of maintenance payments you receive, if you think the circumstances warrant it – for example, if your ex-husband gets a substantial rise in salary, or if your responsibilities increase. If you registered your maintenance order in the Magistrates Court, that is where you apply for an increase. Of course, your ex-husband has an equal right to apply for a reduction in the payments.

Getting maintenance paid

If your husband (or ex-husband) is late making maintenance payments, you can apply to the court to have them enforced. If you don't know where he is, the DHSS may be able to trace him through his National Insurance number and tell the court (but they won't tell you). Alternatively, you can sign over your maintenance payments to the DHSS. The DHSS will pay you supplementary benefit and, if this is more than the amount of the maintenance order, will try to get the money from your husband.

If the order is for more than the SB you get, you have to chase your husband for the rest yourself.

If your husband is in a job (not self-employed) and is more than four weeks behind with payments for no good reason, you may be able to get an **attachment of earnings order**. His employer will then have to deduct the maintenance payments from his pay and send them to the court who will send them on to you.

If maintenance payments get behind, do take action soon. Once they are 12 months overdue, the onus is on you to show that they *should* be paid, not on your husband to show that they should not.

Getting more tax relief

If:

- you have children, *and*
- the maintenance payments are either to you or *for* (not *to*) your children, *and*
- you are paying tax

you could reduce your tax bill (perhaps to nothing) by asking for the wording of the court order to be changed so that the payments *for* your children become payments *to* your children. Your children will then be able to make full use of their personal tax allowances (see page 171).

Don't forget that if you have a child living with you for some of the time you can probably claim additional personal allowance for yourself – see page 362.

Social security benefits

If you are recently divorced and are under 60, you may be able to get **unemployment benefit**, **sickness benefit** or **maternity allowance** even if you have not paid the number of National Insurance contributions usually required. Details are in DHSS leaflet NI.95, *NI guide for divorced women*. Ask at your social security or unemployment benefit office if you think you might qualify.

13

Widowed

In this chapter we cover the main arrangements that will have to be made when your husband dies, and tell you about all the special financial arrangements for widows. This will undoubtedly be a difficult time in many ways, and you will almost certainly need support and advice. Two organisations which will be able to help you are:

- Cruse, the National Organisation for the Widowed and their Children. The address and telephone number of your local branch should be in the phone book or obtainable at your library; if not, ring 01-940 4818 or write to Cruse House, 126 Sheen Road, Richmond, Surrey TW9 1UR, to find your nearest branch.

- The National Association of Widows also has branches in various parts of the country. It only costs £3 to join, and you can then use their advisory service provided by widows for other widows. You can phone or write with your problems, call at your local branch or someone can call on you. They publish a very useful *Handbook for widows* which gives legal and financial advice as well as emotional support (£1.72 including postage). Details from National Association of Widows, Chell Road, Stafford ST16 2QA (tel. 0785 45465).

Both these organisations can put you in touch with other widows in your neighbourhood (which many women find very valuable) and help you with any sort of problems (emotional, financial or practical). There may be other organisations in your area helping widows and one-parent families. You may want to contact your minister of religion, and you can also ask your local authority social services department for a social worker to call and help you. If you want to know more about any of the practical arrangements than is given here – registering the death, obtaining certificates, arranging burial or cremation and funeral – you can get a free leaflet D.49, *What to do after a death*, from any DHSS office or Citizens Advice Bureau (CAB). Rather more information is given in *What to do when someone dies* (£6.95 from Which? Books, Castlemead, Gascoyne Way, Hertford SG14 1LH, or at your local bookshop. *Wills and probate* is also available at the same price, or both books for a combined price of £9.90 including postage).

When your husband dies

Unless someone dies in hospital, you should always call a doctor and, if they seem to have died as a result of an accident or anything other than illness or natural causes, you should call the police. If you are on your own, do not be frightened to call someone you know well at any time of day or night and ask them to help.

The doctor may give you a certificate stating the cause of death in a sealed envelope addressed to the registrar (or may send it to the registrar direct). The doctor will also give you a **notice to informant** telling you about registering the death. You should tell the doctor if you wish the body to be cremated. If your husband wanted to donate any part of his body for transplant or research, or if you want to do so, you will have to act quickly. If the body is to be donated for research, telephone the Inspector of Anatomy (01-636 6811; outside office hours 01-407 5522) without delay.

You should then contact a funeral director to arrange for the body to be taken to a chapel of rest and, over the next few days, make provisional arrangements for the funeral (do not make definite arrangements until you are sure the death will not be reported to the coroner – see below).

You should try to locate your husband's will, which may be at home or may be with your bank or solicitor. If you have any queries about it you may want to contact your solicitor (see page 338 for how to find a solicitor and how to get Legal Aid). You will need to contact whoever your husband has appointed as **executors** (the people responsible for dealing with his money and possessions). If there is no will as far as you can discover, you should get form PR.48 from the Registrar (see below) or from a solicitor. This tells you what you will need to do before you can apply for the **letters of administration** which will give you authority to deal with your husband's estate. There is more information on what happens to your husband's possessions on page 195.

Unless the death is reported to the coroner *and* there is an inquest, the death must normally be registered within 5 days (8 days in Scotland). Registrars are listed in the phone book (under *Registration*) – but phone first saying where your husband died to make sure that you go to the correct office at the correct time. You should take the doctor's certificate, your husband's NHS medical card, any war pension book, some money and, if the coroner has sent you a pink form, take that too. If you do not want to go yourself, the 'notice to informant' your doctor gives you tells you who may go instead. The funeral director will be able to help with registering the death if you ask him to.

The registrar will give you, free of charge, a special **death certificate** which has a form (BD.8) on the back for claiming the death grant and widow's benefits. He will also give you leaflets about these benefits, and a form about dealing with your husband's will. There are three other types of death certificate and you may need several copies of each. It is generally much cheaper to get them at the time of registration than later:

- **standard death certificate** (£1.80) for obtaining probate, for claiming on life insurance policies on your husband's life, and for claiming widow's pensions from his pension schemes (you will need one for each policy and scheme)

- **certificate for certain statutory purposes** (£1.50) for claiming from National Savings accounts and investments in the Trustee Savings Bank when probate is not required (see page 196); for claiming social security benefits and pensions other than death grant and widow's pensions; for claiming death grant and widow's benefits if the free certificate is lost

- **certificate for purposes of Friendly Societies Acts** (£1.50) for claiming benefits from a registered friendly society. Or you can use a standard death certificate for this.

If you take a list of the organisations you are going to have to claim from, the registrar will be able to advise you about how many certificates of each type you need. The types of death certificate are slightly different in Scotland and the charges are different in Northern Ireland. The registrar will also give you a **disposal certificate** (in Scotland a **certificate of registration of death**) which authorises burial or cremation.

The doctor, the police or the registrar (or anyone else who thinks the death might not have been natural) may report the death to the **coroner** (**procurator fiscal** in Scotland). When this happens, there may have to be a post mortem examination and possibly an **inquest** (**public inquiry** in Scotland). In England and Wales the registrar cannot register the death until he gets authority from the coroner. If there is an inquest, you can ask the coroner to give you a written statement so that you do not have to wait to claim your widow's allowance and other social security benefits. The coroner will send the registrar the necessary information for registering the death and the coroner will issue the disposal certificate.

Organising your financial affairs

Although initially you may find you have little ready cash, it is likely that you are entitled to money from a number of different sources over the few months after your husband's death. We look at these in the next section. First we look at what needs to be done with your current financial arrangements.

Things which you owned jointly with your husband normally become yours immediately (unless you have jointly arranged something different). So if you have a joint bank or building society account, you can continue to use it. But there are special rules concerning your home (see below).

Things which are in your husband's name alone become part of his estate, and you will not normally be able to get at them until the estate is settled. For example, a bank account of his will be frozen. But there are some exceptions – for example, you will normally be able to withdraw up to £5,000 from a National Savings, building society or TSB account of your husband's by applying with the appropriate form and death certificate (and possibly marriage certificate).

If your husband owed any money, these debts are payable out of his estate. You do not have to pay them out of your savings though (if the debts are substantial, things may have to be sold to pay them). Specific loans (like your mortgage, bank personal loans and finance company loans) may be covered by life insurance which will mean the loan (or most of it) is paid off by the insurance company.

If you rent your home

Whether the tenancy was in your joint names or your husband's name alone, you have a legal right to take over the tenancy and stay in the home as long as you were living in it before your husband died. You should inform the landlord of your husband's death and ask for the tenancy to be transferred to your name. The terms of the tenancy and your right to stay in your home will be exactly the same as they were before. For more information see Chapter 6.

If you are going to find it hard to pay the rent, ask your landlord if you can delay paying some of the rent until your husband's estate is sorted out. You should also apply for **housing benefits** for help with your rent and rates (see page 56).

If you own your home

If the ownership of your home is in your husband's name only, but he has left it to you in his will, you should have it changed to your own name. Your solicitor (or one suggested by your building society, bank or CAB) can do this for you. If your husband did not make a will or if it is invalid, you will be able to ask for the home to be transferred to you. If your husband has left the home to someone else in his will, you will be able to ask the court to make provision for you out of his estate (see page 197).

If your home is in joint names, the position depends on what kind of joint ownership you had (see page 320). You can find this out from the deeds of the house which are probably with your solicitor or bank for safe-keeping. If you were **joint tenants**, then the home automatically becomes your property (your husband's will cannot change this) and no legal changes are necessary. But if you were **tenants-in-common**, his share in the home becomes part of his estate and he has the right to leave his share to someone else in his will. If this happens, consult a solicitor if you have not yet done so – you will not necessarily lose your home.

If your home is mortgaged

If it was an **endowment mortgage**, there will be a life insurance policy to cover the loan. If it was a **repayment mortgage**, try to find out if there was a life insurance policy specifically to cover the mortgage – the bank or building society or whoever the mortgage is from may well know. If there is, write to the insurance company enclosing a death certificate.

If the mortgage is an endowment mortgage or if it is from a bank, the insurance company will normally pay enough money to pay off the loan directly to the lender. But if it is a repayment mortgage from a building society, the insurance money will normally be paid to you and you can use it to repay all or some of the loan or for whatever other purpose you like. If the mortgage is paid off, the house is then yours and you will have no further mortgage payments to make so you can ask your bank to cancel any standing order. If the amount the insurance company pays is not quite enough to pay off the whole loan, you can either settle the rest yourself or continue making small payments.

If there is no specific life insurance policy for the mortgage, your husband may have other life insurance policies which are sufficient to pay off the loan if you wish. If you plan to continue with the mortgage, write to the lender and tell them you will be making the payments in future. If you are going to find it hard to make the remaining payments, do not worry – you are unlikely to lose your home if you explain the position to the mortgage company. You can ask them to extend the term or if you can pay interest only for a while – if the mortgage has only a few years to run, this will mean a big reduction in the monthly payments. For other help in this situation, see Chapter 4.

If you are going to stay in your home, it is generally worthwhile leaving a very small amount of the mortgage unpaid – £10 or even £1, for example (some building societies have special schemes for doing this). Then if you ever want to borrow money from the same lender for major repairs, modernisation or improvements to your home, it will be a much simpler and cheaper process. This will usually be the cheapest source of money (see page 134).

Tell the tax office

It is important that you tell the tax office that your husband has died so that your tax position can be sorted out as soon as possible. If you have a job or are self-employed or get a pension from a previous employer, write to your own tax office. Otherwise write to your husband's (if you cannot find any tax papers, ask his employer). If neither of you had a tax office, write to or call at your nearest one (in the phone book under *Inland Revenue*). If you do not contact the tax office, you could miss out on a substantial rebate and you could be paying too much tax – or, worse, you could be paying too little and a large bill could be accruing.

Inform the tax office of your husband's death and tell them if any of the following apply:

- you have any children under 16 living with you (or under 18 and in full-time education)
- you have a relative or employee living in your home looking after you or acting as housekeeper
- either you or your husband were 64 or more on the previous 6 April.

If any of these apply, you may get more than the normal amount of income free of tax.

Also tell the tax office that you are getting or applying for widow's benefits (and any other taxable benefits – see opposite). And ask for a copy of leaflets IR.23, *Income tax and widows* and IR.45, *What happens when someone dies*.

Soon after you have told your tax office about your situation, you should get a new **Notice of Coding** (see page 352) showing your new PAYE code and your employer should start to use this.

Income tax in the year you are widowed

In the tax year in which your husband dies, you get very generous treatment from the Inland Revenue. The year is split into two separate periods. In the period from the previous 6 April to the date of your husband's death you get the **married man's allow-**

ance, the **wife's earned income allowance** and any other allowances you are entitled to, to set against your joint income. In the second period, from your husband's death to the following 5 April, you get the **single person's allowance** plus a special **widow's bereavement allowance** (see page 363) to set against your own income. If you have any dependent children, you may also qualify for the **additional personal allowance** (see page 362). As the total allowances you are entitled to in the complete tax year are much greater than in any normal tax year, much less tax will be payable. If you or your husband have already paid some tax (e.g., on earnings or pensions) you will probably be entitled to a rebate.

In subsequent tax years you are taxed like a single person (unless you remarry), so you get single person's allowance. In the tax year following the one in which your husband died you get a further widow's bereavement allowance (as long as you have not remarried by the start of that tax year). And you get additional personal allowance for each tax year that you are a single parent. If you do not get this allowance, you may be able to claim **housekeeper allowance** instead (see page 363). All these allowances can be set against any of your income.

Claiming all the benefits you are entitled to

As we have said, you may be entitled to payments from a large number of different sources after your husband's death. Tracking them all down and filling in all the necessary forms may take some time and some determination, and you will probably find a friend's help invaluable. It is likely that you will be able to get:

- **death grant** (or £30 payment from the state)
- **widow's benefits** (initially £54.20 a week, paid for by your husband's National Insurance contributions), or **industrial death benefit** if your husband died from a qualifying industrial disease, or **war widow's pension** if your husband died as a result of service in the armed forces
- increases to widow's benefits if you have dependent children
- widow's pensions and lump sums from your husband's employer's pension scheme or from personal pension plans he paid into

- lump sums from life insurance policies provided by your husband's employer or taken out by him or by you
- income from a family income benefit life insurance policy
- a lump sum from a personal accident policy, if your husband's death was the result of an accident
- any death or superannuation benefits provided by your husband's trade union or professional body
- other social security benefits, like **unemployment benefit**, **sickness benefit**, **family income supplement**, **housing benefits**, **supplementary benefit** (see Chapter 4)
- a tax rebate (see previous section)
- a reduction in the tax deducted from your earnings, because you get extra allowances
- money, investments and possessions you inherit from your husband.

We look at what needs to be done to sort out your husband's affairs and at how you can inherit from his estate on page 195. But first we look at how you go about claiming the other items in the list above. In practice, it is likely that both these matters will be happening at the same time.

Death grant and widow's benefits

As soon as your husband's death is registered, complete the claim form (BD.8) on the back of the special death certificate the registrar gives you and send or take it to the nearest social security office. You will then be sent two claim forms, BD.1 for claiming death grant and BW.1 for claiming widow's benefits. You should send these back as soon as possible (and certainly within three months of your husband's death) with your marriage certificate, any National Insurance contribution card, any DHSS books of payment orders in your husband's name (e.g., for pension payments), and the funeral director's estimate or bill. But do not delay claiming if you do not have all these documents or if you do not know the answers to all the questions on the form – simply write 'I do not know' or 'To follow'.

Death grant

This is a one-off payment of £30, usually paid to your husband's executors, though it may come to you. Most widows will qualify, but for such a meagre amount the rules are incredibly complicated. If your application is turned down, ask for DHSS leaflet NI.49 where the rules are spelled out.

Widow's benefits

This is a weekly payment which almost all widows will be entitled to for 6 months, and many will get until they retire or remarry. You get extra benefit for each dependent child. Widow's benefits are easy to claim and to get, but as the details are more lengthy we have dealt with them in the next section. If you are over 60 when your husband dies you may get your husband's state pension instead of widow's benefits – again the rules are complicated and we deal with them separately on page 193. It may be three or four weeks before you get your first payments, but they will be backdated to the date of your husband's death.

If an industrial injury or a qualifying industrial disease was one of the causes of your husband's death, you may get industrial death benefit instead of widow's benefits. Although the amount is much the same as you get with widow's benefits, it is worth claiming as there are fewer restrictions on what other benefits may be claimed at the same time. Ask for DHSS leaflet NI.10 at your social security office.

Widow's pensions

If your husband had a job, his employers will tell you what pension and lump-sum benefits you are entitled to when you inform them of his death. Employers' pension schemes are allowed to pay a lump sum of up to four times your husband's annual salary, plus a refund of all the pension contributions he had paid plus interest, though not many schemes are that generous. The money may come to you automatically or the trustees of the scheme may have discretion as to whom it is paid. In deciding, they will take account of the wishes expressed by your husband on a special form they keep. You may also get a widow's pension from the scheme, paid to you for life (sometimes only until you remarry). The maximum the scheme can pay is just under half what your husband was earning, but again few schemes pay this much. The pensions manager at your husband's place of work will explain to you how your pension is worked out. The scheme may also provide a small pension for each of your children as long as they are under 18 or in full-time education.

If your husband had belonged to pension schemes in previous jobs, you will need to write to the pensions managers of each company and ask what benefits are payable – most likely a lump-sum payment.

If your husband had paid into personal pension plans, you should write to each of the insurance companies and claim any return of contributions or widow's pension you are entitled to – the documents should say. If you do not know, write and ask the company what benefits are payable.

If your husband was retired, his pensions from previous employers may automatically provide widow's pensions, generally at half or two-thirds of the rate he received. There are two other possibilities, both of which also apply to personal pensions. The pension your husband received may have been guaranteed for a certain period, generally 5 or 10 years, so that if he dies before the period has elapsed the pension will be paid for the remainder of it (you may get the lot in one payment). Alternatively, if the scheme had no automatic widow's pension or guarantee, your husband may have opted at retirement to take a smaller pension himself so that the pension could continue as long as either he or you were alive (often at a lower rate) – called a **joint-life annuity**. For example, instead of getting a pension of £1,000 a year for as long as he was alive, he may have chosen a pension of £800 as long as you were both alive, followed by a pension of £400 for the survivor.

Claiming on life insurance policies

You may be able to claim the proceeds of some life insurance policies yourself immediately. You can (and should) do so if you are named in the policy as the beneficiary and the policy is **written in trust** – look for a mention of trustees or a **trust declaration** or some mention of the Married Women's Property Act 1882. If you are not sure, ask your solicitor or the insurance agent or company. Money from these policies can be paid to you on sending them a death certificate. If you are named as the beneficiary but the policy is not written in trust, the insurance company has to wait for grant of probate before paying you the money. If you are not mentioned as the beneficiary, the policy becomes part of your husband's estate and the money from it will then be subject to his will or the **intestacy rules** (see page 329).

If your husband had any **family income benefit** life insurance policies, these pay a tax-free income (usually quarterly) instead of a lump sum – though you may be able to have a lump sum instead. The income continues until the end of the term of the policy. For example, if your husband dies in the fifteenth year of a 20-year policy, you get the income for 5 years. With some policies the income increases each year at a pre-set rate.

Personal accident insurance

If your husband's death was the result of an accident, it may be covered by a personal accident insurance policy. As this insurance is cheap, it is sometimes offered as a 'perk' with membership of other organisations. Many credit cards provide benefit ranging from £15,000 to £200,000 if the cardholder is killed on a journey paid for with the card – so it is well worth checking. The money will normally be paid to the personal representatives.

Trade unions and professional bodies

Some of these provide life insurance and personal accident benefits for their members – so again it is well worth writing to them to ask.

State benefits and pensions

There are three social security benefits which are together called widow's benefits. They are yours of right – paid for by the National Insurance contributions your husband paid. Together these benefits can provide you with an income from the death of your husband until you retire or remarry, but this will depend on your circumstances.

If you are under 60 when your husband dies

You get a weekly payment of £54.20 for 6 months (called **widow's allowance**) plus an extra £8.05 a week for each child you are receiving child benefit for.

If you have children or are expecting a baby, after the first 6 months you get a lower payment of £38.70 a week (called

widowed mother's allowance), plus £8.05 for each child. You continue to receive this until your children reach the age of 19 or leave home.

– If you are over 40 when this ends, you get a **widow's pension** of up to £38.70 a week (the amount depending on your age). You continue to get this until you start getting your **state retirement pension** (between 60 and 65). Your basic retirement pension will be at least as much as your widow's pension.

– If you were under 40 when this ends, you get no further widow's benefits.

If you do not have children:

– and you were over 40 when your husband died, after the first 6 months you get a **widow's pension** of up to £38.70 a week (the amount depending on your age). You continue to get this until you start getting your **state retirement pension** (between 60 and 65).

– and you were under 40 when your husband died, you get no further widow's benefits.

The amounts of benefit given here apply from July 1986 to April 1987. The amounts are normally increased by the Government each year in line with rising prices – you can find the most recent rates in DHSS leaflet NI.196.

Do not be reluctant to claim because you feel you do not really need the money – your husband paid National Insurance contributions in order that you could receive these benefits on his death.

You only get the full amount of widow's pension if you are 50 or more when you start receiving it. If you are 40 you only get 30% of the amount (currently £11.61 a week). You get an extra 7% (currently £2.71) for each year that you are over 40 when you start to receive the pension. But the pension you get does not increase as you get older (apart from cost-of-living increases).

The amount you get in widow's benefits is not affected by earnings at all – you can earn as much as you like. It is, however, affected by most other payments from the state that you receive, including grants for education or training allowances. If you remarry, you lose your entitlement to widow's benefits from your former husband. If you live with a man as his wife, the payments stop, but start again when the cohabitation ends.

When you start getting widow's allowance you should tell your tax office as widow's benefits are taxable (though additions for dependent children are not). It is paid weekly. You get a book of orders which you can cash at your post office on the days they are due or within the following 3 months. If you are getting child benefit and it is paid 4-weekly in arrears, you can ask for it to be paid weekly by orders you can cash at the post office. Doing this will help your cash-flow.

You do not need to claim widowed mother's allowance or widow's pension – one or other of these benefits should follow on automatically from widow's allowance. If you think the amount you are being offered is wrong, you can appeal. These benefits can also be paid weekly by orders you cash at the post office. Or you can have them paid every 4 or 13 weeks direct to a bank account, building society account or National Savings investment account. This may save trips to the post office, but these payments are not made until the *end* of the period they cover, meaning you have to wait much longer for your money. If you want to be paid this way, choose 4-weekly payments.

In addition to your widowed mother's allowance or widow's pension you will also get any additional pension your husband earned from the **state earnings-related pension scheme** (commonly known as 'Serps'). The amount you receive will be reduced if you do not get the full rate of widow's pension because of your age, or if you get any widow's pensions from contracted-out pension schemes run by your husband's employers.

If you are finding it hard to manage when your widow's allowance or widowed mother's allowance ends, you may qualify for other social security benefits including unemployment benefit if you are looking for a job, sickness benefit if you are too ill to work, supplementary benefit, housing benefits and family income supplement. See Chapter 4 for more information.

If you were separated from your husband when he died, you are entitled to the same benefits as above. But if you were divorced or your marriage was annulled you cannot claim widow's benefits. However, if you have not remarried and your husband was helping to support any of your children, you can probably get **child's special allowance** of £8.05 a week for each child in addition to child benefit (details are in DHSS leaflet NI.93 and claim on form CS.1).

YOUR NATIONAL INSURANCE CONTRIBUTIONS

If, before your husband died, you had the right to pay reduced-rate National Insurance contributions (often called the **lower stamp**), you can keep the right to do so for as long as you get widow's benefits. Or you can change to paying full-rate contributions. For the pros and cons, see pages 291 to 295 and DHSS leaflet NI.51, *Widows: guidance about NI contributions and benefits*.

WHEN YOU REACH 60

If you are receiving any widow's benefits when you reach 60, you have a three-way choice:

- to continue receiving the widow's benefit you are getting
- to claim your state retirement pension instead
- to give up your widow's benefit and defer drawing your state retirement pensions, in order to get a higher rate of retirement pensions when you do start to draw them.

You should in any case contact your social security office before you reach 60 to find out about claiming your state retirement pension and how much it will be. Whether it will be worth drawing will depend on a number of factors:

- If you intend to continue working after age 60, your basic retirement pension is likely to be reduced (see page 306) whereas widow's benefits are not.
- If you are getting widowed mother's allowance, you can continue to draw this for as long as you qualify. You will also get any graduated pension of your own and half the graduated pension earned by your husband when you retire or reach 65.
- If you are getting widow's pension when you reach 60, you can continue drawing it until you retire or reach 65. The state retirement pension you are offered will be at least the same amount. You get any graduated pensions when you retire.
- If your husband had deferred his retirement, you get any extra pension he had earned by doing so.

See page 302 for more about claiming and deferring retirement pensions.

If you are 60 or over when your husband dies

The benefits you get depend on whether you and your husband were getting state pensions when he died:

Case 1: **If neither of you were getting state retirement pensions,** you get widow's allowance for the first 26 weeks. After that, if you do not have any dependent children you get the total state retirement pension your husband was entitled to. If you do have any dependent children you get widowed mother's allowance for as long as you qualify, plus half your husband's graduated pension entitlement and, when you retire, your own graduated pension.

Case 2: **If your husband was getting a state retirement pension but you were not,** you get a state basic retirement pension worked out as if your husband were getting it but without having to retire (there is no reduction if you continue working). You also get your husband's additional pension and half his graduated pension, and any increase he had earned by postponing his retirement.

In either Case 1 or 2: **when you retire or reach 65, if you are entitled to a basic pension on your own contributions**, you can get this on top of any amount you are already getting, up to the standard rate for a single person. You also get:

- both your own and your husband's additional pensions, up to the maximum for a single person
- your own graduated pension plus half your husband's graduated pension
- any increases that you or your husband had earned by postponing retirement.

Case 3: **If you were getting a state retirement pension but your husband was not,** you get widow's allowance instead of your basic retirement pension for 26 weeks (plus your own additional and graduated pensions). After that, if you have any dependent children you will get widowed mother's allowance, plus half your husband's graduated pension entitlement and, when you retire, your graduated pension. Otherwise you will get the total state retirement pension your husband was entitled to even if you have not retired.

Case 4: **If you were both getting state retirement pensions** and your basic pension was based entirely on your *husband*'s contributions, then the position is the same as in Case 2.

If your basic pension was based entirely or partly on your *own* contributions, you can get your husband's basic pension on top of your own, up to the standard rate for a single person. You also get:

- both your own and your husband's additional pensions, up to the maximum a single person could get
- your own graduated pension plus half your husband's graduated pension
- any increases that you or your husband had earned by postponing retirement.

Your husband's NI contributions

If you are to qualify for widow's allowance, your husband must have paid (credits do not count) either:

- 25 Class 1, Class 2 or Class 3 National Insurance contributions at any time before 6 April 1975 and before he was 65, *or*
- in any one tax year since 6 April 1975, NI contributions on earnings of at least 25 times the **Lower Earnings Limit** for that year. For example, in the 1985–86 tax year the Lower Earnings Limit was £35.50 a week, so if in 1985–86 your husband paid contributions on earnings of at least £887.50 (i.e., £35.50 × 25), then this year will pass the test.

If you are to qualify for widowed mother's allowance or widow's pension, your husband must meet the same conditions, only with 50 substituted for 25 (but substitute 52 for any tax year since 6 April 1978). And to get the full amount of benefit, your husband must have paid (or been credited with) NI contributions for about 9/10 of his working life (since he was 16). If his NI record is not that good, your widow's benefit will be reduced. But you can still get any additional pension your husband had earned. For more information, see DHSS leaflet NP.36, *Your benefit as a widow after the first 26 weeks*.

Sorting out your husband's affairs

If your husband left a will, it will state who he wanted his possessions to go to, and who he wanted to act as his **executors** (**executors nominate** in Scotland) – the people who are responsible for carrying out his wishes, paying his debts and any tax due, and making sure that everything goes to the right people. He may have appointed you as an executor, perhaps the only one.

If you cannot find any trace of a will, you will need to apply for **letters of administration** which will give you the authority to deal with his affairs, and your husband's possessions will be distributed according to the **intestacy rules** (these are given on page 329). In England and Wales, if your husband's estate is worth less than £40,000 (£85,000 if you have no children) things are straightforward because you inherit everything of his. But if his estate is worth more than this, it gets complicated, especially if you have children. If you feel unable to cope, ask a close relative or friend or a solicitor to help. We give only a brief description of what happens here, so that you know what to expect. A detailed account is given in a book called *Wills and probate* (see page 179).

The executor of the will or administrator of the estate is called the **personal representative** (**PR**) of the person who has died. The PR is responsible for your husband's affairs during the **period of administration** of the will – the time from his death until the distribution of the estate is completed. If a solicitor is not assisting the PR or if he is not one himself, the PR should contact a district Probate Registry (in Scotland a Sheriff Court) as soon as possible. The PR may have to attend there, and will be given a form on which to compile a list of all your husband's possessions, whether owned individually or jointly, with valuations (there are rules about how certain assets like shares are to be valued, but you do not need professional valuations for a home or its contents). A list of all your husband's debts is also required, and it is usually necessary to advertise the death, allowing anyone who was owed money by your husband at least two months in which to claim.

Unless your husband's estate was small, the PR will have to sign an Inland Revenue Account of the estate, and will be told by the Registry if any Inheritance Tax is likely to be due. If it is, the amount will be calculated provisionally and the PR must arrange how it is going to be paid (though the proportion of the tax attributable to homes and land need not be paid for 6 months after the death and can then be paid in instalments). Money to pay Inheritance Tax can come from any National Savings accounts or investments of your husband's, or from most building society accounts, or it can be borrowed from a bank. See Chapter 21 for more about Inheritance Tax.

Unless your husband's estate is very small or consists only of cash and personal belongings (like furniture and a car), the PR must apply for a **grant of probate** (or **letters of administration**) – official recognition that the will is valid and that the PR has authority to deal with your husband's affairs. After application, the PR will need to visit the Registry to swear the papers and pay the Inheritance Tax before probate can be granted.

Once probate is granted, the PR can ask for all money belonging to the estate to be handed over, can sell property which is not required and should settle the debts. It is important that the PR settles all your husband's debts including bills which have arisen since his death (like tax demands and solicitor's fees) before distributing any assets. This is because creditors take priority over heirs, and the PR would have to pay out of his own pocket if they had distributed all the assets.

The gifts specified in the will can then be transferred or distributed and receipts obtained, and finally the residue of the estate can be handed over and accounts finalised. The administration of the estate is then complete.

If the PR receives income from investments of your husband's (e.g., share dividends, building society interest) during the period of administration, he may be able to pay some of this to you. If so, he will deduct basic-rate tax from it before paying it to you. If your income in this part of the tax year is not high enough for you to pay tax, you can reclaim the tax deducted from the Inland Revenue (unless it was interest from building societies or banks).

If the estate takes a long time to wind up and you are short of money in the meantime, it is often possible for the PR to make interim payments to you if it is clear that you stand to inherit a reasonable amount from the estate after all taxes and debts have been settled. If a solicitor is administering the estate you should certainly ask him to do this.

If you and the other people who stand to benefit from the will are unhappy with the way your husband has allocated his estate and you can agree on a more acceptable allocation, you can ask your solicitor to draw up a **deed of family arrangement**. You can do this even if your main aim is to reduce the tax bill, and even if assets have been distributed, but you must do it within 2 years of the death and must inform the Inland Revenue within 6 months.

Except in Scotland, certain people are also entitled to ask the courts to assign a larger part of your husband's estate to them than they have been allocated. They include you, a former wife who has not remarried and anyone who has been treated as a child of the family or who was dependent on your husband at the time he died. But the process can be complicated and expensive – get advice from a solicitor.

14

Children

This chapter takes you through the financial side of having and bringing up children – from the benefits and pay you're entitled to while pregnant, to supporting a student son or daughter through college.

Having a baby

Maternity leave and maternity pay

If you are employed, you can take **maternity leave** from 11 weeks before the week the baby is due. You can leave your job before this if you want, but then you won't have any right to **maternity pay**, nor will you have any right to return to your job after the baby is born. You can also carry on working *longer* if you want – but you won't get maternity pay for any week that you're working.

Maternity leave can last for up to 29 weeks after the birth – and unless you work in a small firm (with five or less employees), you may also have the right to return to work at any time up to 29 weeks after the birth. Your firm is allowed to offer you a 'suitable alternative' job – i.e., one with the same wages and conditions.

You have a right to return to work *and* a right to maternity pay if:

- you have worked 16 hours or more a week for the same firm for at least two years, *or* 8 or more hours a week for the same firm for at least 5 years, *and*

- you carry on working until you are 29 weeks' pregnant (it doesn't matter if you are employed but off sick), *and*

- you tell your firm 3 weeks before you stop working that you intend to do this because of your pregnancy. If you want to return to work after the birth, you must also say so in this letter. It is sensible to say you want to return even if you don't – just in case you change your mind. (You can still get maternity pay if you don't go back to work after the birth.)

Your firm may write to you after your baby is born to ask if you *still* want to come back; if you do, you must reply within 14 days saying yes. (If you say yes, you can change your mind later; but once you have said no, you have no legal right to reclaim your job.) Finally, you have to write again 3 weeks before your return, giving the date that you intend to go back.

Maternity pay is paid for the first 6 weeks of your maternity leave at a rate of 90 per cent of your normal wages *less* tax, National Insurance contributions, and the maternity allowance – whether or not you actually get this allowance (see below).

Maternity grant and maternity allowance

Maternity grant is a social security benefit paid as a lump sum to pregnant women who have lived in this country for at least six of the twelve months before their baby is due. It is intended to help pay for things like nappies, baby clothes, a pram, and so on – but it's only £25 so it won't go very far.

You can claim it at any time from the 26th week of your pregnancy up to 3 months after the baby is born. If you are also applying for maternity allowance, however (you use the same form), it's important to make an early claim.

Maternity allowance is a weekly cash benefit which is usually paid for 18 weeks – starting 11 weeks before the week the baby is due, and continuing for 6 weeks after the birth. (If your baby is late, therefore, you may get maternity allowance for longer.) It is currently £29.45 a week – and you may get extra if you support your husband or a person who takes care of any other of your children.

Whether you qualify depends on your previous National Insurance contributions record: the rules are set out in leaflet NI.17A, which is free from social security offices, Citizens Advice Bureaux (CABx) and antenatal clinics. But claim anyway, even if you haven't worked since your last baby was born; the social security office will work out whether or not you're entitled to the allowance.

Claim as soon as possible after the 26th week of your pregnancy, on form BM.4 (available from antenatal clinics, doctors, midwives, health visitors, and social security offices). You won't get the allowance for any week that you're working, but if you have claimed, you will get it as soon as you stop. And don't forget to claim maternity grant at the same time.

If you don't have enough money while pregnant – for example, if you don't qualify for maternity allowance – see Chapter 4 for details of other benefits you might be able to claim.

Diary

- 25th week of pregnancy – if you are taking the maximum amount of maternity leave, write to your firm and say so. Also, tell them whether you intend to return to work afterwards.

- 26th week of pregnancy – claim maternity grant and maternity allowance as soon as possible.

- 29th week of pregnancy – your maternity leave and maternity pay can begin. Also, your maternity allowance can be paid from this week.

- 6 weeks after the birth – your maternity allowance will stop.

- At any time up to 26 weeks after the birth – you can write to your firm giving them 3 weeks' notice that you intend to return to work.

- At any time up to 29 weeks after the birth – you can return to work.

Benefits for mothers and children

All pregnant women and mothers of children under one are entitled to free prescriptions. You can claim using form FW.8 from your doctor, midwife or health visitor; fill it in and send it to your **Family Practitioner Committee** (see phone book). Alternatively, after the baby is born, claim using form P.11, from social security offices or post offices.

All children under 16 are also entitled to free prescriptions simply by signing the declaration on the back of the prescription before giving it to the chemist.

All pregnant women, mothers of children under one, and children under 16 are entitled to free NHS dental treatment – just tell your dentist when you go.

All children under 16 (or under 19 if still in full-time education) can have free glasses, and free treatment from an optician. Ask the optician for form F.1, fill it in, and send it to your local social security office.

For more details, see:

- leaflet P.11, *Free prescriptions*
- leaflet D.11, *NHS dental treatment*
- leaflet G.11, *NHS glasses*

all available from social security offices.

Child benefit

This is a weekly benefit payable for each child under 16 (or under 19 if still at school or college and studying up to A-level or OND standard) – provided you have lived in this country for six of the last twelve months before you claim. It's currently £7 a week for each child.

Claim as soon as possible after you have registered your baby's birth, on forms CH.2 and CH.3. If these forms weren't sent to you when you claimed maternity grant, you can get them from social security offices. Return them together with your baby's birth certificate.

For more details on child benefit, get leaflet CH.1 from social security offices.

Single mothers

If you are bringing up a child on your own, you are entitled to **one-parent benefit**. This is a weekly payment (currently £4.60) which is made at the same time as child benefit. You can't get more than £4.60, however many children you have – and you won't get it at all if you are living with someone as a couple, even if you aren't married. If you do qualify, however, make sure you claim, using form CH.11 (which also gives more details on the benefit).

Single mothers are also entitled to the **additional personal allowance**. This is an extra tax allowance (of £1,320 in the 1986–87 tax year) – which could mean that you don't have to pay so much income tax. You can claim the allowance if you are single, separated, divorced or widowed – even if you are living with someone as a couple – provided you are bringing up a child.

The Inland Revenue has produced a leaflet called *Income tax and one-parent families* (IR.29), available free from local tax offices, which contains lots of useful information on your tax position. For more details on the additional personal allowance, see page 151 – and for organisations which provide advice and support for single mothers, see the list on page 337.

Educational benefits for children

- **travel to school** If the nearest school is two or more miles away (for children under 8), or three or more miles away (for children of 8 or over), you may be able to get some help from your local education authority (LEA) – perhaps a free bus pass or free school bus. Contact your local education department or education welfare department (see phone book) for more information.

- **school milk and meals** LEAs no longer have to provide school milk or meals – with one exception: they must provide a *free* meal to every child whose parents get supplementary benefit or family income supplement (see pages 50 and 52).

- **school uniform** LEAs may at their discretion provide uniforms and other school clothing (or grants towards these). Contact your local education department or education welfare department to find out whether this help is available, and whether you qualify.

- **education maintenance allowance** Some LEAs will pay an allowance to parents of children who stay on at school after the age of 16. More details from education departments.

Going back to work

The first thing you have to do is to make childcare arrangements. If you are one of the lucky few whose firm provides a nursery or creche, you will be taxed on this perk if:

- your firm pays some or all of the costs, *and*
- you count as **higher-paid** (broadly, if you earn more than £8,500 a year – but the rules are more complicated than this, so refer to page 225).

If both of these things apply to you, you'll be taxed on how much your firm pays towards the perk – so if they pay £500 a year, and you're a basic-rate taxpayer, you'll have to pay 29% of £500, i.e., £145 in tax. Of course, this is still preferable to having to make your own nursery arrangements.

Other women may have a relation who can take care of their child while they're at work – but if not, the options are:

- a childminder
- a day nursery
- a home-help or nanny.

A **childminder** is anyone (other than a relation) who is paid to look after your child, in their home, for more than two hours a day. Childminders are legally obliged to register with the social services department, so contact this department (see phone book) for a list of registered minders in your area. And for more information, contact the National Childminding Association (13 London Road, Bromley, Kent BR1 1DE).

Day nurseries may be private, or run by the local authority. Your chances of getting a place for your child in a council nursery are very slim, unless you are a single parent – and even private nurseries may have long waiting-lists, so put down your name as early as possible. Again, the social services department will be able to tell you about all the nurseries in your area.

If you can't find a place for your child, it's possible to get together with other parents and set up your own nursery, staffed by paid professionals and run by a parents' committee. For more information, see *Self-help day care schemes*, a pamphlet from Gingerbread (35 Wellington Street, London WC2E 7BN).

A third option is to take on a **home-help** or **nanny** to look after your child in your own home. Wages vary considerably, depending on how experienced the nanny is – look at ads in magazines like *The Lady* for an idea of current rates.

Agencies such as The Nanny Service (Oldbury Place, London W1) specialise in finding nannies, or you can advertise yourself – or try your local Jobcentre or employment agency.

Paying for private schools

If you want your children to go to private school, the golden rule is: start saving as early as possible. There are several investment plans on the market which are aimed specifically at providing money for school fees. You may invest a lump sum right at the beginning, or a payment every month for a number of years – or a combination of the two.

The schemes are usually based on a series of life insurance policies which **mature** (come to an end and pay out a sum of money) in successive years – so that each year you have money for the fees. But you normally have to start saving well in advance. If you are considering such a scheme, bear in mind the following points:

- it may be quite *inflexible*. You don't know how your financial circumstances might change in the future, so find out what would happen if you could no longer afford to pay the monthly premiums

- there's no guarantee that you'll get enough money to pay the fees. These schemes simply pay out a sum of money at regular intervals – which may turn out to be less than, or more than, enough. (To give you an idea, over the past few years day-pupil fees have increased by over 12% a year, and boarding fees by over 14% per annum.)

See Chapter 5 for information on other ways of investing for the future – and to find out more about school fees and the investment plans on the market, contact the Independent Schools Information Service (56 Buckingham Gate, London SW1E 6AG).

Your children's money

Pocket money

One of the odd laws of nature is that 'other children' *always* get more pocket money than yours! Recently an annual survey of pocket money was published (by Birds Eye Wall's Ltd.) – so at last you can check out this claim. In 1985 the average amounts were as follows:

5–7 year-olds	50p. a week
8–10 year-olds	72p. a week
11–13 year-olds	£1.28 a week
14–16 year-olds	£1.88 a week

Your child's income and tax position

For tax purposes, a child is treated in exactly the same way as an adult. A child gets the **single person's allowance** (£2,335 in the 1986–87 tax year) to set against his or her income, so each child can have an income of up to £2,335 without paying any tax. Income includes any money the child earns (e.g., from part-time jobs) and any income from investments (e.g., interest or dividends) but not money the child is given as a present, or education grants and scholarships (see page 344 for a full list). If the child's income is more than the allowances he or she can claim, there will be some tax to pay on the excess. If the child gets income from which tax has already been deducted (e.g., share dividends) and his or her income is too low to pay tax, the tax can be reclaimed from the Inland Revenue (except with income from banks, building societies and certain other investments).

There is one exception to the above. If a child under 18 gets more than £5 income in a tax year from things given to them by their own parents (whether single, married, separated or divorced), the income counts as the parents', not the child's. This is to stop you avoiding tax by putting investments in your child's name. However, there is one (rather complicated) way out of this – see page 207.

Covenants

If a grandparent (or any other generous friend or relation) wants to supplement your child's income, they can do so through a **deed**

of covenant – and get tax relief on their payments. You can't get tax relief on a covenant payment to your own child, however, unless he or she is over 18 (or married) – see page 208 below.

A covenant is a legally binding agreement under which one person promises to make a series of payments to another. The person who makes the payments can get tax relief at the basic rate only (currently 29%) provided that:

- neither they, nor their husband or wife, gets any benefit from the payments, *and*
- the covenant is drawn up so that it can last for more than six years (even though it may be ended before then).

HOW A COVENANT WORKS:

Suppose a grandparent wants their grandchild to have £100 a year. The grandparent deducts 29% (the tax relief) from the £100, and hands over only £71 to the grandchild. The grandparent can keep the £29 deducted, provided they pay at least that much tax on their own income.

If the grandchild's income (including the 'gross' amount of £100) isn't high enough for them to have to pay tax, they can claim back from the Inland Revenue the £29 deducted. So, for a cost of only £71 to the grandparent, the grandchild has gained £100.

To claim back the tax, the grandparent must each year get form R.185AP from the Inland Revenue, fill it in, and give it to the grandchild. The grandchild (or their parent if they're under 18) must then send the completed form back to their tax office.

The covenant must be properly drawn up if the payments are to qualify for tax relief, so get advice from your local tax office.

Part-time jobs

Another way your child might consider supplementing his or her pocket money is by getting a part-time job – a paper round, for example. Broadly speaking, no child under 13 is allowed to have a job, although there are special rules for children in the entertainment business. There are also restrictions on the hours children can work, and the type of job they can do – so it's worth checking with your local education welfare department (see the phone book) first.

Investing for children

Choosing investments for your child is very much like choosing them for yourself – you have to ask the same sort of questions. For example:

- how much money is there to invest?

- how long is it to be invested for?

- how much of a risk are you prepared to take with the money, in the hope of getting a very good return?

See Chapter 5 (page 67) for how to work out an investment strategy.

Because children can have income of up to £2,335 (in the 1986–87 tax year) before they have to pay tax, the two points to bear in mind are:

- with some investments – notably building society accounts and most bank deposit accounts – the interest is paid out after tax has been deducted, *and the tax can't be claimed back*. So even if your child shouldn't have to pay any tax, he or she is effectively doing so. In this case, a different type of investment – for example, a National Savings investment account – might be better, as the interest is paid out without tax being deducted.

  You'll have to compare the **net** (after-tax) interest on, say, a building society account, with the **gross** (before-tax) interest on other investments, to work out which is better.

- if you give your child investments which provide income of more than £5 a year, it will usually be taxed as *your* income. The exception is if you set up an **accumulation trust** for your child, and the interest is accumulated (i.e., not spent) until the child reaches 18 or gets married. However, the rules about trusts are very complicated, so you should consult a solicitor if you're thinking about doing this.

There are some investments (such as National Savings) which children can have in their own name right from birth (although they can't generally withdraw money until they reach seven or so). With others (for example, shares and premium bonds), there is a minimum age for investing – though you can invest money in your child's name if he or she is too young. The money can then only be used for the child's benefit.

These days banks, building societies and others are trying to attract children at a very young age (in the hope of keeping them for life), and so are offering all sorts of incentives. Don't necessarily be swayed by the offer of a free piggy bank! Follow the guidelines in Chapter 5 to choose the investment which will give your child the best return.

Students

If your child wants to go on to college or university, find out whether or not they qualify for a grant. A booklet called *Grants to students* (free from your local education authority) sets out the rules. Even if they do qualify, you might still be expected to make a contribution towards the grant. Broadly, the size of your contribution (if any) depends on:

- how much the student needs to live on (an amount fixed by the Department of Education, according to where the student will be living), *and*
- your income (after making certain deductions – such as interest on your mortgage).

You'll have to fill in a form giving details of your finances, and then the LEA will tell you whether or not you're expected to contribute – and if so, how much. A couple of points worth noting are:

- If you've got two children very close in age who are both planning to go to college, you could be better off if they went at the same time. Any contribution you're expected to make isn't doubled – it's simply divided between them, and the LEA pays any extra.
- If you're separated or divorced, the income of one parent only is taken into account when working out the size of any parental contribution. This is usually (but not necessarily) the income of the parent who has custody of the child – ask your LEA for more information.

The best way for parents to make contributions is through a **deed of covenant** (see page 206). Covenants for students usually stop after 7 years *or when the student ceases full-time education, if this is earlier*. Although most university and college courses last less than six years, full-time education *could* last longer, so this wording is acceptable. The Inland Revenue has produced a special form, (IR.47), for drawing up the covenant – and another form (IR.59) explains all about students' tax position, including how to reclaim the tax deducted from the covenant payments. These forms are free from tax offices.

15

Protecting Yourself and Those Who Depend on You

Insurance is a way of protecting yourself and your family against possible future hardship. For example, could you cope if you suffered a long illness and had to give up your job? Or if you became disabled and could no longer look after the home and the children? This chapter describes how to insure both your life and your health – and how to make sure you choose the best policy.

Insuring your life

The first question to ask yourself is whether you need any life insurance at all. If you are single and without any dependants (children, perhaps, or an elderly parent), then the answer is probably no – unless you have any debts which wouldn't be repaid on your death. However, if there is anyone who would be financially worse off as a result of your death, then you should take out some life cover.

If you live with a partner and have a job, your earnings are probably an important part of your joint finances. Even if you don't have any earnings (perhaps because you've given up your job while the children are small), your contribution in the home would still be expensive to replace – nannies and home-helps aren't cheap. And if you are a single parent, or responsible for providing for an elderly relative, then it's crucial that you have adequate cover.

How much you need

If you've decided that you should take out life insurance, the next question to ask yourself is how much cover you need.

First, you should make sure that your dependants would have enough money on your death to cover immediate and short-term expenses – the cost of your funeral, for example, or any tax you owe. And secondly, you need to think about the *longer-term*. This means working out how much income they would gain on your death – and how much they would lose. Income they would gain might include a widower's pension for your husband from your job; and if your mortgage is covered by insurance on your life there will be no further payments to make. Income they would lose might include your earnings, or any maintenance payments you get from an ex-husband. Don't forget to allow also for any *extra* income which would be needed after your death; for example, the cost of paying a childminder.

You should aim to take out enough cover to ensure that your dependants wouldn't be worse off as a result of your death. For example, you might have worked out that they would be worse off to the tune of £6,000 a year. You can take out a policy which will provide them with an annual income of this amount (paid in monthly or quarterly instalments), or you can take out a policy which will pay out a (much larger) lump sum. This could then be invested, and the interest used to provide them with the necessary income.

You should also think about *how long* the money will be needed for. For example, if you have very young children, they will probably be dependent on you for another 15 or 20 years, so you might choose a policy which lasts for 20 years. Finally, you need to make sure that the amount of cover you take out now will still be enough in the future (£6,000 will be worth only £1,550 in 20 years' time, if inflation is 7%). One way of coping with this is to take out insurance which is **index-linked**: your cover goes up each year in line with inflation. However, there are many other types of policy on the market, too, so below we explain how they work, and how to find the policy to suit your needs.

Which type of policy?

Broadly, there are two main types of life insurance. With pure life insurance (often called **term insurance** or **protection-only life insurance**) the insurance company will pay out only if you die within a set number of years (the term of the policy). With the second type of life insurance, you pay much larger amounts to the insurance company; some of this is used to buy life insurance, but most of it is invested for you, and the accumulated investment is paid out at the end of a fixed period or when you die. If your aim is simply to provide protection for your dependants, choose term insurance instead – it's a lot cheaper. If you do want a way of saving, too, look at other forms of investment: you may well get a better deal, and much more flexibility, if you keep your insurance and investments separate (see Chapter 5).

How term insurance works

You choose the term of the policy (say, 10 or 20 years), and if you die within that period, the insurance will be paid out. There are policies which pay out a **lump sum**, or policies which pay out a **family income benefit** – a tax-free monthly or quarterly income. This is normally payable only till the end of the term, so if you died in the ninth year of a 10-year policy, your dependants would get an income for one year only. A lump-sum policy will provide the same amount whether you die in the first or last year of the term, so this is generally better value. However, if your dependants are unused to handling large sums of money, they could lose everything if they invested the lump sum unwisely – so they (and you) might feel happier with the regular income from a family income benefit policy.

With standard term insurance, the amount of cover stays the same throughout the whole term, but because of inflation, after a few years this might not be enough to meet your dependants' needs. In this case, you should choose an increasing or **escalating** policy where the amount you are insured for escalates each year, perhaps by 5 or 10%, or in line with inflation.

These days, term insurance can be very flexible – for example, there are policies which allow you to increase your cover every few years, and policies which can be converted into a different type of insurance. However, you might not actually *need* all this flexibility, so don't be talked into buying a more complicated policy than necessary (there's no point in paying extra for options you are unlikely to use). A straightforward escalating policy, lasting for as long as you are likely to have dependants, and which would provide sufficient income for them to live on, may well be your best bet.

If you and your partner are both taking out life insurance, you may find it is slightly cheaper to have a **joint life policy**. But for a number of reasons we would recommend you to have individual policies, particularly as a joint life policy can be much less flexible if your circumstances change in the future.

If you are self-employed, have freelance earnings or are in a job but are not a member of your employer's pension scheme, you can get full tax relief on the premiums you pay for term insurance. You will need to ask for a special policy called a **Section 226A policy** – see page 289 for details. This is well worth doing as it will normally mean that each £10 of premiums costs you only £7.10.

How to get insured

Decide which type of policy you want (e.g., an escalating family income benefit policy); how long you want it for (e.g., 20 years); and how much cover (e.g., £6,000 a year). Then look at the most recent report in *Which?* magazine (available in your local library) for the companies that are recommended. Contact several of these and ask for details and quotes for the premiums. Two insurance companies which are often amongst the cheapest (partly because they pay no commission to middlemen and so do not deal through brokers) are Equitable Life (tel. 01-606 6611) and London Life (tel. 0272 279179).

Instead of approaching the companies yourself, you could go through a professional adviser (such as your solicitor or bank manager) or through a broker (a registered insurance specialist). To find a broker, look in Yellow Pages under *Insurance brokers*, or contact the British Insurance Brokers' Association (see Chapter 22), who will send you a list of brokers in your area.

Once you have chosen a company, you will have to fill in a **proposal form**: a questionnaire which asks you specific questions, for example, about your health. You must answer everything honestly, otherwise the company could refuse to pay out a claim in the future. You also have to disclose any other 'material facts' – anything else which may be relevant.

If you know who you want the insurance money to go to if you die, it is well worth asking the company to have the policy **written in trust**. This costs no extra, and means a special wording will be used so that the money can be paid promptly, after your death (without waiting for probate) and it will be completely free of Inheritance Tax – see page 321 for more information.

You may be asked to send off your first premium with the proposal form; alternatively, the company may send you an acceptance letter first. You usually have a choice about whether to pay monthly, quarterly, half-yearly or yearly. The more frequent the payments, the more you will pay out in total each year, but if it will help your budgeting to pay in instalments then do so. Don't forget to ask whether any discounts are available – for example, some companies give discounts to members of certain trade unions or professional associations.

INFLATION CHART: WHAT £10,000 WILL BE WORTH IF:

inflation averages 5%	after 5 years	£7,835
	after 10 years	£6,139
	after 15 years	£4,810
	after 20 years	£3,769
inflation averages 10%	after 5 years	£6,209
	after 10 years	£3,855
	after 15 years	£2,394
	after 20 years	£1,486

Life insurance which includes investment

Policies which include investment work in different ways. Some, like term insurance, last for a set number of years, and will pay out if you die within that period. However, unlike term insurance, they will also pay out if you survive to the end of the period: *you* will get the lump sum, so these policies are really a way of saving for the future, as well as getting life cover. On the face of it, then, they sound like a good deal. The drawbacks are, firstly, they are a lot more expensive than term insurance (see the table on page 215); secondly, they tie up your savings for a long time (if you wanted to get at your money before the end of the term, you could lose out); and thirdly, you may well be able to get a better return from another form of investment.

Whole life policies are not for a set period – they will pay out on your death *regardless* of when that happens. With some, you have to pay the premiums for the whole of your life; with others, the premiums stop after you reach a certain age. Despite their name, these policies are also used as a way of saving – though if you needed to get at your money and so *cashed in* the policy, you could find the amount you get back is quite low (particularly in the early years). And again, whole life policies are more expensive than term insurance.

Endowment policies last for a set period. A **non-profit** endowment policy guarantees to pay out a set amount at the end of the period (or on your death). A **with-profits** endowment policy also guarantees to pay out a set amount, but this grows over the years as the insurance company adds bonuses to it. However, these bonuses can't be predicted in advance and might in any case be worth a lot less by the time you get them, because of inflation.

Unit-linked policies may last for a set period or for the whole of your life. Part of your premium pays for life cover, and the rest is invested by the insurance company. The amount you get back at the end of the period (or on your death) depends on how well the investments are doing *at that time*: their value can go down as well as up, so this is a more risky way of saving.

THE COST OF DIFFERENT TYPES OF LIFE INSURANCE

	woman age 29	*woman age 44*
Example yearly premium for term insurance[1]	£50	£200
Example yearly premium for with-profits endowment insurance[2]	£1,000	£1,100

[1] for a 20-year escalating policy, paying a lump sum of £20,000 in the first year. This increases each year by 5%.
[2] for a 20-year policy guaranteeing a lump sum of £20,000. This increases each year as bonuses are added to it.

Insuring against long illness

Death isn't the only thing which can cause financial hardship: so can a long illness. You might be unfortunate enough to contract a serious illness which takes a year or two to clear up, or you might even become *permanently* disabled – and in either of these cases, you could find yourself very short of money.

If you have a job, check how much sick pay you would get from your employer – and for how long. Some employers have very generous sick-pay schemes, and will continue paying you for as long as you are too ill to work (right up to retirement age, if necessary). Others will only pay you for a few weeks, however, and after that you might have to manage just on state benefits. If you are self-employed, a long illness could be even more disastrous financially; and even though you aren't able to earn, you might still need to pay for a home-help or childminder.

If you think a long illness could cause you financial hardship, consider taking out **permanent health insurance** (**PHI**) – insurance which pays you an income while you are too ill to work.

How PHI works

Permanent health insurance usually pays you an income while you are too ill to do your normal job and not able to do any other. (A few companies will pay out only if you are too ill to do *any* job for which you are 'reasonably' qualified.) In addition, you can often get a reduced income if you can only return to work part-time, or in a lower-paid job, because of your illness. It's called *permanent* because it can't be cancelled by the company, no matter how many claims you make or how long you claim for.

When you take out a policy, you choose a 'waiting period' of perhaps three or six months, which means that the company won't pay out for the first three or six months of any illness. The longer the waiting period, the cheaper the premiums, so work out for how long you could cope before running into financial difficulties, and choose a waiting period of that length of time. You also choose how many years you want the policy to last – perhaps until you reach the age when you will get a pension.

How much cover?

You decide how much income you want the policy to pay out – within certain limits. The insurance company will want to make sure that you are not actually better off during illness, so it will set a limit of, say, three-quarters of your previous earnings (including money you get from other sources, such as state benefits while sick). Not many companies will insure women who don't have earnings – two that do are Permanent (tel. 01-636 1686) and Phoenix (tel. 0272 277788). There is usually a financial limit for women who aren't earning: for example, they might pay out a maximum of £50 a week. Unless you have lots of other sources of income, however, you should probably insure for the maximum allowed by the company.

It may be a long time before you make a claim, and when you do, your illness may also last for a long time. For these reasons it's important that your policy offers some protection against inflation – both *before* a claim, and by increasing the insurance paid to you *during* a claim. With a few policies, both of these increase automatically in line with inflation each year, and although such policies may be more expensive, they could be well worth it.

Choosing a policy

Again, your starting point should be *Which?* magazine (in your local library). Contact several of the recommended companies for details of their policies and quotes for the premiums. These are the main points to bear in mind when making your choice:

- **the cost** Premiums depend on a number of factors: your age, your health, and your occupation, for example. Some jobs are considered to be more risky (to your health) than others, and so carry higher premiums. However, not all companies use the same definition of a risky job, so it's worth shopping around. The cost can also depend on your *sex*: most companies charge women higher premiums because they say women are more likely to claim than men. The Equal Opportunities Commission disagrees, saying that the companies' statistics on this are out-of-date – but in a recent court case, the judge ruled that women could continue to be charged more. You can ask any company what *loading*, or extra charge, it puts on women's premiums (one or two don't put on any, so as a point of principle you could choose one of these). Alternatively, just shop around for the lowest premiums for *you* – a company which does load might still work out cheapest.

- **protection against inflation** Find out whether the cover before a claim increases each year, and if so, by how much. Some companies increase the cover only every few years – so if you claimed at the 'wrong' time (just before an increase was due), you could find yourself under-insured. Others do increase the cover each year, but only by 3%, say – so if inflation stays at its present level, your cover would soon start to look on the low side. Also, avoid policies where the income paid *during* a claim doesn't increase (or increases, but not by much).

• **the exclusions** Most policies have several exclusions, or specified circumstances where they won't pay out. If you intentionally injure yourself and then try to claim, for example, you are highly unlikely to succeed. However, companies differ on their other exclusions, so it's worth comparing the policies carefully – particularly if you think you may become pregnant in the future. Some policies won't pay out for *any* illness connected with pregnancy or childbirth, but others will at least pay out if you are still ill several months after the pregnancy ends.

YEARLY PREMIUMS
for an index-linked policy, paying an income of £100 a week

waiting period	*woman aged 29*	*woman aged 44*
3 months	£115	£220
6 months	£100	£190
1 year	£85	£170

Insuring against accidents

You can take out **personal accident and sickness** insurance, which usually provides five different kinds of benefit:

• an income if you are unable to work because of an accident or illness – usually, for up to 2 years.

• a lump sum if you are permanently disabled in an accident – but not if you are disabled through illness.

• a lump sum if you lose one or more limbs (or eyes) in an accident.

• a lump sum to your dependants if you die in an accident – but not if you die because of an illness.

• a cash payment for each day you spend in hospital, or a contribution towards your medical expenses.

These policies may sound like a good deal, but they also have their drawbacks, and a combination of **term insurance** (see page 212) and **permanent health insurance** (see page 216) is probably a better option for most women. Here's why:

• You take out an accident and sickness policy for a set period (often a year), but if you claim during that time, the company may refuse to let you renew the policy. With PHI, the company can't cancel, no matter how many claims you make.

• If you are still ill at the end of the two years, you are unlikely to get any more money – whereas PHI will continue to pay out for as long as you are unable to work.

• PHI will pay out for disablement caused through illness, as well as accident, if it prevents you from working.

• You are highly unlikely to lose a limb or an eye in an accident – other injuries are much more common – and in any case, the lump sum under an accident and sickness policy is often quite low. If the injury prevented you from working, a PHI policy would pay you an income.

• Term insurance will pay out to your dependants if you die because of illness, as well as because of an accident.

However, it might be worth taking out an accident and sickness policy *in conjunction* with PHI: this would mean you could choose a two-year waiting period, as the accident and sickness policy would pay out for the first two years of illness. Check whether this would work out cheaper than just taking out a PHI policy with a shorter waiting period.

EARNING MONEY

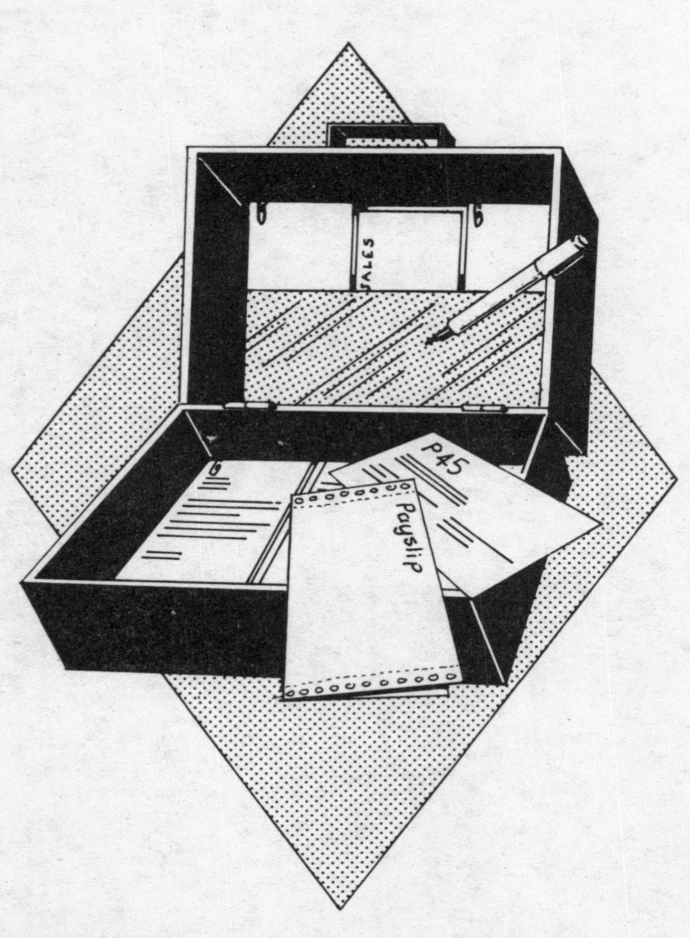

16

Your Job

Finding a job

With over three million people unemployed, finding a job may seem a daunting task – but use as many sources as possible in your search:

- the Jobcentre or (for more senior jobs) the Professional and Executive Register (PER)
- employment agencies – both general and specialist
- national and local newspapers
- trade and other specialist magazines
- ads in shop windows or by factory gates
- local radio
- contacting firms on spec
- asking friends, family, colleagues and old business contacts if they've heard of any vacancies
- advertising *yourself* – e.g., in the local newspaper.

There are agencies which can help you to prepare your job applications (or *curriculum vitae*), but they are often very expensive, and there's no guarantee of success. Your local Jobcentre or PER office will probably give just as good advice – free. And they'll also have details of training courses in your area.

Your contract of employment

Once you've found a job, there are several things you should check about your terms and conditions of employment. Provided you work 16 or more hours a week, your firm must give you a written statement including details of:

- your pay
- your hours
- your holiday entitlement
- your sick pay
- any pension scheme run by the firm
- your notice period.

The details of your pay should set out not only how much you're paid (and how often), but also whether you're eligible for overtime, bonuses or commission payments. And it's well worth checking if there are any perks (e.g., luncheon vouchers) which come with the job.

By law you should get the written statement within 13 weeks of starting work but you'll probably want to find out about these things at the interview to enable you to decide whether or not to accept the job.

Starting work

If it's your first job, you'll have to be introduced to the mysteries of the payslip. Every employee has a right to an itemised pay statement which sets out:

- the **gross** (before deductions) amount of your pay
- the deductions (for example, income tax)
- the **net** amount of your pay – what you actually take home.

The most important deductions are for income tax (explained in Chapter 23), and National Insurance contributions (see page 275).

These contributions are paid by everyone who earns £38.00 a week or more. The money collected goes towards providing things like unemployment benefit, sickness benefit and (perhaps most important), state retirement pensions (see Chapter 19). Once you've paid a certain amount of National Insurance contributions, you become entitled to these state benefits – so that if you're unlucky enough to lose your job, say, or have a long illness, you'll get some money from the state to help you out.

If you belong to the firm's pension scheme, your monthly contributions to the scheme will also be deducted from your pay. Provided it's a **statutory** or **approved** scheme (nearly all are), your contributions aren't taxable – so they'll be deducted before the tax on the rest of your pay is worked out. Chapter 19 explains more about firms' pension schemes.

Perks of the job

Many jobs come complete with certain perks (or fringe benefits) – for example, luncheon vouchers. Some perks are tax-free, and so don't affect your tax bill at all. The most common tax-free perks are:

- luncheon vouchers of up to 15p per working day
- canteen meals
- free or cheap tea or coffee
- free life insurance
- free sick pay insurance
- free overalls, or other clothes specially needed for your job
- staff outings.

Other perks, however, have what's called a **taxable value**. This means that the Inland Revenue decides the perk is the equivalent of an extra amount of pay – which you have to pay tax on. The rules for working out the taxable value of these perks depend on whether or not you count as **higher-paid**.

Broadly speaking, you count as higher-paid if your earnings and perks over the year add up to £8,500 or more. In this case, the taxable value of any perks you get is normally the amount they cost your firm. So if you get a perk which costs your firm £100, this figure will be added to your wages, and you'll probably have to pay tax on it.

If you don't count as higher-paid, the taxable value of the perk is normally its **secondhand value**. Many perks – for example, free hairdressing at work – don't have a secondhand value, so you won't have to pay any tax on them.

There are special rules for some perks – for example, company cars and cheap loans (for a season ticket, say):

• **company cars** If you *don't* count as higher-paid, the taxable value of your company car is nil, so you won't have to pay any tax on it.

If you *do* count as higher-paid, the taxable value of your company car depends on its age, the engine size, and how much it cost when it was new. Your employer will have the relevant figures.

If your firm pays for any petrol for *private* use of the car, this also has a taxable value, but only if you count as higher-paid. The taxable value depends on the engine size of the car, not on how much petrol you get.

• **cheap loans** If you *don't* count as higher-paid, you won't have to pay any tax on cheap loans your firm gives you.

If you *do* count as higher-paid, you won't have to pay any tax on loans which qualify for tax relief. For example, if you work for a bank and your employer gives you a cheap mortgage, this might qualify for tax relief (see Chapter 7) – so you wouldn't have to pay tax on it. If the loan doesn't qualify for tax relief, however – if it's for a season ticket, say – the taxable value is the difference between the interest you pay the firm, and the amount you would pay if you were charged the **official rate of interest** – currently 12%.

However, if the taxable value of all your cheap loans is £200 or less, you do not have to pay any tax on them.

Redundancy

If your firm makes you redundant, you are entitled to at least one week's notice, provided you've worked for the firm for at least a month. If you've worked for at least 2 years, you're entitled to 2 weeks' notice; if you've worked 3 years, you're entitled to 3 weeks' notice; and so on, up to a maximum of 12 weeks. If your employment contract gives you a longer notice period, however, you're entitled to that longer period.

You should get any wages, holiday pay or maternity pay owed to you (all of these are taxable) – and you should also be paid during the notice period. If you work out your notice, this pay is taxable; if your firm agrees *in writing* that you don't have to work out your notice, the pay is tax-free.

Provided you've been with the firm for at least 2 years since you were 18, working not less than 16 hours a week, you're probably entitled to a minimum lump sum **redundancy payment**. (Some workers – for example, women over 60 – aren't entitled to this payment, however. See the Department of Employment *Booklet 16* for more details – free from employment offices.)

Redundancy payments are normally tax-free if they total £25,000 or less; you'll have to pay tax on any excess over £25,000. If you have any disagreements with your firm over redundancy, get advice from your trade union or local Citizens Advice Bureau.

Part-time work

If you work part-time, you often have fewer employment rights than your full-time colleagues. For example, we said above that you're entitled to a written statement giving details about your pay, hours, etc. – provided you work 16 or more hours a week. If you work between 8 and 16 hours a week, however, you're not entitled to this statement until you've been with the firm for at least five years! And if you work for less than 8 hours a week, you're not entitled to a written statement at all.

Another example relates to your rights during pregnancy. Part-time workers can take time off for antenatal care – but they may not always get maternity pay, nor may they always have the right to return to their job after the baby is born. See page 198 for more details.

If you earn less than £38.00 a week, you don't have to pay any National Insurance contributions – which means you may lose out on state benefits (see Chapter 4) and a state pension (see Chapter 19).

The Department of Employment has published a leaflet, *Advice for those interested in part-time work*, which outlines rights at work for part-timers, and tells you where to go for more information. The leaflet is free from employment offices.

17

Earning Money at Home

In this chapter we look at ways of earning money by working at or from your home. This may be for just a few hours a week, or may take up more of your time than a full-time job. But we assume that all you need to start are you, the abilities and knowledge you have, your home, and some fairly basic equipment.

It's possible that your work at home may develop into something rather bigger. Or you may have ideas about starting a more fully-fledged business from the outset. We look at these possibilities in the next chapter – though if the business is run from your home, much of this chapter will apply too.

Is working at home for you?

Working at home is appealing for a number of reasons. You are independent, and can fit your working hours around other things you have to do. You don't waste time and money travelling to work every day. You can still take the children to school and collect them. You can attend to family emergencies during your working hours, and cope with work emergencies out of office hours. And using your home is very much cheaper than renting other premises from which to run a business, entailing another phone, a second rates bill, more furniture, and so on.

But there can be serious difficulties with working at home. You may need to reorganise your private life quite considerably to be able to cope. You will need the support of your partner and family, and they may need to agree to take over some of the jobs that you have previously done. You may find it very lonely working on your own, and may get depressed when things aren't going well. You will need to be well motivated and will probably have to set yourself strict working hours during which you will not let yourself be distracted. The more you can cut yourself off the better.

Using part of your home exclusively for work could mean some liability for Capital Gains Tax when you sell it. Under the current rules though, the amount of tax you have to pay is likely to be very small, if anything at all. However it is best to use a specific part of your home *mainly but not exclusively* for your work (e.g., you work in it 40 hours a week and the family uses it for 5 hours on average). Your Tax Inspector may then allow you to claim a proportion of the rates (and rent) on your home as a business expense, without incurring a Capital Gains Tax liability when you sell the home. But there is no guarantee the Inspector will allow this – it depends on your circumstances.

What can you do?

You may have no doubts about the type of work you want to do at home. You may know exactly how it will run – who your customers will be, how much you'll charge and how much you'll make. You may have several skills you could use, or you may have a strong desire to try your hand at something of which you have no previous experience but which you feel confident you could do. Formal qualifications aren't essential. You will be judged by the quality of what you produce. But if you are a qualified teacher, typist, linguist, musician, hairdresser, mechanic, potter or chef, you may well be able to put your experience to good use. Below we look briefly at some of the most common ways of earning money at home, but you will find a lot more ideas in any of these books:

Making Money at Home by Olga Franklyn (Futura, £3.95)
Spare-Time Income by Peter Farrell (Kogan Page, £4.95)
Earning Money at Home (Consumers' Association, £6.95)
Working for Yourself by Godfrey Golzen (Kogan Page, £4.95)

It's probably easier to make money out of providing a service (e.g., typing or teaching) than by selling things you have made.

This is because people expect to pay you for the time you spend doing their work and, unless expensive equipment or materials are involved, most of the money you get goes into your pocket. But if you are making cuddly toys or dolls' houses, people are inclined to think in terms of the cost of the materials and forget about the time involved in making them. You must ask yourself whether you can make the things *and* sell them *and* get a decent amount for your time.

CRAFTS

A crafts venture is likely to be most successful if you don't try to compete directly with the shops but aim instead for something different. People will pay more than standard shop prices for hand-thrown pottery or hand-knitted sweaters, but only for something better, more attractive and more individual than they can buy elsewhere.

TEACHING

If you are a qualified teacher or have specialist knowledge, you may find there is a demand for private coaching at home for both children and adults. In a city there are likely to be people from abroad who want to improve their spoken and written English. You could write to local firms and colleges offering to tutor their trainees and foreign students. Teaching will be far more profitable if you can teach two students or even a small group at the same time, rather than individually. You can also expect students to provide all their own books and materials.

TAKING IN LODGERS

If you have one or more spare rooms in your home, taking in lodgers can be a reliable way of getting some extra cash without spending too much time or effort. If you find your lodgers privately, you need do no more than inform your house contents insurance company and consider what extra cover you need. But if you are offering the rooms publicly (e.g., in a local newspaper or at a local college) you should check with your local planning and housing departments on their requirements. If you have a mortgage you should get permission from the mortgage company and if your home is rented you should ask the landlord. If you intend having more than six lodgers you must also get a fire certificate from your local Fire Prevention Officer. If you are offering holiday or tourist accommodation, your regional Tourist Board will be able to give you help and information (in Northern Ireland registration is essential). You should always have a written agreement with tenants, preferably drawn up by a solicitor, who will also be able to tell you about your own and your lodgers' rights. These will depend on the extent to which your lodgers have exclusive use of part of your home or whether they share your home, meals and so on with you. You may find it useful to get the following *Housing Booklets* from your local Citizens Advice Bureau (CAB): *The Rent Acts and you, Letting rooms in your home* and *Shorthold tenancies*. Like working at home, letting part of it can lead to a small Capital Gains Tax liability when you sell the home, but not if your lodgers share your living rooms and generally eat with you. If they live separately, the CGT liability will be lowest if you have used the lodgers' accommodation as your own at some time, even if only for a short period. See page 138 for more information.

LOOKING AFTER CHILDREN

If you are considering looking after other people's pre-school children at your home, contact the local authority social services department to talk it over first. They can explain to you their requirements and what you will need to provide to qualify for registration. They may know of a short course you can attend. You will need to have adequate facilities at your home and may need to buy cots, pushchairs, small chairs and tables, a playpen and toys. The National Childminding Association (13 London Road, Bromley, Kent BR1 1DE) will also be able to send you useful information, supply standard agreements and arrange public liability insurance.

Three kinds of work we don't recommend

BEING A MAIL ORDER AGENT

Mail order catalogues are usually sent free in reply to an advertisement in the press. You can order things for yourself or your friends. Your friends pay the prices in the catalogue and you are paid 10% commission by the company (or you can have goods to the value of 12½% of your orders). There is quite a lot of paperwork to do, and catalogues give your customers the option of paying in weekly instalments over 30 weeks or more – which means you have to collect money from them each week. The goods ordered are normally delivered to you and you have to take them to your customers. If a customer decides against something, you have to send it back. So there's a lot of work to do for little reward – £1,000 worth of orders will only bring you £100 in commission, but could mean you delivering 50 items, sending 20 back and collecting a total of 900 payments from people. This could also be a fast away to lose friends!

SELLING PARTIES

Some companies use 'parties' as a way of demonstrating and selling their products – most commonly kitchen equipment, clothes and jewellery. As an organiser you have to arrange these parties in your own home or find other people to run them, and demonstrate and sell the products. Orders are usually delivered to you and you take them to the buyers and collect the money. The company pays you commission on what you sell. Because you can't keep asking the same people to have parties selling the same things, this is likely to be a job that lasts only a few months. And a lot of people object to selling methods where they feel obliged to buy things they don't really want – so again you could lose a few friends.

BEING A 'HOME WORKER'

This is work done at home directly for a manufacturer, and is usually paid on a piece-work basis – i.e., you are paid for the amount you do, not how long it takes. The pay is often very low, and you get no automatic right to any of the normal advantages of employment – paid holidays, sick pay, maternity rights, redundancy pay. And while you may save on fares to work, you may have to provide your own equipment and materials. You may also have equipment and materials around the home which are dangerous to children, pets or people unfamiliar with them. This type of home-working is very cheap for the manufacturer who pays low wages and has no overheads, and is often regarded as exploitation of people desperate for money.

Making a plan

If your main intention is to occupy your time rather than make money, you may be happy just to start your work and see how it goes. But if earning some money is going to be important to you, then it's essential you make a plan which answers these questions:

- **What are you going to do? Who are your potential customers?** (make a list). **How many customers do you need and how will you find them?**

- **How much is it going to cost you to get going?**

Think about – equipment you need to buy
– things you need to rent (e.g., phone)
– materials you need to buy
– the cost of advertising or getting cards or leaflets printed

Have you got all this money, or are you going to have to borrow some of it?

- **What will the regular expenses and overheads be?** (for example, cost of materials and stationery, telephone and postage, use of your car)

- **How much are you going to charge?**

Are you going to undercut other people in order to get sales, or offer a better-quality service at a higher price? How much do you need to charge to cover your costs and your overheads and make a profit?

- **How soon will you be making money?**

Work out how much income you'd get in the first 6 months and the first year if the business goes as well as you hope. Then subtract all the expenses you've listed and see what's left. Then do the same again, but this time assume things don't go anything like as well as you hope. Could you still manage?

If the money side of your business is simple (e.g., you're taking in lodgers or giving piano lessons and charging each half-term) this plan will be straightforward. If your business involves assembling components bought from a number of suppliers and sold to a number of different outlets, you may need to spend a while playing around with the figures until you find a framework which is workable. In doing so, you will be making decisions about the scale on which you are going to start your business. If it is going to cost you quite a bit to get established, you will probably need a bank loan. You should draw up a chart showing how much money is likely to come in and go out each month and the monthly balance – called a cash-flow. This is quite straightforward and is explained on page 249.

What to call yourself

You can call your business or your products pretty well anything you like. There are a few words you cannot use without permission (like *Royal, British, National, Society, Trust* or anything which implies a connection with the Government or a local authority). You should avoid registered trade marks (usually shown by a small R or TM in a circle) and also names being used by other people in your area for the same type of business (check in Yellow Pages). You don't have to register the name of your business with anyone (there isn't any register, except for companies) and no one else can stop you using the name you choose (as long as you don't try to feed on their reputation or imply that the things you make or the services you supply are in fact made or supplied by someone else).

However, there are rules you must follow if you trade under any name which is not simply your real surname (your husband's surname if you are married), with or without your first name or initials but with nothing else added. If you use any other name (e.g., your maiden name, or something like *Jane's Antiques* or *Evans Jewellery*), you must show your real name (or the names of all the partners) and a permanent address on all your business letters, order forms, invoices, receipts and demands for payment. The address must also be displayed prominently in any premises you use.

Going it alone, or with someone else?

There are three ways of going into business – on your own (called a **sole trader**), **in partnership** with one or more people, or by forming a **limited company**. A limited company is expensive to set up and will almost certainly be unnecessary for you starting off at home. Details about companies and also co-operatives and franchises are in the next chapter.

There are no formalities at all in starting a business as a sole trader other than those in the previous and next sections. It's sensible to keep the business money completely separate from your personal money. But you own the business so it's all your money. This also means that the business's debts are *your* debts and, in the last resort, your personal possessions including your home could be sold to pay them.

If you are starting your business in partnership with someone else, you share the profits (usually in proportion to the amount of money you each put in) but *each* of you can be held liable for *all* the business's debts. For this and other reasons, it's often said that choosing your business partner is at least as important as choosing your marriage partner. You must feel convinced that your partner is as dedicated to the project as you are, that you are aiming at the same goals, that you agree about procedures and that you can get on on a day-to-day basis. It is also important that your partner's skills, knowledge and experience make up for the gaps in your own. For example, if you are an excellent potter but don't much like dealing with people or figures, an ex-sales director might well make a better partner for you than another potter. It is *essential* that you have a partnership agreement between you, drawn up by a solicitor, stating:

- the name, address and type of business of the partnership
- the date it starts and the conditions under which it can end
- the amount of money each of you is putting in and under what conditions
- the partnership's bank account and directions about its money
- how profits are to be worked out and divided between you
- what accounts are to be prepared
- how disagreements between you will be settled
- what happens if one of you retires, dies or becomes bankrupt or the partnership is dissolved for some other reason
- the conditions under which the partnership agreement can be altered.

Either a sole trader or a partnership can employ other people. If you are thinking of doing so, read the booklets *Employing people* from the Small Firms Service (see below), *Thinking of taking someone on?* and *Employer's guide to PAYE* (Inland Revenue leaflets IR.53 and P.7, free from tax offices) and *Employer's guide to National Insurance contributions* (leaflet NP.15 from DHSS offices). The Department of

Employment publishes a series of leaflets on employment law, which are available from Jobcentres.

Help and advice

A large number of sources of information and advice are listed in the next chapter. In particular it would be worth your while to contact the Small Firms Service (see page 252), considering whether you would benefit from a free **Self-Employment Course** (see page 253) and seeing whether you qualify for the **Enterprise Allowance Scheme** which pays you an income of £40 a week for up to a year while you get your business going (see page 253).

Who needs to know?

Whether you need any permission before you can start working at home depends largely on what you'll be doing. If you're writing a book or giving Spanish lessons, you'll need to do no more than tell the Inland Revenue, the DHSS and your insurance companies. For some types of business you may need a licence or special insurance arrangements. And if you want to convert your front room into a shop, your garage into an industrial workshop and your front garden into a car park, then you'll need more extensive permission. Details of these requirements are given below.

Using your home

If you own your home, check that there aren't any **restrictive covenants** which prevent it being used for a business. These will be stated in the deeds of your home, and should also be explained in letters you had from your solicitor when you bought it. If you have a mortgage, you should get permission from the mortgage company. They won't mind you doing freelance work at home, but may well object to you turning your home into commercial premises.

If you rent your home, check what the lease allows you to do and ask the landlord if necessary.

Planning permission

You may need planning permission just to change the *use* of part of your home – e.g., from living accommodation to an office or from a garage to a store – even if you aren't altering it at all. You may also need permission for extending your home, for changing it structurally, for building anything in the garden or for putting signs up. Any building work will also need to comply with the **Building Regulations** (see page 132). Before getting any plans drawn up, it's advisable to call at your local planning authority and discuss informally what you've got in mind – you'll probably find you get a lot of free help and advice.

Do you need a licence?

For most types of work you won't need a licence, but for some you probably will. It's sensible to check with your local council, who will be able to tell you what you need to do if you want to start any of the following (unless a different authority is shown in brackets):

- a shop, if you employ anyone
- a mobile food shop (environmental health department)
- taxi hire
- an employment agency or employment business (it is illegal to run one of these without a licence from the Department of Employment; but if the agency is only for qualified nurses and midwives, ask your local authority)
- looking after children (social services department)
- a nursing home
- a caravan site
- a pet boarding or breeding kennel (environmental health department)
- a riding establishment.

Insurance companies

Before you start working at home you should write to the insurance companies which insure the structure of your home and its contents and tell them what you're up to. Don't try to play it down or hide anything – if you don't tell them the full story they could refuse to pay you a penny on any claim at all. The companies may not change your policy or charge you any extra if they don't think the risk is any higher.

The DHSS

As a self-employed person, you will normally be liable to pay National Insurance contributions. These are made up of two parts:

- a flat-rate **Class 2** contribution (£3.75 a week in the 1986–87 tax year) paid to the DHSS on a weekly or monthly basis

- an earnings-related **Class 4** contribution, worked out and collected in arrears by the Inland Revenue at the same time as the income tax which is due on your profits (see next section).

Class 2 contributions entitle you to a limited range of social security benefits – but they give you *no* entitlement to unemployment benefit and qualify you only for a *basic* state pension, not additional (Serps) pension (see page 273). Class 4 contributions don't give you any extra entitlement at all – they simply mean that people who earn more pay more. Details are given in leaflet NI.41, *National Insurance guide for the self-employed* from your local social security office.

When you start working for yourself, you should write to your local DHSS office and tell them. They will send you an application form for paying Class 2 contributions. If you only do occasional bits of freelance work you only have to pay these contributions for the weeks you work. If you are normally self-employed, you have to pay them each week. But you won't have to pay them at all if one of the following applies:

- you are over 60, *or*

- before 5 April 1978 you were married or widowed and chose **reduced liability** and you haven't given it up (or lost it) since (see pages 292–3 for the pros and cons). If this applies to you, you should have a **Certificate of Election** (form CF.383). If you don't know whether this applies to you, ask your local DHSS office, *or*

- you expect your earnings from your business to be less than a certain amount in the current tax year (i.e., in the period from the last 6 April to the next 5 April). In the 1986–87 tax year, the earnings limit is £2,075. *Earnings* means your takings, less what you spend in the course of running the business on things like rent and rates, insurance, printing and stationery, postage and telephone, petrol and fares, etc. If this applies to you, you can apply for 'exception' from paying Class 2 contributions (get leaflet NI.27A, *People with small earnings from self-employment*, complete the form in it and send it to your social security office). But, unless you also have a job in which you are paying Class 1 contributions or qualify for **Home Responsibilities Protection** (see page 276), you may be better paying your Class 2 contributions, as not doing so could affect the amount of state pension and other benefits you are entitled to.

You can pay Class 2 contributions by buying a stamp each week at the post office and sticking it on a card given to you by the DHSS. But if you have to pay each week it is very much easier to pay by direct debit from your bank or National Girobank account, by filling in the form in leaflet NI.255. Your contributions will then be taken automatically from your bank account once a month in arrears.

The tax office

When you start your own business, however small, you should write to your tax office (your local one or your husband's if you don't have one already) and ask for a copy of leaflet IR.28, *Starting in business*. This includes a form for you to return giving the Tax Inspector information on what you're doing; alternatively you can write a letter describing your business. If you use a specific part of your home *mainly but not exclusively* for your work, say that this is the case (see page 229). If your earnings are small, it won't matter if you don't tell the tax office about your new source of earnings until the end of the tax year (on 5 April); if you are sent a Tax Return you can post it back with a letter describing your business. You should certainly tell the Inland Revenue about your income by the end of the following tax year; if you don't, you may well have to pay a £100 penalty plus interest on tax you owe. See the final section of this chapter for what figures you need to send, and when.

The VAT office

VAT is a tax added to the price of most goods and services supplied by VAT-registered businesses. The standard rate of tax is 15%, so something sold for £10 has £1.50 VAT added to it, making a total price of £11.50. But some things are exempt from VAT, and others are zero-rated. If you are registered for VAT, you charge VAT on VAT-able goods and services you supply and have to pay this over to the Customs & Excise every three months. But you can also reclaim from the Customs & Excise all the VAT that you pay on things you buy for your business. In practice, you simply pay over or reclaim the difference between the two. If you are not registered for VAT, you must not charge VAT at all, nor can you reclaim any.

It is most unlikely that you will have to be registered for VAT when you first start your business. You need only register if the turnover of your business (all your businesses if you have more than one – but not including any of your husband's) is more than £7,000 in any quarter (ending 31 March, 30 June, 30 September and 31 December) or more than £20,500 in the past four quarters, or if at any time you have reason to believe that your turnover could exceed £20,500 over the coming 12 months. If one of these applies it is very important that you get in touch with your local Customs & Excise office straightaway, as you will be liable to pay VAT from the date you should have registered, and if you haven't charged it to your customers you will have to find it out of your own pocket.

If some of your supplies are exempt from VAT you may not need to be registered even if your turnover exceeds the limits above. And there are some occasions when it can be worthwhile being voluntarily registered for VAT, even though your turnover is below the limits (e.g., so that you can reclaim the VAT you pay on things you buy for your business). For details see these following leaflets (available from your local Customs & Excise office):

700/1 *Should I be registered for VAT?*
700/15 *The ins and outs of VAT*
700 *The VAT guide* (this includes a list of all the other VAT leaflets and publications)
700/12 *Filling in your VAT return*
700/21 *Keeping records and accounts*

There may well be a leaflet especially for the line of business you are in, for example:

700/16 *'Party plan' selling and 'direct' selling*
709 *Catering, hotels and holiday services*
727 *Retail schemes* (these are ways of accounting for VAT if you sell direct to the public and it's impracticable to give each customer a separate VAT invoice)
727/6 *Choosing your retail scheme.*

Keeping track of the money

The simplest way of keeping your business money separate from your personal money is to have a separate bank account for it. If you need to ask your bank for a loan for your business, they may insist you have a separate business current account with them.

But business bank accounts normally cost quite a bit more to run than personal accounts. If you do not get more than a few receipts each day and make only a few purchases, you don't need a separate account. But it is essential to keep accurate records. For many small businesses run from home all you need to do is buy a proper cashbook and list all the money your business takes down each left-hand page and all the money your business spends down each right-hand page. Always enter the date, the amount and details. Start a new double-page each day, each week or each month – whichever is most convenient for you. If the transactions are few in number, mark each of the outgoings with one of the following categories; if they are many, have a separate double-page for each category:

stock bought for resale
materials bought for processing
money taken out of the business ('drawings')
tools and minor equipment bought for use in the business
vehicle expenses
other travel and subsistence costs
rates
insurance
telephone, etc.

You must keep bills and/or receipts for all your expenses (or as many as is practicable). If there are a lot of them, keep each month's or each week's receipts in a separate envelope. Where an item is shared with your personal life (like use of your car and your phone) the cost should also be shared. For example, if two-thirds of your car mileage is for business and one-third for private use, then over the year you should take two-thirds of the total cost of running the car out of your business (this includes road tax, insurance, MoT, servicing, petrol, oil and an allowance for depreciation). Again, you should keep all the bills so that you can show the total expense and how you have portioned it.

At some stage you will need to decide when your accounting year is going to end. For tax reasons, if it is likely that your income from the business will be low in the first year or two, it is best that your accounting year ends shortly *after* 5 April – the end of April, May or June is ideal, but if your trade is seasonal don't choose a time when you'll be at your busiest. Your first accounting period does not have to be an exact year – it can be longer or shorter. On the day you've chosen you must close your books and start anew. You must then total up your year's business and draw up a profit-and-loss account, something like this:

Total sales		**£3,455.60**
Cost of materials		– £832.00
Gross profit		**£2,623.60**
Overheads		
Minor equipment	£212.00	
Vehicle expenses	£430.00	
Other travel costs	£56.00	
Rates	£45.00	
Insurance	£29.00	
Electricity	£85.00	
Telephone	£140.00	
Depreciation	£160.00	
		– £1,157.00
Net profit:		**£1,466.60**
Drawings		– £1,250.00
		£216.60

In this example, £216.60 is left in the business to provide some working capital for the next year. Your income tax will be assessed on this amount (your **taxable profit**) as well as the amount taken in *Drawings* (a total of £1,466.60 in our example).

If you are registered for VAT, you will have to keep detailed records of all your transactions (or each day's takings) for your VAT returns. There is a lot of paperwork involved in VAT and this may determine the form in which you keep the rest of your accounts.

Tax on your earnings

How you are taxed on the income depends on your circumstances. There are few hard-and-fast rules here, but the most likely procedures are as follows:

If you have a full-time job and the work you do at home is closely related to it, for example, if you're a teacher and in your spare time you mark examination papers, it is likely that tax will already have been deducted from your spare-time earnings under the Pay-As-You-Earn system (PAYE) before you get them.

If you have a job with an employer in which tax is deducted from each pay-packet under the PAYE system, and if your earnings from the work you do at home are small in comparison, it is likely that the tax office will collect the tax due on your sideline earnings by reducing your PAYE code. They may do this in the same tax year as you get the sideline income (by guessing initially how much it will be), but if you're lucky they will collect the tax over the following year. For example, suppose you earn £500 from your sideline in your first tax year and write to tell your tax office at the end of the tax year (in April): the tax office are very likely to subtract £500 from your allowances when working out the next year's PAYE code. This means that over the next tax year you will pay tax on £500 of income which would otherwise have been free of tax. If the same happens each year, you are paying tax one year in arrears all the time – which is clearly to your advantage. But your tax office could decide to send you a bill for the tax owed for the first year, guess the profit you were going to make in the second year, and knock this off your next year's tax allowances. This would mean you are paying tax at the same time as (or even before) you earn the money, which is disadvantageous, especially if the profit you actually make turns out to be rather less than the tax office estimated. So if this happens it would be worth trying to get the tax office to treat you as self-employed (see below) for your sideline earnings. If they are reluctant to do so, some of the following may help to persuade them:

- being able to show that you are basically in control of the work you do and how, when and where you do it
- being able to show that you are personally responsible for any losses you make
- having a separate bank account for your sideline earnings
- writing to them on headed notepaper
- paying Class 2 National Insurance contributions every week or month
- having an accountant submit your accounts
- being registered for VAT.

If you don't have a job with an employer, and your earnings from working at home are small, the tax office is entitled to send you a tax bill each December (or soon after) asking you to pay the tax on the current tax year's profits on 1 January (or within 30 days). Because the current tax year doesn't end until the following 5 April, neither the Inland Revenue nor you know what they will be. So the tax office will send you a bill based on their estimate of your profits. If you don't agree with their estimate, you must write back within 30 days saying why you think the estimate is wrong *and* you must ask to postpone paying the tax demanded. If you are married, they may send all these to your husband (unless you have asked for **separate assessment** – see page 157). If you think all this is pretty unreasonable, you are not alone. Again, the way out of this situation is to try to get the tax office to treat you as self-employed. See the previous paragraph for suggestions which might help to achieve this.

If your earnings from your business are £2,000 or more, and if you don't also have a job with an employer, the tax office should treat you as self-employed. Details of how the self-employed are taxed are given in the next chapter. What is very strange about these rules is that each tax bill is based on an amount of profit you made in some former period. Even stranger is that some of these periods overlap, so that it looks as though you are being taxed twice on the same income. When you close a business, there is a period in which the profits don't come in any tax assessment. But all this is to your advantage if, as often happens, the profits from your business are small to start with and gradually build up (especially if there is a lot to buy when you start). Most of the time the tax bill you will be paying will be based on your (much lower) profits of a couple of years earlier.

Losses

Of course it's possible that the money going out of your business in your accounting period will exceed the money coming in. A loss is not necessarily bad news for your business, and can be good news as far as tax is concerned as it can mean you are repaid tax you have paid on other income. You have much the greatest flexibility if you are treated by the tax office as self-employed – see page 264. If you are being taxed in some other way (e.g., because you are paid fees as a freelance and have few expenses) you may find it hard to persuade your tax office that it is a genuine loss.

Class 4 National Insurance contributions

If the profits from your business exceed a certain amount, you will be liable for Class 4 National Insurance contributions as well as Class 2 (unless you are 60 or over at the start of the tax year). 'Profits' here normally means the same as 'taxable profits' for tax purposes (see page 266 and Inland Revenue leaflet IR.24 for further details). The amount you have to pay is worked out by the Inland Revenue on your tax assessments and collected along with your income tax. You don't have to pay any Class 4 contributions if your taxable profits being assessed (from all your businesses if you have more than one) are less than a certain amount which, for the 1986–87 tax year, is £4,450. Above that, the contributions are 6.3% of your profits up to £14,820, above which no further contributions are charged. So if, for example, your taxable profits are £6,000, you pay contributions on £6,000 *less* £4,450, i.e., on £1,550; the amount you pay is 6.3% of £1,550 which is £97.65. If your taxable profits are £14,820 or more, the amount you pay is £653.31 (the maximum for the 1986–87 tax year).

If you are married, the limits above apply to you and your husband separately; but, as with income tax, it will normally be your husband who is asked to pay your Class 4 contributions, unless you have asked for separate assessment or to have your own earnings taxed separately as if you were single.

If you are employed in a job in which your employer deducts Class 1 National Insurance contributions from your pay, it's worth knowing that there are two overall yearly limits to the total contributions you have to pay. For the 1986–87 tax year, if you have paid:

- more than £852.56 in Class 1, 2 and 4 contributions, *or*
- more than £1,361.16 in Class 1 and 2 contributions,

you can apply for a refund. If you are a married woman paying Class 1 contributions at the reduced rate, the limits will be lower. To claim a refund, write to the DHSS Class 4 Group, Newcastle-upon-Tyne NE98 1YX, giving details, not later than 2 years after paying the contributions.

But it's not very satisfactory paying and claiming back. Far better not to pay at all. So if it looks as though you are going to pay more than £10 over one of these limits in the coming tax year, you can ask to defer payment of all your Class 4 contributions (if over the first limit above) and all your Class 2 contributions (if over the second limit) until the end of the tax year when the DHSS can work out how much you actually owe. You should apply for this deferment before the start of the tax year (though late applications will be considered). You can only apply if you expect to be employed *and* self-employed during the tax year, and expect your earnings as an employee to be substantial. To apply, get DHSS leaflet NP.18 and send in the attached form CF.359. If you get deferment, the DHSS and not the Inland Revenue will collect whatever contributions are due from you at the end of the year. You must reapply for each future year.

If you make a loss in your business, there will be no Class 4 contributions to pay for that accounting period and you can reduce what you have to pay in future years by setting the loss off against future business profits. You do not have any other options, unlike tax (see page 265). Nor, if you are married, can you set your losses against your husband's profits or vice versa.

A partnership will normally get the bill for all the Class 4 contributions due from all the partners, as with income tax.

18

Starting Your Own Business

In the previous chapter we looked at starting a business in a fairly small way at home. In this chapter we deal with starting a more fully-fledged business, which may need more money, special premises, additional people or other resources. However, much of the information in the previous chapter will also apply to any sort of business and we suggest you read it first.

You and your business will almost certainly need more information and advice than can be given here. There are now a huge number of sources of help for people starting businesses, which means it should be easier than it has been for some time. And, interestingly, the number of women taking advantage of these opportunities is increasing fast and is now running at over half a million a year.

Making a business plan

It is very important to set your plans out on paper so that you can see where the flaws are and so that you have something to present to other people you may need to approach for help, advice or money. Your plan is not rigid – you are likely to modify it continually – but will provide the framework in which you are working.

Putting together a plan which answers the following questions (extremely honestly) will make sure you have researched your business idea and have a clear idea of where you want to get in the first year or two and how you intend to get there:

- What do you want to do?
- Why do you want to do it?
- How do you propose to do it?
- What knowledge and experience do you have of:
  - this line of business?
  - the product you intend to make or the service you intend to offer?
  - raising money?
  - advertising?
  - selling to customers?
  - dealing with complaints?
  - keeping accounts?
  - paperwork and administration?
  - dealing with the authorities?
  - dealing with employees?

- Will you be a sole trader, or are you forming a partnership or a limited company?

- Who forms the potential market for your product or service, how large is it, and what percentage of these people can you expect to buy from you? How are you going to sell to them?

- Who are your competitors, who do they sell to, and how much do they charge? Why should people buy from you rather than your competitors?

- How are you going to make your product or provide your service? Do you need premises, machines, employees, offices, equipment?

- What things do you need to arrange and what organisations do you need to approach? (Make a list – there is a useful checklist in the Small Firms Service booklet, *Setting up a new business*.)

- How much money will you need, and when? Where will it come from? How soon will your business be in profit? You will need to make a detailed financial plan – see below.

• Finally, are you reasonably confident you can carry out this plan? If not, get more information or help, or revise the plan.

You are likely to find the reference section of your nearest central library (usually in your county town) very useful for some of your research – they often keep a large number of trade directories and other relevant information. Ask there too about other such sources – e.g., your local Chamber of Commerce.

Your financial plan

The only sure way of seeing how your business finances might work out is to draw up a realistic **cash-flow projection**. This simply means a chart showing what money is likely to come into and go out of your business each month. If you need to borrow money to get your business going, the lender is almost certain to want to see such a chart. It is not difficult to draw up but will take time. You will need to make a chart like the one below, filling in the relevant figures for at least the first 12 months of your business. Don't expect the figures to come out right the first time – keep adjusting them with a pencil and rubber until you have a formula that works. If you or a friend has a home computer with a *spreadsheet* program, you can create your cash-flow chart on that. This has the great advantage that when you change a figure, the computer will immediately recalculate all the figures that depended on it, which saves a lot of time once you have set it up. In the example cash-flow below, we have put in some very simple figures just to show how the figures relate to each other across the chart. The closing balance (**E**) of each month becomes the next month's opening balance (**A**).

The cash-flow projection shows whether the business makes a profit or a loss in each individual month of trading (**D**). Unless your business gets a lot of money at the outset (from a bank loan, say, or because you withdraw savings and pay them into your business bank account), it is very likely that during the first few months it will show a deficit, as it will be spending money on materials, equipment, stationery, advertising, etc., but getting little back from sales. The cash-flow projection therefore shows a second thing about the business which is vitally important. When the figure at **E** changes from negative to positive, the total money your business has received since it started is at last more than the money it has paid out (in our example figures, this happens most unrealistically in the third month!).

Surprisingly, a business which continues to grow steadily from its formation can be in for a much harder time than one which quickly finds a reasonable level of activity and sticks there. For the latter business, the capital expenditure will have been made, and the income from sales will more than cover the outlay on materials. But for the expanding business, the head can be chasing the tail for several years. There is a continual demand for more capital expenditure, new product development and more staff, while the money coming in relates to the smaller turnover of some months previous and may not even be enough to cover the materials needed to produce your planned future output. Thus the business finds it owes more and more money. This problem is often most acute when the business has been going for two to four years, and is part of the reason why many business failures occur around that time.

CASH-FLOW PROJECTION

		month 1	*month 2*	*month 3*
Opening balance[1]	**A**	**0**	**(200)**	**(700)**
Receipts				
Capital[2]		2,000	0	0
Sales		0	100	1,500
Other income		0	0	0
Total receipts	**B**	**2,000**	**100**	**1,500**
Outgoings				
Raw materials		800	200	200
Staff salaries[3]		0	0	0
Own drawings		100	100	100
Advertising		250	50	50
Insurance		100	0	0
Rent & rates		80	80	80
Light & heat		0	0	100
Telephone & postage		20	20	20
Travelling & entertaining		100	50	50
Office & admin expenses		200	50	50
Capital expenditure		500	0	0

CASH-FLOW PROJECTION – *cont.*

		month 1	*month 2*	*month 3*
Loan repayments		30	30	30
Bank charges & interest		6	6	6
Tax		0	0	0
National Insurance		14	14	14
Accountant's fees etc.		0	0	0
Dividends[4]		0	0	0
Total outgoings	**C**	**2,200**	**600**	**700**
Net profit (loss)[1] for month (= **B**–**C**)	**D**	**(200)**	**(500)**	**800**
Closing balance[1] (= **A**+**D**)	**E**	**(200)**	**(700)**	**100**

[1] a loss or negative amount is normally shown by brackets
[2] for example, money you put in the business or borrowed from your bank
[3] you should add employer's National Insurance contributions of between 5% and 10.45% to the salaries you intend to pay
[4] if a limited company (see page 258)

Sources of help and advice

If your business will involve a substantial turnover or borrowing money or employing people or renting premises, you would be well advised to consult:

- Your bank manager – for advice on running and financing your business.

- An accountant – for advice on whether your business idea is viable, help with preparing a business proposal and cash-flow projections, advice on keeping records and accounts for tax, VAT and management purposes, and guidance on financial decisions.

- A solicitor, for advice on buying an existing business, forming a company or partnership, renting premises, contracts, employing people, etc.

The earlier you approach these people, the more help they will be able to give. If you don't already have a solicitor or an accountant, ask local people (preferably running small businesses) who they use and what they think of them.

The **Small Firms Service** was set up by the Government to encourage small businesses. It produces a useful series of free leaflets (including *A big help to a small business, Starting your own business*, and *Running your own business*) and also provides private counselling sessions (up to a whole day) with an experienced business person for people starting a business or thinking of doing so. The first three sessions are free, each additional one costs £30. For leaflets or counselling, ring *Freephone Enterprise*.

Your local authority may be able to give you a lot of assistance. As well as being able to advise you on planning requirements, licences and controls on the goods or services you provide (**Trading Standards**), they may well have specific schemes for assisting new businesses.

In many areas there is a local **Enterprise Agency** which can offer a range of help (normally free) with finding premises, business planning, getting grants, product development and so on. Ask at your library, Citizens Advice Bureau (CAB) or Jobcentre.

If you live in a rural part of England, the **Council for Small Industries in Rural Areas** (**CoSIRA**) may be able to assist you with finding premises or getting a grant, or provide training or specialist assistance and advice (telephone 0722 336255 for details).

There are various government Development Agencies which can provide access to grants, special assistance and financial concessions. These may be considerable if you are in a Development Area, Assisted Area or Enterprise Zone. Ask the Small Firms Service for details.

You will probably find it worthwhile joining the local Chamber of Commerce, one of the national associations for the self-employed and a national association for people in your particular trade. All of these are likely to provide information and services which you will find useful.

Learning to run a business

It is most unlikely that you have all the skills you need to make your product (or provide your service) *and* sell it successfully *and* run a business. The **Manpower Services Commission** (MSC) runs three main types of courses which will train you in the skills you need. These courses are all free and, what's more, full-time attenders get paid a training allowance of £38 a week:

- **Self-Employment Courses** are 2–6 weeks long and are for people wanting to run a one-person business
- **Small Business Courses** last 6–10 weeks and are for people whose businesses will employ other people
- **New Enterprise Programme** courses run for around 16 weeks and are for people who want to start a business which has real potential for growth.

All these courses include help with getting your particular business going. Ask for the leaflet *Planning to set up your own business?* at your local Jobcentre.

Many business and management schools and colleges, technical colleges, colleges of further education and local Enterprise Agencies run courses on starting up a business. At least one runs courses specially for women (Women's Enterprise Programme, 11 Bridgeman Terrace, Wigan WN1 1SZ).

The Open University runs a correspondence course called 'Start Up Your Own Business' requiring around 50 hours of study-time. You are allocated to a business adviser for up to 9 months. It costs £350, but sponsorship may be available. For details write to the Associate Student Central Office, The Open University, PO Box 76, Milton Keynes MK7 6AN, or ask at your OU Regional Office. The National Extension College runs a correspondence course called 'Be Your Own Boss' which costs only £58.50; details from NEC, 18 Brooklands Avenue, Cambridge CB2 2HN.

Some financial help from the Government

If you qualify under the **Enterprise Allowance Scheme** you can be paid £40 a week by the Government during your first year of self-employment or starting a new business. If your business is a partnership, co-operative or company, it is possible for each partner or shareholder (up to ten people) to get the allowance (as long as at least half of the group get it). The main qualifications for each person are:

- You must not have worked for more than 8 hours in any of the last 8 weeks on the day your application is received. Sometimes time spent working but under a formal redundancy notice can be counted in the 8 weeks.
- You must be receiving unemployment benefit or supplementary benefit on the day your application is received.
- You must have £1,000 in a separate bank account for your business before you can be accepted.
- You must be over 18 and under 60, and prepared to work in the business for at least 36 hours a week.
- The business must be:
  – new (you must not start it before you are accepted on to the scheme, and none of your partners must be in a similar type of business)
  – small (employing less than 20 people in the first three months)
  – independent (not connected with any other business, so agencies and many franchises are unacceptable), and
  – suitable (nightclubs, casinos and political campaigns are out).

For details, get the leaflets EPL.124, *Enterprise Allowance Scheme – a guide*, and EPL.140, *The Enterprise Allowance Scheme* from your Jobcentre or Manpower Services Commission area office. But the rules and time-limits for getting on to the scheme are not given in full in these leaflets. As they are tight, and you can only ever apply once for the scheme, we go into some detail about getting on to it.

Ask your local Jobcentre to include you in the next Enterprise Allowance Scheme information session (you may have to ring your area office of the MSC). This is the only way to get an application form. You must send the form in within 6 weeks of the date of the session. You must say on the form when you want to start the business, which must be on a Monday within 6 weeks of your form being received (partners must all start within 6 weeks of the *first* of their forms to be received). Before you can start you must have got any necessary planning permission, licence, etc., and you must have had an individual interview, to which you must take proof of the business bank account with £1,000 in it (a partnership account must have £1,000 in it for every partner whether they are all in the scheme or not). So you will need to open the account as soon as you have sent off your form (not before), and should ask the bank to send you a statement and a letter showing the account name and number, bank sort code and balance. Before the interview, the MSC will check with the unemployment benefit office or DHSS about your work record and benefit entitlement.

Don't be put off by all the rules – your chance of being accepted on to the scheme is very high if you qualify. But it's important not to start any business activities which could bar you from qualifying before you have signed the agreement (see leaflet EPL.140). Once this is done, £80 will be paid into your business bank account at the end of each fortnight for up to one year. For tax purposes it will be treated like any other business receipt. If you are receiving unemployment benefit when you start on the scheme, tell the benefit office – you may be entitled to a 'week in hand' payment. While on the scheme you will be offered free counselling sessions with the Small Firms Service. You may be visited after 3, 6 and 9 months and asked to re-sign the agreement. You are allowed to take time off for training up to an average of 5 hours a week (it should be possible to take a Small Business Course without losing entitlement). You are also allowed up to 4 weeks' holiday and can do up to 8 hours a week part-time work outside the business. If your business or your personal circumstances change, you should inform the MSC. You can take on a partner during the year, but they will not qualify for the scheme. If you break any of the rules, the allowance may be stopped. If you are 60 during the year, the allowance will stop. If you leave the scheme, you cannot normally rejoin it.

BOOKS

Be Your Own Boss – Starter Kit by D. S. Watkins (National Extension College, £5.95)

The Small Business Guide by Colin Barrow (BBC Publications, £6.50)

Work for Yourself: a Guide for Young People by Paddy Hall (National Extension College, £2.60)

Starting Your Own Business (Consumers' Association, £6.95)

How to Manage Money by G. D. Donleavy & M. Metcalfe (Business Books, £5.95)

Law for the Small Business by Patricia Clayton (Kogan Page, £5.95)

Consumer Law for the Small Business by Patricia Clayton (Kogan Page, £5.95)

Kogan Page publish a number of books on running particular kinds of businesses (list from Kogan Page, 120 Pentonville Road, London N1 9JN)

Raising the money you need

Whatever your line of business, you will need a certain amount of money to start it – for equipment, stationery, materials, legal costs, etc. These costs are fairly easy to estimate. But your business will also need money to:

- cover the time-lag between buying materials and being paid for the finished product – usually several months
- allow you to spend more now to increase your output in the future, even though the money coming in relates to your much smaller output some months ago
- cover the repayments and interest on any loan you had to start off the business, as well as all the other overheads
- cover the fact that everything takes twice as long as you thought it would – because we all imagine we can do a full week's manufacturing *and* a full week's selling *and* half a week's administration all in one week
- give you some money to live on in the period before your business gets into profit.

The need for this funding is very often under-estimated, and shows the importance of drawing up a realistic cash-flow projection. In the very simple example on pages 250–1, you can see that although the business starts with £2,000 in the bank, its account is £200 overdrawn at the end of the first month. In the second month, the expenditure has gone down to £600, but the overdraft has gone *up* to £700. In real life, this situation could continue for some time. Don't let this put you off – if you are aware of what is likely to happen you can plan for it; if it takes you by surprise, it could well mean your business fails.

You will certainly have to provide some, if not most, of the money you need to get your business under way. This could mean withdrawing savings, using your redundancy money, selling things or taking out a second mortgage on your home (though this would be very risky). If you have a life insurance policy which involves investment (e.g., an endowment policy) which you've been paying into for a number of years, you could cash it in or ask the insurance company for a loan on the strength of it. If you ask friends or relations to lend you money, you should draw up a proper agreement between you and ask your solicitor to look it over.

But it's more than likely that at some stage you will have to approach your bank or another financial institution for funding. It's sensible to talk over your plans with your bank manager at an early stage, but if you're going to need a lot of money it may be better not to apply for funds until you have a professional-looking proposal to put forward. The bank will advise you on how to present your case, but you will almost certainly need an accountant's help in drawing it up – and this is itself likely to cost a few hundred pounds. You will need to decide whether you want a loan (usually given to buy particular assets and repaid at an agreed time) or an overdraft (usually best for covering working capital) or both. The bank will normally want some security – most often arranged with a mortgage (or second mortgage) on your home or by depositing a life insurance policy with an investment value – or a combination of both. If your business is a limited company, you may have to sign a personal guarantee saying that you will repay the loan out of your own money if the bank wants its money back and the business doesn't have the resources. If you can't provide security or a personal guarantee, the bank may still be able to lend you up to £75,000 under the **Small Firms Loan Guarantee Scheme**. Under this scheme the Government will repay 70% of your loan if you default, but you have to pay for this guarantee.

You may be able to reduce the amount of money you need initially by buying equipment on hire-purchase or leasing it. With hire-purchase you will have to pay an initial deposit and rental for a fixed period, at the end of which it becomes yours. With leasing there is no deposit and the leasing company usually pays for maintenance. Your accountant can advise you on this.

If you form a limited company, you might at some stage consider **equity-funding** from a venture capital company. This means you issue shares in your business in return for an injection of money. The disadvantages are that the investor is likely to want some control over your business and will be taking a share in the profits. On the other hand, this can mean getting someone with a lot of financial experience on to your board, and equity-funding has the great advantage that your business does not have to repay the money injected. Many venture capital companies are generally only interested in providing fairly large sums (£50,000 or £100,000 or more), though some will provide as little as £5,000. You could also invite friends or relatives to buy shares in your business – they can normally get full tax relief on what they invest (details are in leaflet IR.51, *The Business Expansion Scheme*, free from tax offices).

Two books which contain comprehensive lists of sources of loans, grants and equity finance are:

Money for Business (£3 from The Bulletin Group, Bank of England, Threadneedle Street, London EC2R 8AH)
Official Sources of Finance and Aid for Industry in the UK (£5.50 from branches of NatWest Bank).

What type of business?

We looked at the implications of what it means to be a sole trader or in a partnership in the previous chapter. Here we look at limited companies and co-operatives, and also take a look at buying an existing business and setting up a business under a nationally-known franchise.

A limited company

A limited company is different from an unincorporated business or partnership in that in law it has an existence all of its own. If a partner leaves a partnership, that is the end of the partnership; a new partnership can be started with those who remain. But a company still continues to exist even if every person in it changes. This means that the company's money is its own, quite separate from its owners' or directors' money. Similarly, its debts are its own. One of the main reasons for setting up a company is that if it goes bust, your *personal* liability is limited to the amount you paid for your shares, however much money the company owes (though you will be liable to repay any loans which you have guaranteed personally). Two other reasons are that if your business income is high enough for you to be paying tax at higher rates, converting to a company can reduce your tax rate to 30% (by a combination of factors on which your accountant should be able to advise you).

And it can be easier for a company to raise finance than for a sole trader or partnership. But forming a company involves a good deal of legal work and is not cheap. The company will have to be registered with the **Companies Registration Office**, which involves submitting its Memorandum and Articles of Association properly signed and witnessed. Its accounts will have to be drawn up in a certain form, be audited and be available to the public. The owners of the company are the shareholders, of whom there must be at least two, acting as director and company secretary. Directors are paid salaries by the company (just like any other employee), but as shareholders they can also benefit from dividends paid on the shares and, if the company does well, from the value of their shareholding increasing. You can get a free pamphlet, *Notes for guidance: incorporation of new companies*, from the Registrar of Companies, Companies House, Crown Way, Maindy, Cardiff CF4 3UZ. If the company name is not your own name, the names of the directors must be shown on your stationery and premises.

An alternative to setting up a company is to buy one that is already registered but not operating. You do this through a **Company Registration Agent**. You become the new directors of the company, and can change its name and other details if you want to.

Whether it is worth you incorporating your business (i.e., turning it into a limited company) depends on a number of factors, on which you will need the advice of your accountant and solicitor.

A co-operative

A co-operative is a business which is owned and controlled by the people who work in it. Each person has a vote in all the major decisions. Technically, a co-operative can be either:

- a limited company, formed by two or more members
- an Industrial & Provident Society, formed by seven members, which can have limited liability like a company
- a partnership.

With the first two options, you can choose between each of the workers owning their own shares, or all of the shares being collectively owned.

You will only be interested in forming a co-operative if you agree with the basic philosophy. Your business will not consist of the normal two groups of managers who make all the decisions and employees who carry them out. You will have to be prepared to share the responsibility and the rewards with other people. But because everyone has a direct interest in the success of the business (unlike employees), it is claimed that workers in a co-operative are very much more committed, they manage themselves much more efficiently and strive to maintain high standards.

The National Co-operative Development Agency can provide information, advice, training and support for co-operatives. It can also provide model rules and Articles of Association for various kinds of business which you can adapt to your own requirements. Ask for the leaflet *Working together the co-operative way* from your local library or CAB, or send £1.50 for the booklet *How to set up a co-operative business* to the Co-operative Development Agency, Broadmead House, 21 Panton Street, London SW1Y 4DR. There may well be a local co-operative development agency in your area which can help you set up and run a co-operative – for example, in developing your business idea, finding other people, finding premises, raising money and legal matters.

Franchising

Franchising is a way of buying a small business with a nationally-known name. Most branches of businesses like Wimpy, The Body Shop, Prontaprint, British School of Motoring, Singer, Pronuptia, Pizza Express and Budget Rent-a-Van are in fact small independent businesses using a national name. The business itself may be a partnership or a limited company or you may be self-employed.

In return for a hefty down-payment (usually £5,000 to £20,000 but sometimes £100,000 or more), you get the right to use the franchise company's name and sell its products, help with finding premises and setting up the business, and training and advice. There will almost certainly be other costs to find (e.g., for premises, shopfitting, a van, stocks, equipment, insurance and employing extra staff). When the business is running, you have to pay the company royalties out of your turnover or commission on stock you buy – sometimes both – whether or not your business is making a profit. Franchise companies normally reckon that you will get back your initial investment in 1–4 years, but there is no reliable information on how many people do so.

It is very important to get good advice before you decide to take up a franchise, and find out everything you can about the franchise company and how other franchisees have got on. For further information, read the report in the November 1983 issue of *Which?* in your local library, and get the British Franchise Association's information pack (£2 from Grove House, 628 London Road, Colnbrook, Slough SL3 8QH). You could also look at *Taking Up a Franchise* by G. Golzen, C. Barrow and J. Severn (Kogan Page, £5.95). And ask your bank about any special schemes they have to support people taking up franchises.

Buying an existing business

An existing business is not likely to come cheap, even if it is not doing particularly well at present and needs money to be invested in it to build it up. To get an idea of what is available and at what price, look in *Dalton's Weekly* magazine. It is essential that you get your accountant to look very carefully into the finances of any business you are thinking of buying, and your solicitor to look at the legal side. If you will need financial help from your bank (as is most likely), you will need to draw up much the same kind of financial plan as for a new business.

Business premises

If you need to find premises for your business, it would be sensible to contact your local authority, local Enterprise Agency and the Small Firms Service (see below) and any other organisation in your area which may be able to assist. There may be special concessions or grants available which you will not want to miss out on.

The main factors to take into account when finding premises are:

- how suitable they are for your intended use
- whether the location will enhance your business prospects, and is satisfactory for access and transportation
- the cost
- whether planning permission is necessary (you may well need

permission for *change of use* even if you are not intending to make any structural change to the buildings)

- whether the premises will be affected by any planned development
- whether the premises are expandable if your business does well.

Consider getting premises professionally surveyed and valued, and do take your solicitor's advice on the lease or purchase. You may well need to get a fire certificate – you should in any case consult the local Fire Prevention Officer before signing anything and make sure you can comply with his requirements.

The Small Firms Service produces a leaflet *How to find premises* (ring *Freephone Enterprise*) which gives more advice and lists agencies who may be able to help.

Insurance

There are a number of risks in running a business which appropriate insurance can lessen. The main ones to consider are:

- Damage to your premises, equipment or stocks from fire, flood, explosion, vandalism, etc.
- Theft of equipment or stocks, and damage done by thieves.
- Loss of or damage caused to goods in transit.
- The loss of business caused by one of the above happening (called **consequential loss insurance**).
- Loss or theft of money, cheques, postal orders etc. from your office, home, till or on the way to the bank.
- If you employ anyone (other than your own family and help in the home) you must by law be covered for claims an employee could bring against you for injury or illness arising in or from their work – called **employer's liability insurance**. (You can get a leaflet called *Short guide to the Employers' Liability Act* from the Health & Safety Executive, 1 Chepstow Place, London W2 4TF).
- Claims a member of the public might bring against you for injury caused by your or your employees' actions (**public liability insurance**) or by a fault in one of your products (**product liability insurance**).

• **Motor insurance** is, of course, required by law. You can also take out insurance which will provide you with a chauffeur if you lose your driving licence.

• You can get insurance which will provide you with an income if you cannot work through illness or as the result of an accident (**permanent health insurance** – see page 216). If you would need a private room in hospital to be able to carry on your business, you could consider **private patient's insurance**. If the death of a partner or someone you employ would mean loss of business and/or having to buy their share of the business, you can insure against this (**key person insurance**).

Of course there may be other specific risks in the business you are contemplating. It would be sensible to discuss these with an insurance broker or company representative to see what cover is available and at what cost. With every type of insurance, costs vary considerably between companies so it is worth getting several quotes.

Keeping accounts and paying tax

In the previous chapter we looked at ways of keeping records and accounts for a simple one-person business. For a larger business you will need to set up a much more elaborate system which meets your needs. It would be sensible to ask your accountant for his suggestions in some detail. There are books available (e.g., Collins' *Self-Employed Account Book*) which have clearly laid-out forms and records for all your business transactions – these are very useful if they suit your purposes. It might be worth computerising your accounts from quite early on. There are now systems available which require you to do little more than enter the money you spend and the orders you get; the computer then compiles your accounts, sends out invoices, prints out your VAT returns and so on. This can save you a lot of time and mean a lower accountant's bill. But it's very important that you get a system which is appropriate to your business needs, for which you will need some good independent advice.

We also looked in the previous chapter at VAT and National Insurance contributions. There remains the thorny business of income tax on earnings from self-employment or a partnership. So take a deep breath . . .

How the self-employed are taxed

As a self-employed person, you will get an income tax assessment for each tax year you are in business (though if you are married the assessment will be sent to your husband unless you ask for **separate assessment** – see page 157). A tax year runs from 6 April one year to 5 April the next. But the assessment will be based on your business accounts, and your accounting year is unlikely to correspond with the tax year. Also, you are taxed on the profits you make, and these won't be known until after the end of your accounting year. So once your business has been going for two complete tax years, each year's tax assessment will normally be based on the profits you made in the accounting year ending in the previous tax year (see below). Therefore the assessment you get for the 1986–87 tax year asks you to pay the tax due on the profit your business made in the accounting year which ran between 6 April 1985 and 5 April 1986. This system is called **preceding-year basis**.

But this doesn't mean there is no tax to pay for the first couple of tax years you are in business. As we said above, there is an assessment for each tax year. So the first three years have special rules, which are shown in diagram 2. Similarly, there have to be adjustments when you close down a business – see diagram 3.

The odd effect of these rules is that certain periods of trading at the start of your business will form the basis of more than one tax assessment. (Similarly, at the end of the business, there will be

Diagram 2: **Accounting periods when a business starts . . .**

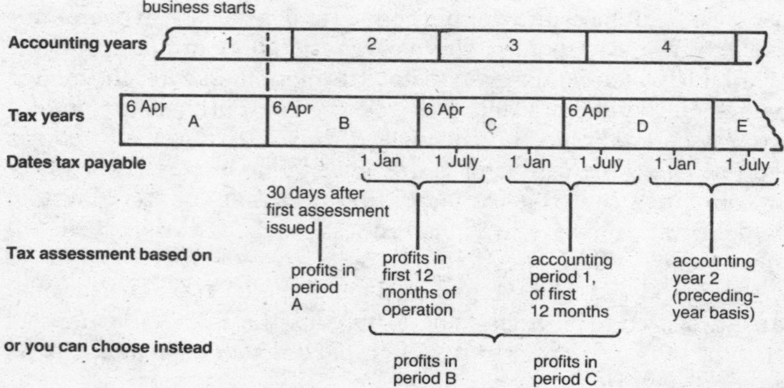

Diagram 3: ... and when it closes

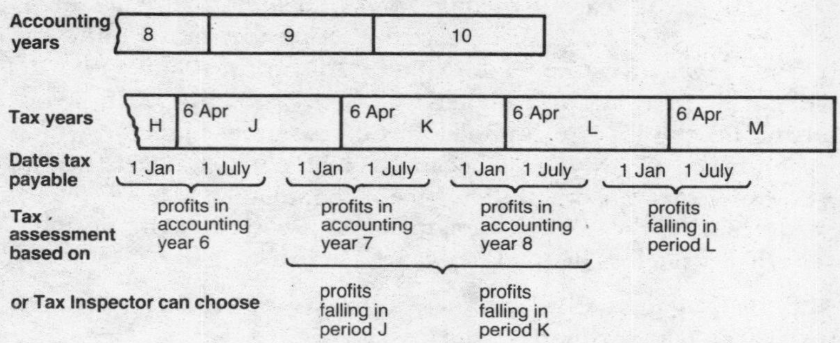

periods which aren't used for any tax assessment.) There is a definite advantage in this system for you: if your profits in, say, the first two or three years of trading are low, it means low tax bills for the first four or five years of your business.

Each tax assessment has to be paid in two instalments, on 1 January in the year of assessment and on the following 1 July. But if the assessment is sent out late and a date has already passed, the tax due must be paid within 30 days.

The first assessment you get when you start a business is nearly always sent out late. The Tax Inspector will wait until you have been in business for 12 months to see what profits you are making. At the end of your first accounting period you should send in your accounts fairly promptly. You will then probably receive the assessments for the first two tax years together. The first will be based on the profits attributable to the tax year in which you started up, and the second on the profits in the first 12 months of trading. If the Tax Inspector doesn't have enough information to make an accurate assessment, he will estimate your profits, and you must appeal if you don't agree. Full instructions about how to appeal are sent out with each assessment. Don't be frightened of appealing – many people do it as a matter of course. But you must still pay the tax demanded on the due date unless you also apply to postpone doing so.

If you make a loss in any of the first 4 years in which you start a business, you can set off the trading loss and any capital allowances against any taxable income you received in the previous 4 tax years. This means you will get a rebate (plus tax-free interest) of tax you paid in those years, which can be highly advantageous.

The loss must be set off against the earliest year first, and in each year against your earned income *before* your investment income. If you are married, you can restrict the set-off to your own income (earned *before* investment) or extend it to your husband's (worthwhile if he paid tax at a higher rate than you). But try to avoid setting off the loss or capital allowances against income which wasn't taxed anyway (e.g., because it had Wife's Earned Income Allowance or some other allowance set against it).

Alternatively, you have the same options with a loss in the first 4 years as with a loss in any later year. These are:

- to set it against other income you (or your husband) get in the tax year in which you make the loss, *or*

- to carry it forward to set against profits from the same business in future years.

If, during the 3 tax years before you started trading, you incurred expenditure which, had you started your business, would have counted as an allowable business expense, it gets the same options as a loss made in the tax year in which you start up your business.

The amount of tax to pay on your taxable profits is worked out in exactly the same way as income tax on other income (see Chapter 23). Your profits are added to other income you have, your personal allowances are subtracted, and tax is calculated on what is left.

How the profit or loss is worked out

The profit or loss shown in your end-of-year accounts may not be the figure on which the Tax Inspector bases his assessment. Because of the tax rules, a number of adjustments may have to be made. The basic calculation for tax purposes is broadly:

your takings during the year
plus any increase in the value of your stocks during the year (or *less* the decrease in value)
less cost of materials and stock purchased
less business expenses and overheads.

The result may have to be adjusted to take account of money owed by your business and owing to it at the beginning and end of the year. From this result you may deduct:

- capital allowances you are entitled to (see below)
- half the amount you pay in Class 4 National Insurance contributions
- the premiums you pay for a personal pension plan (see page 285) or special life insurance policy (see page 289)
- any losses carried forward from earlier years.

Not all business expenses are deductible for tax purposes. The general rule is that the expenditure must be legitimately spent in the course of the business, but there are no hard and fast rules. Your accountant should have a good idea of what will be allowed for your type of business. You will find a comprehensive list in *The Tax-Saving Guide* published with *Which?* magazine each March (in your local library).

Capital expenditure (on cars and major equipment and things which will last rather longer than one year) has its own rules. Basically, you can claim **capital allowances** of up to one-quarter of the cost in the first year, and one-quarter of what is left in each subsequent year.

If you use anything partly for business and partly privately, you can claim the proportion of the cost or capital allowance that represents business use.

How partnerships are taxed

For tax purposes, the profit or loss made by a partnership is worked out in exactly the same way as for a self-employed person. And the same rules apply about which accounting period each tax assessment is based on. But in working out the amount of tax payable, the Inspector divides the partnership's profits for the accounting period in the same proportion as they are in fact being shared between the partners in the current tax year. He then works out how much tax each partner would individually have to pay on that share, and adds these up to get the total tax bill for the partnership. (It is up to the partners to decide how they actually split the bill between them.)

If a partner leaves or a new partner joins, technically the partnership ends and a new one begins. This normally means that the rules shown in Diagrams 2 and 3 come into play. Alternatively, if everyone before and after the change agrees, the partnership can be regarded as continuing. Depending on the pattern of profits and losses in each year, which alternative you choose could make a substantial difference to your tax assessments, so ask your accountant to recommend the best one.

YOUR FUTURE

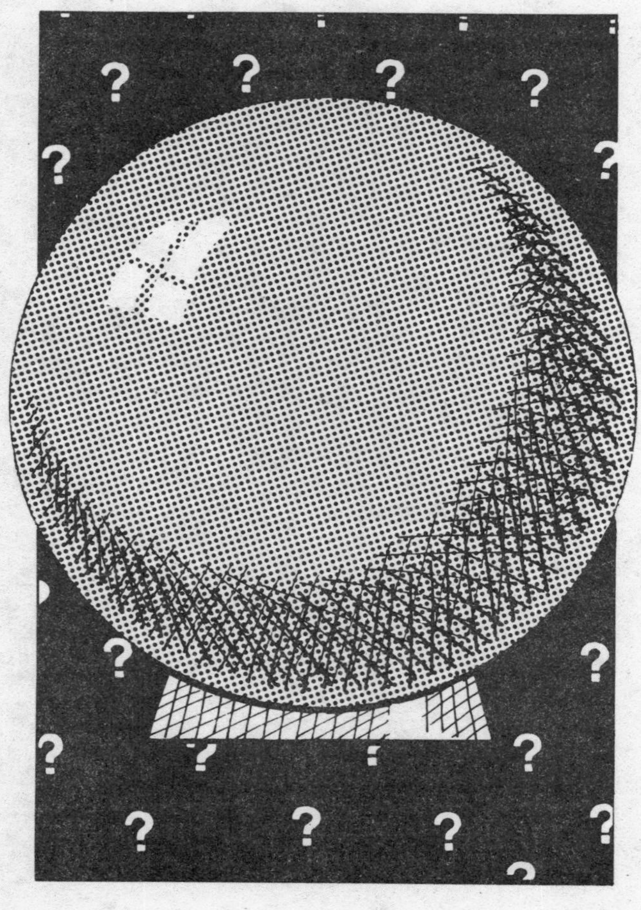

19

Planning for Retirement

The biggest problem with retirement planning is this. If you retire at 60, you can expect to live another 21 years (this is the average for women) and will need an income to live on for the whole of that time. As your working life is probably rather less than 40 years, it is clear that quite a substantial amount of money needs to be put aside for you during your working life to have something to draw on in your retirement. On the other hand, until you are pretty close to retirement, it is almost impossible to know how much money you will need, let alone how much you will get. This is partly because of inflation and partly because of the intricacies of pension schemes.

A pension scheme is simply a way of saving money while you are working so that, when you retire, an income can be paid back to you for the rest of your life. Generally, the more money you have paid in, the longer you have belonged to a scheme and the higher your earnings, the greater will be the amount of each pension. There is a state pension scheme which is compulsory – anyone who earns more than a certain amount has to pay National Insurance contributions, part of which go towards providing state pensions. If you have a job, your employers may run a pension scheme which you may have to join. If you do not belong to your employer's scheme or if you are self-employed, you can arrange an individual pension plan with an insurance company. So when you retire you may be entitled to pensions from several different sources.

While there are no precise answers to the problem of knowing how much you should be setting aside for the future and at what stage, there are certain things you can and should do:

- Make sure you will qualify for a basic state retirement pension in your own right. If you also qualify on your husband's contributions, that is a plus.

- While you are in a job, join the firm's pension scheme if it runs one.

- Use **personal pension plans** and **additional voluntary contributions** to top up your retirement income.

- Invest spare money carefully and acquire assets you would be prepared to sell to boost your income in retirement.

We look at each of these in detail in the following pages. There are other ways of providing an income for yourself in retirement and these are dealt with in the last part of this chapter. The next chapter includes a section on ways you may be able to increase your income after you retire.

Pensions are even more of a minefield for women than they are for men because what you get often depends on your marital status. To add insult to injury, a woman's pension entitlement is likely to be lower than a man's because:

- women's working lives are shorter, because they retire earlier and often have a number of years when they are not working

- women's retirement is longer, because they retire earlier and live longer

- women's pay is lower

- many pension schemes used to exclude women. This is now illegal, though it means many working women have missed out in the past. And it is quite legal for a company to have a poorer pension scheme or none at all for lower grades of workers – which may in practice mean mainly women.

It is no accident that three-quarters of the pensioners who have to claim supplementary benefit because they do not have enough to live on are women.

There are one or two small compensations which work in favour of married women. The state schemes and many firms' schemes provide a pension for a man's widow after his death, whether this is before he retires or afterwards. And your husband's contributions to the state pension scheme also qualify *you* for a state retirement pension. If you are married you will want to take these rights into account when deciding what provision you should make for yourself (more details on page 295).

To keep things as simple as possible, we look first at the pension provision you can make for yourself. We then look at the pension entitlement a married woman may gain from her husband's National Insurance and pension contributions.

Your state pension

There are really two state pension schemes, one providing a basic pension and the other an additional pension. Both schemes are paid for by National Insurance contributions. You may qualify for just a basic pension, just an additional one, or both.

If you have paid enough National Insurance contributions over your working life, you will get a **basic state retirement pension**. This is a **flat-rate** pension, meaning that everyone who qualifies for a full pension gets the same amount. Most people who pay National Insurance contributions, whether in a job (Class 1 contributions) or self-employed (Class 2 contributions) will get some sort of basic pension. Periods of registered unemployment, maternity leave and time spent at home looking after dependants will not normally lose you any basic pension, even though you do not pay contributions during this time.

Then there is the **state additional pension scheme** which has come to be known as 'Serps' – the state earnings-related pension scheme. How much you get depends on your earnings in the years since 1978 (when this scheme started) – the more years you have worked between 1978 and retirement, and the higher your earnings, the more additional pension you will get. The only way you can earn entitlement to additional pension is by having a job and paying Class 1 National Insurance contributions (contributions paid by the self-employed do not count). But if your firm runs a pension scheme which is as good as Serps or better, it can make you join that instead (called **contracting-out** of Serps); for these years you are building up your entitlement to the firm's pension, not additional pension. Or the firm can let you (or make you) contribute to its own scheme as well as Serps.

It is the additional pension scheme (Serps) that the Government has been thinking of cutting back, because of fears about how much it will cost to run in future.

Before Serps started in 1978, there was a scheme called the **graduated pension scheme**. Many people who worked in a job between 1961 and 1978 will get a small pension from this scheme when they retire.

Shortly before you are 60, the DHSS will work out how much of each type of state pension you are entitled to. When you retire, you will receive the total of all your state pensions in one payment each week or month – and this weekly or monthly rate will normally be increased each year by the Government in line with inflation, so that its value remains much the same. You may have to pay some tax on what you get.

We cover the main aspects of the two state schemes below, but not every condition or exception. You will find further information in the following leaflets, obtainable free from social security offices:

NP.32 *Your retirement pension*
NP.32A *Your retirement pension if you are widowed or divorced*
NP.32B *Retirement benefits for married women*
NI.1 *Married women – your National Insurance position*
NP.27 *Looking after someone at home? – How to protect your pension*
NI.42 *National Insurance – Voluntary contributions*
NI.48 *National Insurance – Unpaid and late paid contributions*
NI.51 *Widows – Guidance about NI contributions and benefits*
NI.95 *NI guide for divorced women.*

Your basic state retirement pension

This is a pension of £38.70 a week, with possible additions of £23.25 a week if another adult (not your husband) is dependent on you, and £8.05 for each dependent child. These figures apply from July 1986 to April 1987, but they are normally increased in line with inflation each year.

The route to a basic pension is to collect as many **qualifying years** as you can during your working life. If you were born after 4 July 1932, you will normally need 39 qualifying years to get a full pension. If you are older than that, you may need fewer than 39, but you may find that any contributions you paid before 1948 do not carry any pension entitlement (see leaflet NP.32).

But the number of qualifying years you will need is reduced by the number of years for which you get **Home Responsibilities Protection** while you are looking after someone at home (see below for details). For example, if you have 10 years of Home Responsibilities Protection you only need to collect 29 qualifying years instead of 39 for a full pension.

If you do not have enough qualifying years for a full basic pension, you may be entitled to a reduced amount (details in leaflet NP.32).

The way you get a qualifying year has changed over the years. The number of qualifying years you collected before 6 April 1975 is simply the total number of weekly flat-rate NI contributions you paid before that date, divided by 50. If there is any remainder, it counts as one more qualifying year. For example, if you paid 270 of these weekly contributions at any time before 6 April 1975, you accumulated 6 qualifying years.

Since 1975, each tax year (i.e., from 6 April one year to 5 April the next) has been looked at individually. For a tax year to be a qualifying year, you need to pay either:

- 52 weekly Class 2 contributions (if self-employed), *or*
- 52 weekly Class 3 (voluntary) contributions, *or*
- if you are in a job, an amount equal to 52 weeks of Class 1 contributions on the **Lower Earnings Limit** for the year (see below), *or*
- a mixture of these.

Between 1975 and 1978, the relevant number in each case was 50, not 52.

If you are in a job, you do not have to pay National Insurance contributions for weeks in which you earn less than the Lower Earnings Limit. For the 1986–87 tax year this limit is £38.00. Once your earnings reach £38.00, your employer has to deduct 5% of them in NI contributions. If your pay was the same as the limit for 52 weeks, it would total £1,976. Your total contributions would be 5% of £1,976 which is £98.80. So 1986–87 will be a qualifying year if you pay at least £98.80 in Class 1 National Insurance contributions. If you earn a lot more than the Lower Earnings Limit, you will pass this test quite quickly. For example, if you earn £100 a week, your employer will deduct 9% in contributions – i.e., £9 a week; so you will pass the test in 11 weeks (because you will then have paid £99).

Any contributions you pay in Northern Ireland or the Isle of Man count in the same way. Contributions you pay in certain other countries can also count – see leaflet NI.38, *Social security abroad*, and check with your social security office.

At certain times you may be credited with contributions instead of having to pay them. This happens if you are:

- unemployed; but if you are not getting unemployment benefit (e.g., because you have been out of work for more than a year) you may have to sign on at the unemployment benefit office each week
- sick (but if you are not getting sickness benefit you may have to send in sick notes to your social security office)
- getting maternity allowance, invalid care allowance, or unemployability supplement
- on an approved full-time training course to help you get a new job (see leaflet NI.125)
- a young person aged between 16 and 18 who has left full-time education but is not yet working.

Although you must actually have paid all the contributions needed for at least one qualifying year, it does not actually matter how many of the rest of the contributions in your working life were credited rather than paid.

Home Responsibilities Protection (HRP)

You can – and should – claim this for any complete tax year since 6 April 1978 in which you have stayed at home to look after children or a sick or elderly person. Each year for which you get HRP reduces the number of qualifying years you need by one (but can't reduce it to less than 20). For example, if you would normally need 39 qualifying years but have 17 years of HRP, you only need to have collected 39 *less* 17 = 22 qualifying years to get a full basic pension. If you had 23 years of HRP you would need 20 qualifying years (the minimum) to get a full pension. If you have fewer qualifying years than you need, your basic pension will be reduced proportionately.

To get HRP for a tax year, your NI contributions must have

been too low for it to be a qualifying year. Also, for the whole of that year (from 6 April to 5 April) you must have either:

- been getting **child benefit** for a child under 16, *or*
- been getting **supplementary benefit** so that you can stay off work to look after an elderly or sick person at home, *or*
- spent 35 hours a week looking after someone who gets **attendance allowance** or **constant attendance allowance**, and you do *not* get invalid care allowance, *or*
- a combination of these at different times in that year.

In the first two cases you get HRP automatically; in the last two cases you have to claim it (fill in the form in leaflet NP.27).

Not enough qualifying years?

If, when you are 60, you have not collected enough qualifying years to get a full basic pension, you may still qualify for a reduced pension. The proportion you will get is shown in leaflet NP.32. Alternatively, at any time before you are 60 you can, if you want to, convert a recent tax year into a qualifying year by making **voluntary contributions** (Class 3 contributions). You must normally pay these within 2 years of the end of the tax year, though if you were a student you have up to 6 years, from the end of the tax year in which the course ended, to pay them. If you did not pay any contributions in the tax year, you will need to pay 52 weeks' worth of Class 3 contributions. If you paid some contributions, you need only pay enough to make the tax year up to a qualifying year. If you pay within 2 years of the end of the tax year, you pay at the rate which applied to that tax year. If you pay later than that (because you were a student), you pay at the rate then in force, unless the rate has been higher in the interim. In the 1986–87 tax year, these contributions are £3.65 a week.

Before you decide to pay voluntary contributions, check with your DHSS office that you will benefit from doing so. They should be able to tell you how much difference it would make to your basic pension. Remember you can still get a basic pension even if you do have gaps in your contributions (because most people need only 39 qualifying years, while you may have over 40 years between leaving school and age 60, and because HRP may reduce the number of qualifying years you need).

Your additional state retirement pension (Serps)

The state **earnings-related** scheme is entirely separate from the state basic pension scheme. You may get a basic pension or an additional pension or both. The only time you build up entitlement to an additional state pension is when you are working for employers and:

- over the tax year your weekly wages are more than the Lower Earnings Limit for that year, *and*
- you are not in an employer's pension scheme which is contracted-out of the Serps scheme.

Class 2 and 4 NI contributions paid by the self-employed do not count towards an additional pension. Nor do Class 3 voluntary contributions. Nor do Home Responsibilities Protection, periods of unemployment, training, sickness or unpaid maternity leave. As the rules stand at the moment you only need to contribute to this scheme for 20 years to get the full benefit. However, the Government has proposed basing the pension on your lifetime's earnings, with special arrangements for married women, lone parents, disabled people and those looking after them.

Diagram 4: **Class 1 NI contributions from April 1986**

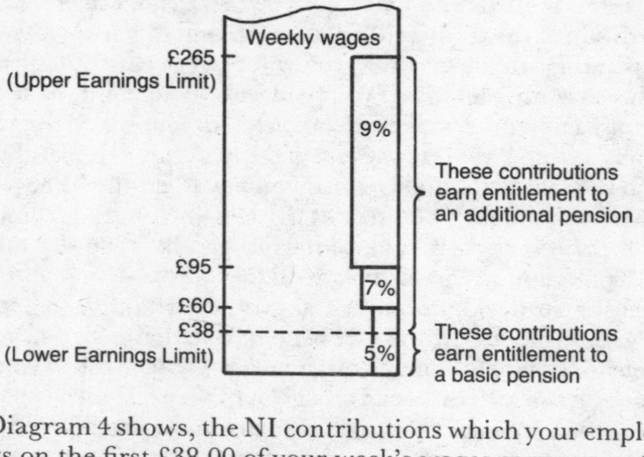

Weekly wages
£265 (Upper Earnings Limit)
9%
These contributions earn entitlement to an additional pension
£95
7%
£60
£38 (Lower Earnings Limit)
5%
These contributions earn entitlement to a basic pension

As Diagram 4 shows, the NI contributions which your employer deducts on the first £38.00 of your week's wages earn you entitlement to a basic pension. The rest of the contributions he deducts earn you entitlement to additional pension. The more you earn, the more you will pay in contributions and the more additional pension you will eventually get (though earning more than the Upper Earnings Limit will not earn you any extra pension).

Unfortunately, the scheme is still young – it only started in 1978 – so the pension you get from it is likely to be modest for anyone retiring in the next few years. The rules for working out how much pension you will eventually get are complicated, and if the Government's current proposals come into effect the calculation will in some cases depend on the year in which you retire. But to take a simple example, suppose you have paid into the scheme since it started and your earnings are currently £100 a week and your employer gives you a pay rise each year in line with inflation until you retire in the year 2000. At that time your weekly wage will still buy what £100 will buy today. The amount your pension will be worth (still in today's money) will be a quarter of the difference between £100 and the Lower Earnings Limit (£38.00), i.e., a quarter of £62.00, which is £15.50 a week. Combined with a full basic state pension which should still be worth £38.70 a week, you will get £54.20 a week – a big drop from your £100 a week earnings.

Pensions from your job

A company pension scheme is a way of having money saved for your retirement. While you are working, you and the company put money into the scheme which is then invested, mainly in shares, property and Government stocks. When you retire, the scheme pays you an income for life. If you work in the public sector (e.g., as a nurse or teacher) your pension scheme will be much the same.

Companies do not have to run pension schemes for their staff, but most larger firms do. The firm may only allow certain staff to join its scheme, or may have different schemes for different grades of staff. Each scheme has its own rules about who can join, how much money is to be paid in and what the benefits are. The rules are laid down by the company, perhaps after negotiations with trade union or staff representatives. But the Government lays down minimum standards which every scheme must keep, and also the maximum benefits it can provide (so that schemes do not try to promise too much or get used as a way for the company to avoid tax).

One of the main safeguards is that the pension scheme's money is kept entirely separate from the company's money. It does not even belong to the company – it belongs to the scheme. Each scheme is technically a trust fund, administered by a group of trustees. These trustees may be the firm's managers, or may include staff and pensioner representatives (they may sometimes be an outside trust company). Whoever they are, they have a legal obligation to act in the interests of all the members of the scheme, not in their own or the company's interests. The rules of each scheme are set out in a **Trust Deed** and other documents.

Each pension scheme should have a booklet explaining how it works. It should say who can (or has to) join, how much you and the firm pay in, and what benefits you are entitled to when you retire. It should also say what happens if you leave the company before retirement. Many schemes incorporate other benefits like life insurance and pensions for dependants, and the booklet should explain these too.

If you are within a few years of retirement or are thinking of changing your job, it is important that you ask for a statement showing the benefits you have earned in the scheme.

How a pension scheme works

With most schemes, your firm deducts a percentage of each of your pay packets (usually around 4%) and pays it into the pension fund. You do not have to pay any tax on this money. So if you earn enough to be liable for tax, each £100 you contribute costs you only £71 (because if you didn't pay the £100 into a pension scheme you would have to pay tax on it and would only get £71).

Your firm also pays money into the fund – often two or three times as much as you pay. The result is that a lot more money is invested than the cost to you (often four or five times as much). With some schemes (called **non-contributory**), the firm pays the whole cost and you pay nothing. The money in the fund is invested, and a special concession means that pension funds do not pay any tax on the profits they make from their investments. The result is that a pension scheme is likely to be a much more profitable way of saving for your retirement than most other investments.

Even if you are very young and do not intend to stay in the job long, it can still be worth joining your firm's scheme. The reason in this case is that many schemes allow you to withdraw your contributions if you leave the firm within 5 years of joining the scheme, and you may get a very high return on them – see below.

Most schemes set a normal retirement age (often 60 for women, 65 for men) when you will become eligible to start receiving your pension. If you retire earlier you can start receiving your pension earlier as long as you are at least 50 or are too ill to work again, but the weekly or monthly rate will be lower. If you postpone drawing your pension you will eventually get a higher rate.

With most schemes, the amount of pension you get is based on the number of years you contributed to the scheme and on the amount you were earning before you retired (or when you left the scheme). These are called **final pay schemes**. For example, a generous scheme may give you a pension of 1/60th of your 'final pay' (though 1/80th is more common) for each year you contributed to it. So if you contributed for 40 years, you would get a pension of 40/60ths (i.e., 2/3) of your 'final pay'. 'Final pay' may mean your salary in the final year, but often it is more complicated – the average of the three best years in the last ten, or something like that.

You can see that the pension you get from a final pay scheme can be quite good if you have spent most of your working life with one firm. But suppose you worked for a firm for five years when you were young and then left. The pension you get when you retire many years later will be 5/60ths (or 5/80ths or whatever fraction is used) of your final pay *when you left the job*. Thirty years ago, your pay would probably not have been more than £500 a year, so the pension you would get if you were retiring now would be 5/60ths of £500 which is only £41 a year. Inflation over the 30 years your pension has been frozen has made it almost worthless. However, if you leave a job after 1 January 1986 and leave your money in the scheme, the pension entitlement which you earned after 1 January 1985 has to be increased by 5% a year (or by the rate of inflation, if that is lower) for each year until the pension is payable. (You do not always have to leave your contributions in the scheme – see below.)

Money purchase schemes are rather different from final pay ones. In effect, each member of the scheme has an individual account. The money you and your employer pay into your account remains invested until you retire (even if you leave the job). At your retirement, the money is 'taken out' and is used to 'buy' you a pension at the going rate. Often the yearly amount of pension you get will be around 13% of the money in your 'account'. So if there is £10,000 in your account, you might get a pension of around £1,300 a year.

You can see that in the past money purchase schemes have been better for job-changers than final pay ones, as the money you have paid in continues to earn interest and profits from being invested, rather than being frozen on your salary at the time you left the job. But for people who have spent most of their working lives in one job (or the last 20 years of it, say) money purchase schemes have often not provided as high a pension as a good final pay scheme. If you had had a free choice, it would have paid you to go for money purchase schemes if you were under 40, say, and not intending to stay in the job for more than 10 years, but to opt for final pay schemes if you were over 50 or intending to retire from the job. Now that final pay pensions cannot be frozen, the difference is less marked.

Links with the state additional pension scheme (Serps)

The pension you get from your firm may be additional to both the state basic and additional pensions. But many final pay schemes are **contracted-out** of the additional pension scheme. This means that you (and your firm) pay lower National Insurance contributions. In return, your firm has to guarantee that the pension it eventually pays you will not be less than the additional state pension you would have received if you had contributed to the additional pension scheme in the same period. This part of your pension is called the **Guaranteed Minimum Pension** (**GMP**). Like additional pension, when the GMP is paid to you it will be increased each year in line with inflation *unless* at the time of contributing you are married or widowed and have kept the right to pay the **lower stamp** (i.e., the lower rate of National Insurance contributions – see page 291).

Earning extra pension

Your firm is quite entitled to pay extra into its pension fund in order to provide additional benefits for individual members. This is a fairly common tax-free 'perk' for valued employees and directors, particularly if they joined the company late in life and have not earned much pension entitlement. So one way of getting a higher pension is to ask your employer to make a special contribution for you.

The alternative is to pay in extra yourself. If your scheme allows it, you can make **additional voluntary contributions** (**AVCs**). This is particularly worthwhile in the five to ten years before you are due to retire, especially if your pension entitlement is otherwise on the low side. In fact, in this period AVCs are probably the best investment you can make. The effective return can be well over 20%, because the interest paid on AVCs is usually fairly high to start with *and* you get tax relief on what you pay *and* there is no tax on the interest they earn. At retirement, you can normally choose which of the possible retirement benefits you want your AVCs to top up – e.g., your pension, your tax-free lump sum or your dependants' pensions. To get the tax advantages you must make regular payments until you retire, though if you stop paying you will not lose the tax concessions if you have paid regularly for at least 5 years or if it would cause you hardship to continue. The total contributions you pay into your firm's scheme (regular contributions plus AVCs) cannot be more than 15% of your earnings. If you are considering paying AVCs, talk to your firm's pensions manager and check what benefits your firm's scheme could provide from them.

When you leave a job

What happens to your pension rights when you leave a job depends on the scheme's rules and what choices are allowed to you. The main possibilities are:

- **Your pension rights are preserved for you for when you retire.** We have described what happens in this case under final pay schemes and money purchase schemes above.

- **You transfer your pension rights to your new employer's scheme.** You can do this if you are moving to a new job straightaway, and the rules of the new scheme allow transfer. Your old firm's scheme will put a **transfer value** on your pension rights, which is the amount of money it is prepared to hand over. If it was a money purchase scheme, this is simply the value of the investments in your 'account'; transfer values for final pay schemes have normally been lower, but should improve when new regulations are introduced. If your new employer's scheme is a money purchase one, the money handed over goes into your new 'account'. If it is a final pay scheme it buys you so many years of service (almost certainly fewer than you had actually contributed for).

• **Your pension rights are transferred to an insurance plan.** In this case the transfer value is paid to an insurance company which invests the money for you. When you retire, the money that has accumulated is used to buy you a pension.

• **You withdraw your contributions.** You can only do this if you have been a member of the scheme for under 5 years and if the scheme's rules allow it. You can only withdraw what *you* paid in, not your employer's contributions. The scheme may add some interest to what it pays you (though the yearly interest rate is usually under 5%), and it has to deduct tax at a special rate of only 10%. The tax concessions on pensions mean that what you get back is equal to a return to you of at least 12% and possibly much more – even over 25%. Withdrawing contributions can be a useful option if you have been in the scheme for under a year or are a young person who wants to have enough for the deposit on a first home, say. But unless you have a terminal illness, you should not withdraw pension contributions for a frivolous purpose, nor once you are past the age of 30.

When you retire

On retirement, you collect the pensions you are entitled to from the various schemes you have belonged to. Most schemes allow you to exchange part of your pension for a tax-free lump sum – see page 303 for details.

If you have worked in the public sector, the pension you get is likely to be increased each year in line with inflation from the time you retire. With other contracted-out schemes, the GMP part of your pension (see page 282) will get the same yearly increases as other state pensions. But there are no other requirements for pensions to be increased. Some schemes guarantee to increase pensions by a fixed amount each year (e.g., 3% or 5%). Others may not have any provision for increases. However, in either of these cases the firm may decide to make a discretionary increase from time to time to all its pensioners (the firm pays for these, not the pension scheme). The best firms have made regular discretionary increases which have kept up the value of their pensions with rising prices.

Problems with a firm's pension?

If there are aspects of your firm's pension scheme you do not understand or which concern you, talk to the firm's pensions manager or one of the scheme's trustees. The Company Pensions Information Centre (3 Old Park Lane, London W1Y 3LJ) can give general information about pension schemes and produces a series of booklets including *How to understand your pension scheme, How a pension fund works* and *Pensions for women*. The Occupational Pension Advisory Service (Room 327, Aviation House, 129 Kingsway, London WC2B 6NN) is able to answer individual enquiries to scheme members and their widows and dependants. It may be able to advise you if you are unhappy with the information, advice or decisions you get from the scheme manager or trustees.

Personal pensions

A personal pension is a pension you arrange with an insurance company and pay for yourself. You pay money out of your earnings to the insurance company, either a lump sum or a regular amount each month or year or, with some plans, any amounts at any time. The insurance company invests your money until you decide you want to start drawing a pension. Part of the money that has accumulated for you can then be withdrawn as a tax-free lump sum, while the rest is used to buy you a pension.

Personal pensions are a very worthwhile way to invest for retirement because they get much greater tax concessions than most other forms of investment. You get tax relief on the money you pay in, so that investing £100 only costs you £71 (because you would otherwise have to pay tax on that £100 and be left with only £71). Your money is invested in the insurance company's pension fund, which does not have to pay any tax on the investment income it gets or the profits it makes when it sells investments. If you decide to give up part of your pension in exchange for a lump sum, you get this completely free of tax. And the pension you receive is treated by the Inland Revenue as earnings, not investment income; this makes a difference if you are married, as it means the income is treated as yours, not your husband's, and up to £2,335 of it can be tax-free because of your Wife's Earned Income Allowance. In return for these tax concessions, the main restriction on these plans is that you cannot normally get any of your money out again until you are at least 60, and most of it must then be used to provide a pension. You can, however, stop paying into a plan, and may be able to get a loan on the strength of the money that is invested for you.

Paying money in

There are well over a hundred different personal pension plans available, and they come in all shapes and sizes. Over your working life you may collect a number of different plans. Some are **single-premium** policies – i.e., you just pay in a single lump sum, though with certain of these you can pay in further amounts later. Some are **regular-premium** policies – i.e., you agree to pay so much each month or each year. Some are more flexible than others – with some you can miss a certain number of payments or pay lower amounts without being penalised. Some plans are completely flexible – you can pay what you like when you like.

Money you pay into these plans has to come out of your earnings (from a job or from self-employment or freelance work). Broadly, you are allowed to pay up to 17½% of your **Net Relevant Earnings** for each tax year into personal pensions. But there are times when you can pay more than 17½% – see below. You can make the payments in the tax year they are for or the following year.

If you are self-employed or have freelance earnings or are a partner in a partnership, the Class 2 National Insurance contributions you pay qualify you for a basic state pension but no additional pension. Your Class 4 NI contributions do not entitle you to any pension. So a personal pension plan is very important for you if you want to have more to live on after retirement than a basic state pension. Your Net Relevant Earnings for a tax year are the **taxable profits** on which you are being charged tax in that year. For example, if your Tax Inspector sends you a Schedule D Notice of Assessment for the 1985–86 tax year, your Net Relevant Earnings for 1985–86 will normally be the trading profits shown there (plus any balancing charge), *less* the capital allowances, losses and business interest shown. Personal allowances are not deducted, nor are National Insurance contributions or pension or life insurance premiums you have paid.

If you are in a job where you work for an employer, but are not a member of the firm's pension scheme, you can use personal pensions to top up your state pensions. You cannot pay premiums out of earnings which come from a job where you belong to the firm's scheme. So your Net Relevant Earnings for the tax year are your earnings in the tax year (including the taxable value of any fringe benefits, but less anything you have spent on allowable expenses – see page 356) from any jobs in which you do not belong to the firm's pension scheme. In the past, if you had a choice between joining your employer's pension scheme and taking out a personal pension plan you would generally have done better to join the firm's scheme because the firm would normally pay most of the cost, whereas it would contribute nothing to a personal pension. But the Government has proposed that, from April 1988, if you choose to have a personal pension your firm should pay into it too. This could tip the balance in favour of having a personal pension in your early working life if you are likely to change jobs more than once every five years, say. But if you are older and likely to be in the same job for the last ten years of your working life and the firm has a good pension scheme, you would probably be best joining it.

If you have more than one job, business, or source of freelance earnings, your Net Relevant Earnings for the year is the total of the Net Relevant Earnings from each.

If you are married, you have your own Net Relevant Earnings – your husband's earnings do not count.

You will normally be able to pay more than 17½% of your Net Relevant Earnings into these plans in a tax year and still get tax relief on the full amount you pay if you were born before 1934 or if you have not paid the full 17½% of your Net Relevant Earnings in any of the last seven tax years. You can also pay last year's premiums this year, if you have not already used up last year's full 17½% allowance (plus any unused from previous years). The insurance company or broker you deal with will help you work out how much you are allowed to pay. They will also give you a **Self-Employed Premium Certificate** showing how much you have paid in premiums. You send this to your Tax Inspector to claim your tax relief. If the payments you have made relate to different tax years, you should ask your Tax Inspector for a form 43 on which you can show how the money is to be allocated.

How the plans work

Most plans are either with-profits or unit-linked. They work rather differently:

- With a **with-profits plan**, the company decides how it can most profitably invest your money. It guarantees at the outset to pay you a certain amount of pension at a certain age (or it may guarantee a certain amount of money being available to buy you a pension at a certain age). The guaranteed amounts are not very high, but as time goes on and the company makes profits on its investments it increases the guaranteed amounts by adding 'bonuses'. So your pension (or fund of money) gradually grows – its value cannot fall.

- A **unit-linked plan** is more like a unit trust. You can say where you want your money invested – e.g., in shares, property, Government stock and so on, or in a mixture of these. The value of your stake goes up and down with the total value of the investments in the fund. This means that how well you do depends very much on *when* you invest and withdraw. Ideally, you would invest when the value of the fund is low and withdraw when it is high, but unfortunately it is only possible to see these peaks and troughs in retrospect.

So unit-linked plans are more risky than with-profits ones; while the best unit-linked plans have done much better than the best with-profits ones, the worst ones have done much worse. The best way of hedging your bets may be to have both with-profits and unit-linked policies, if you can afford it.

Some companies offer two other types of policy:

- **non-profit policies** These are like with-profits policies except that they guarantee higher pensions initially but there are no bonuses added to increase the guaranteed amounts. You should not consider one of these unless there are only a few years to go before you intend to retire and you want to be extra-cautious.

- **deposit administration policies** These work much like a bank deposit account, paying interest on the money you have invested. They can be useful in the last few years before retirement if interest rates are high and you want to be certain you do not lose any money.

The benefits you get

Most plans allow you to start taking the benefits at any time between your 60th and 75th birthdays. If you are in an occupation which traditionally has a younger retiring age (e.g., a nurse or midwife) or you become too ill to work again, you can start taking the benefits then. The age at which you actually stop work does not matter, nor will earning money affect the pension you get in any way. (When we say 'retire' in this section, it is just shorthand for 'starting to take the benefits of the policy'.) If you have several pension plans, you can start taking the benefits from each at different times if you want to – this is a way of gradually increasing your income in the first few years of retirement. Of course, the earlier you start taking the benefits from a policy, the less you will get – because your money will have been invested for a shorter period and the pension will be paid for a longer one. If you have had the plan for only a few years, taking the benefits one year earlier will reduce them substantially.

As we have said, you can transfer all the money that has accumulated in your plan to whichever company is offering the best pension deal at the time. A life insurance broker with a computerised quotation service is likely to be the best person to find this company for you. You can also give up part of your pension in exchange for a tax-free lump sum. For example, instead of having a pension of £3,000 a year you could have a tax-free lump sum of perhaps £6,000 and a pension of £2,000 a year. You cannot normally exchange more than about ⅕ to ¼ of your pension, and the lump sum will not usually be much more than three times the reduced pension.

Some plans treat a small amount of the premiums you pay as life insurance, so that if you die before you start taking the benefits of the plan the company will pay back the total premiums you have paid, perhaps with interest. Other plans do not pay anything. However, if you qualify for one of these plans you also qualify for full tax relief on life insurance premiums you pay on special **Section 226A policies**. You can pay premiums of up to 5% of your Net Relevant Earnings for these policies each year, and get full tax relief as long as these premiums *plus* your personal pension premiums do not come to more than 17½% of your Net Relevant Earnings for the tax year. If you ask for the policy to be **written in trust** for the person you want the money to go to on your death (who should be named in the policy), the money paid out will be free of Inheritance Tax.

Choosing your personal pension plans

Because of the vast range of plans available, the complexity of them and the importance to you of getting a good pension, you will need to do some homework. If you find it hard to decide between the enormous number of features they offer, there is a thorough survey in Chapter 18 of *The Which? Book of Saving and Investing* which should be in your library.

Do *not* take out the first plan you see advertised in the newspapers, or leave it all up to a life insurance broker. Get leaflets from a number of insurance companies and see what they offer. But do not be too impressed with the enormous pensions and funds they promise. The figures ignore a vital factor – inflation. If you want to compare the main details of all the schemes available, ask for an up-to-date edition of a book called *Self-Employed Pensions* published by Financial Times Business Publishing Ltd.

With a regular-premium policy or one which allows future payments to be made, make sure that any guarantees (e.g., about pension entitlement, amount of fund, charges, unit allocation or annuity rate) apply to all payments you make, not just the first, and preferably even if you increase the amount you pay in. If they do not, you would probably do better with single-premium policies as the amount of commission paid to the broker who arranges it for you is much lower – so more of your money is invested. But a few life insurance companies do not pay any commission to brokers anyway – so are not likely to be recommended by a broker. It is worthwhile getting information from two of these companies whose plans have produced good pensions in the past – Equitable Life (tel. 01-606 6611) and London Life (tel. 0272 279179). Equitable Life have an excellent with-profits plan which is very flexible – you can pay in what you like when you like – and the guarantees in the policy apply to all future payments.

Pensions for married women

As a married woman, you can build up your own entitlement in exactly the same way as anyone else:

- to a basic state pension of your own by paying Class 1, 2 or 3 National Insurance contributions, or being credited with contributions (though for at least one tax year they must have been *paid*), or since 1978, by getting **Home Responsibilities Protection**;
- to a state additional pension by paying Class 1 contributions on earnings above the Lower Earnings Limit;
- to company pensions by joining your employers' schemes; *and*
- to personal pensions by paying money into these plans.

But as a married woman, you will want to take into account in your pension planning the benefits your husband will get from the pensions he has earned entitlement to. You should also be aware of what benefits his pension schemes would provide for you if he were to die, and how all these benefits would be affected if you were to separate or divorce. There are also differences in the contributions paid by some married women. We look at these points in this section.

The 'lower stamp'

This section only applies to you if you still have the right to pay married women's reduced rate National Insurance contributions (once commonly known as the **lower stamp**), or the right not to pay any Class 2 contributions. If you do not have this right, please skip to page 295.

Before April 1978, women who were married or widowed could choose to pay special lower National Insurance contributions. Having the right to pay these lower contributions is called **reduced liability**. When in a job, you pay a smaller percentage of your earnings in contributions. When self-employed, you pay no Class 2 contributions. In return, while you have reduced liability you get no entitlement to a state basic pension, or state additional pension, or any social security benefits which depend on NI contributions.

No one can choose reduced liability now, but if you chose it before April 1978 *and* it hasn't been taken away from you since, you still have the right to pay special lower contributions. Alternatively, you can change over to paying normal contributions at any time.

The right to pay special lower contributions is taken away from you if:

- you ask to pay normal contributions, *or*
- you get divorced or your marriage is annulled, *or*
- your husband dies (but not until the end of the tax year in which your widow's benefit ends); *or*
- for any two consecutive tax years since 1978 you have neither been self-employed, nor in a job in which National Insurance contributions were payable.

If you are not sure whether you have reduced liability, ask your DHSS office.

If you once had the right to pay special lower contributions but lost it and have not worked since, your pension rights may qualify for Home Responsibilities Protection for the period since you lost that right or since 1978, whichever is later – see page 276. If, for example, you had reduced liability 8 years ago when you gave up work to have a baby, and you have received child benefit since, you will get HRP for the last 6 years. You cannot have Home Responsibilities Protection for any period in which you still had reduced liability (the first 2 of those 8 years in our example). Nor, for that period, can you be credited with any NI contributions, nor can you pay any Class 2 or Class 3 contributions.

If you still have reduced liability, you do not need to be earning to change to full liability. You can change at any time. You might then be able to get future contributions credited straightaway, or pay enough Class 3 contributions to make the current tax year a qualifying year. If you qualify for HRP, it can start on the following 6 April.

IF YOU STILL HAVE REDUCED LIABILITY, SHOULD YOU CHANGE TO PAYING FULL CONTRIBUTIONS?

The table below shows the main differences in the benefits you get:

full liability	*reduced liability*
1 **Unemployment benefit** (Class 1 contributions only)	No entitlement
2 **Sickness** and **invalidity benefits** and **maternity allowance** (Class 1 or 2 contributions)	No entitlement

3 Your own **state basic retirement pension** (Class 1, 2 or 3 contributions)	No entitlement to a pension of your own. You will have to rely on a **wife's state pension** based on your husband's contributions
including the right to: • have contributions credited during sickness or unemployment • **Home Responsibilities Protection** if you are at home looking after someone • pay Class 3 contributions to fill gaps in your record	You have no right to these while you have reduced liability
4 **State additional pension** (Class 1 contributions only, and only if you earn more than the Upper Earnings Limit)	No entitlement to your own additional pension

or: **if you are in a firm's pension scheme which is contracted-out:**

The GMP part of the pension you earn will, when it is paid, be increased each year by the Government in line with rising prices.	A level pension only. None of the pension you earn during this period will be increased after retirement.

There are some benefits which are not affected, because they do not depend on National Insurance contributions. These include child benefit, family income supplement, supplementary benefit and maternity grant. Widow's benefits are not affected (because they depend only on your husband's contributions). Nor is **state graduated pension** affected – you get what you have earned when you retire, whether or not you have reduced liability.

POINTS TO CONSIDER ARE:

• The more you earn and the more years you will have worked between 1978 and reaching 60 the more worthwhile it is to change to full liability, because you will then earn yourself a state additional pension. If you will have worked for something approaching 20 years in that period, the amount of additional pension you get should be a good return on your money.

• If you are older than your husband or less than 5 years younger, you will have to wait until he is 65 before you can get a wife's state pension on his contributions. But you can get your own pensions starting when you are 60.

• If, by the time you are 60, you have 24 or more **qualifying years** (see page 274), you will have earned more basic pension on your own contributions than the maximum wife's state pension you could get on your husband's contributions. If you have had Home Responsibilities Protection for any years since 6 April 1978, you will need fewer than 24; to find out how many, subtract the number of years of HRP from 39, multiply by 0.6 and round up. For example, if you have 9 years of HRP you need more than 30 × 0.6 = 18 qualifying years to get more in your own basic pension than a full wife's basic pension. But if you have 19 or more years of HRP, you will need 12 qualifying years.

• If you are in your fifties and do not have a very good contribution record in the past, it may not be worth your changing to full liability.

• If you are planning to have your first child, you should change to full liability, preferably in time to qualify for maternity allowance. You will then be able to get Home Responsibilities Protection from the 6 April after the birth of your child.

• If you are going to stop work for a few years to look after a relative and you will qualify for supplementary benefit to do so, you should change to full liability before the next 5 April and you should apply for HRP for each of the following tax years.

• Remember that to get *any* basic pension of your own, you must have actually *paid* enough contributions for one of your qualifying years. They cannot *all* be credits and HRP.

• Only you can judge whether the entitlement to the social security benefits is something which may be of value to you.

• If you are self-employed, the benefits of full liability are much less, because Class 2 contributions do not carry the same benefits.

For many working women, the extra basic pension *and* the additional pension you will get by paying full contributions will make it worth your while to do so. You can ask your social security office to advise you on the best course in your circumstances.

HOW TO CHANGE

You can change to full liability at any time. The current tax year may be able to count as a qualifying year. Details and the necessary form are in DHSS leaflet NI.1, *Married women: your National Insurance position*. Once you have made this change, you can't change back.

Pension entitlement from your husband

BASIC STATE RETIREMENT PENSION

The National Insurance contributions which your husband will have paid over his working life (whether in a job or self-employed) will entitle him to a state basic retirement pension and you to a smaller **wife's state pension**. When he is 65 (but not before, even if he retires earlier), he will be entitled to start drawing a basic pension for himself. If you are then under 60, he will be able to get an increase for you. Once you are 60, the increase will stop but you will be entitled to your own wife's state pension, earned by your husband's NI contributions. The amount you get will normally be about 3/5 of what your husband gets. Your entitlement is not affected by being separated from your husband, but *is* affected by divorce.

From July 1986, the full amount of basic pension your husband can get is £38.70 a week and you would get £23.25, a total of £61.95 a week. If you have any children still dependent on you, you can get an extra £8.05 for each. So far the Government has increased these amounts each year roughly in line with rising costs. As long as they continue to do so, you can take it that the basic pensions you and your husband eventually get will be *worth* about the same amount as they are now.

Of course, once you are 60, you may be entitled to a state basic pension you have earned on your *own* National Insurance contributions. You cannot get a wife's state pension as well as your own basic state pension – you get whichever is the larger amount, though if each pension is less than £23.25 a week, you can get both of them, but not more than £23.25 in total. If your husband is not yet 65 you should claim your own pension anyway. Once he is 65, you will be told how much wife's state pension you would get. If this is more than your own basic pension, claim the extra.

IF YOUR HUSBAND DIES

There may be substantial benefits you can get from the various pension schemes your husband has contributed to, whether he dies before or after he has retired. See Chapter 13 for details.

IF YOU SEPARATE OR GET DIVORCED

Separation and divorce do not affect your entitlement to any pensions you have earned yourself. Nor does separation affect your entitlement to state pensions based on your husband's National Insurance contributions, but divorce can reduce these. Separation or divorce may well end your entitlement to any pension or widow's benefits from your husband's company pension schemes and personal pension plans. This can be a substantial loss. See page 174 for details.

20

Retirement

Approaching retirement

Most people have less to live on after retirement than they had before. Some people have very much less. Even if you have been in work for a good many years, the pensions you are entitled to are likely to be a lot less than your earnings before you retired. You will need a substantial amount of savings to be able to draw a worthwhile income from them without running them down.

But it is not all doom and gloom, for there are a number of reasons why you may need less after retirement, and a number of ways in which you can save money:

- If you own your home, you are likely to have paid off any mortgage you had, so you will not have those payments to make each month. As you no longer need to live near your place of work, you may also be able to move to somewhere smaller or cheaper; this would raise some money which you could invest, as well as meaning smaller rates and heating bills in the future. Alternatively, you can raise money on the value of your existing home (see page 309).

- You will not have any fares to work to pay.

- You will not have any National Insurance contributions or pension contributions deducted from what you get.

• Once you (or your husband) are 64, a special tax allowance means that less of your income is likely to be taxed.

• Your reduced income may mean you are entitled to benefits you could not claim before – for example, a rent or rate rebate.

• Your local authority may provide day centres, home-helps, meals on wheels and cheap travel.

• You will qualify for discounts on a range of services and entertainments. Prescribed medicines will be free.

• Younger, healthier or wealthier members of your family may be able to help you out in various ways.

• You will have more time for doing jobs around the home yourself, rather than paying someone else to do them.

When can you draw your pensions?

When you look at your pension entitlement, you may find that you can start drawing different pensions at different ages. For example:

• pensions for women from firms' schemes will normally start when you are 60, though some start at 65. However, you can usually choose to retire earlier or later than the normal date (if your employer agrees)

• you can draw your own state basic, additional and graduated pensions when you are 60 as long as you count as 'retired', but you can defer drawing these for as long as you like until you are 65

• if you are married, you are entitled to a wife's state pension (based on your husband's National Insurance contributions) when your husband is 65 (as long as he counts as 'retired' and is drawing his own pension and you are then over 60)

• many personal pensions can be drawn at any age between 60 and 75. But in certain occupations (e.g., nursing) you can draw the pension earlier.

To count as 'retired' for state pensions, *any* of the following conditions must apply:

• you will not be doing any paid work, *or*

- you will only be working occasionally, *or*
- you will not be working more than 12 hours a week, *or*
- you will be earning less than £75 a week, *or*
- you expect to earn more than £75 a week only occasionally.

Once you are 65 (70 for a man), you count as retired regardless of any work you do.

You do not have to start drawing your various pensions at the same time. The longer you put off drawing any pension, the higher the amount you will get when it starts to be paid. So it may make sense to delay claiming some of your pensions. Your income over the first few years of retirement can then show a steady increase as you draw more.

Retiring early

Retiring early is likely to mean a lower pension, because you will be paying fewer contributions. And if you also start to draw the pension sooner, the amount will be lower still because it will have to be paid for that much longer. So before you decide to take early retirement, do check what effect it will have on all your pensions.

If your employer agrees, once you are 59 you can choose to retire from your job (or work part-time only) and receive a weekly tax-free payment under the **Job Release Schemes**. Your employer has to agree to take on an unemployed person to take over the work you give up. The rules of the schemes change slightly from year to year, but full details are in the leaflets *Job Release Scheme*, *Part-time Job Release Scheme* and *Advice for those interested in part-time work*, available free at your Jobcentre. Until March 1986 you would have got a tax-free payment of £49.95 a week if you gave up a full-time job or £28.95 if you changed from full-time to part-time (between 16 and 29 hours a week). You could get slightly more if you were married and your husband's income was less than £13 a week. You cannot join the scheme if you are being compulsorily retired by your employer within 6 months and, with minor exceptions, you do not get the allowance if you earn any money or get any social security benefits. While you are getting the allowance, enough National Insurance contributions will be paid or credited for you to protect your state basic retirement pension. But you could well lose out on entitlement to state additional pension or your pension from your employer's scheme – so check this carefully before agreeing to early retirement.

Putting off retirement

With most employers' pension schemes, if you retire late you stop making contributions when you reach the scheme's normal retirement age and the pension you eventually get will be higher. With state pensions it is all rather more complicated.

You do not have to pay any National Insurance contributions once you are 60. You can ask your local social security office for a **Certificate of Age Exemption** to give to your employer, which entitles you to have no contributions deducted from your pay. If you are self-employed, you stop paying Class 2 contributions when you are 60 and the last Class 4 contributions you pay will be for the year of assessment in which you are 60.

You can defer drawing all your state pensions (basic, additional and graduated) for up to 5 years. This is normally worth doing if you are intending working after you are 60, as earnings you get can reduce your state basic pension (see pages 274–7). Even if you have started to receive your state pensions, you can (just once) cancel them and decide to take them later. In either case, the amount you eventually get from all your state pensions will be around 7½% higher (plus the Government's cost-of-living increases) for each year you defer. But there is no increase for any period in which you get certain other state benefits, such as unemployment benefit, sickness benefit or widow's pension.

If you cancel your retirement and go back to work for an employer who is paying you a pension which is **contracted-out** (see page 282), the **Guaranteed Minimum Pension** part of what you get may be stopped. It will be resumed when you stop this work, and the amount of pension you then get will be increased in the same way as deferred state pensions.

If you are married, you can defer or cancel your **wife's state pension** (based on your husband's contributions) in exactly the same way as your own pensions. If any part of your pension is based on your husband's contributions and he wants to defer taking his own pension, you must give your consent when he applies, as it will mean that this part of *your* pension is also deferred until he starts to draw his own pension. And if in the meantime you receive any state pension of your own (basic, additional or graduated), your wife's state pension will not be increased during your husband's deferment.

If you are a widow, there are some special rules which are described in Chapter 13.

To defer taking your state pensions, see page 302. To cancel a pension you already receive, use the form in DHSS leaflet NI.92, *Earning extra pension by cancelling your retirement*, which contains further information.

Giving your pensions a last-minute boost

Apart from deferring a pension, there are two other ways you may be able to earn yourself a higher pension before you stop work:

- If you are in a job and a member of the firm's pension scheme, paying **additional voluntary contributions** to the scheme is very worthwhile in the last few years before retirement – see page 283.

- If, in any of the last 7 years, you have earnings from self-employment or from a job in which you did not belong to the firm's pension scheme, and in the last 2 years you have paid tax on your earnings from these sources, it can be worth paying money retrospectively into a **single-premium personal pension plan**. For example, if you have other money saved up or a lump sum from another pension scheme which you want to use to produce income, you could pay this money into one of these plans. You could then get a tax rebate of 29% of the amount you paid in, and you can pay this in as well if you have enough earnings. You can start drawing an income straightaway or at any time before you are 75. This switch costs nothing and can mean a higher income for life, but you will have to watch the figures very carefully. A life insurance adviser should be able to advise you on how to arrange your payment for the maximum advantage.

Selling a business

There is a valuable exemption from Capital Gains Tax if you sell (or give away) a business when you are 60 or over, or earlier if you have to retire due to ill-health. If you have owned the business for 10 years or more, £100,000 of the taxable gains you make will be exempt from Capital Gains Tax. If you have owned the business for less than 10 years, £10,000 of gains will be exempt for each complete year you have owned it. You only get one £100,000 exemption however many businesses you have, but you do not have to sell everything up at once.

The exemption applies to gains you make when you dispose of land, buildings, plant, machinery and equipment, but not trading stock. It also applies to disposals of:

- the business itself
- your share in a partnership
- shares in a family trading company of which you are a full-time working director (subject to certain conditions) as far as these are represented by the value of the business's assets.

For more about Capital Gains Tax, see page 364. For more information about retirement relief, see Inland Revenue leaflet CGT.6, *Retirement: disposal of a business* (free from tax offices).

At retirement

Claiming your pensions

If you are retiring from a job with a pension, there should be little problem claiming the pension. But if you are entitled to deferred pensions from other firms' pension schemes you have belonged to in the past, you will have to contact them individually. When you want to start drawing a personal pension, you simply write to the insurance company and tell them (you will need to be in the age-range allowed by the policy, unless your health is poor enough to justify drawing it earlier).

To claim your state pensions, the DHSS will normally send you a form about four months before your 60th birthday. If you have not received one three months before then, write and ask for it. If you are married and are entitled to any pension on your husband's contributions, *you* must be the one to claim it. Even if you do not want to start drawing your pensions straightaway, you *must* make a claim (saying on the form that you want to defer it): if you do not claim you may well miss out on some of your pension entitlement.

If you have deferred or cancelled drawing your pension and now want to start drawing it, ask the DHSS for a new claim form about three months beforehand.

You must say on the claim form whether you intend to continue working and how much you will be earning. If this is more than a certain amount and you are under 65 you will be told that you cannot draw your state pensions yet because you do not count as retired (see below). Otherwise you will be told the amount of your pension and how it is made up, and can appeal against this if you disagree. There is more information on your entitlement to state pensions in Chapter 19. Also see DHSS leaflet NP.32, *Your retirement pension.*

Should you exchange part of your pension for a lump sum?

Many firms' pension schemes and personal pension plans allow you to exchange part of your pension for a tax-free lump sum. With a company **final pay scheme** you will generally get around £11 for each £1 of yearly pension you give up. With a **money purchase scheme** or **personal pension plan** you may get less – particularly if annuity rates are high at the time.

There are restrictions on the amount you can exchange:

- With a firm's pension scheme, your lump sum cannot be more than 1½ times your annual salary at the time you retire, and that is only if you worked for the firm for 20 years or more. If you worked there for a shorter period, the lump sum will be less. And if the scheme is contracted-out, the remaining pension cannot be less than the Guaranteed Minimum Pension.

- With a personal pension plan, the lump sum cannot be more than three times the pension which remains (or, with some plans, three times the highest level pension payable under the plan, even if you take an increasing pension).

Whether you should take a lump sum is largely a personal decision. Even if you only want income, there are two cunning ways of using the lump sum to get a higher income than the one offered by the pension scheme:

- Using the lump sum to buy a single-premium **personal pension plan**, getting a tax rebate and then using the tax rebate in the same way. It is not a bad idea to defer taking the pension you get from this money for a few years – it will then be quite a bit higher. See *Giving your pensions a last-minute boost* on page 301 and *Personal pension plans* on page 285 for more details and to see if you qualify.

- Using the lump sum to buy an **annuity** (see page 307). You will not get a tax rebate, but part of the income you get from an annuity is tax-free. Again, you could choose an annuity which starts to pay out income in a few years' time and get a much higher income.

The firm's pensions manager or the insurance company should be able to tell you which is the most advantageous path for you. Remember to ask how much income you would get *after* any tax has been paid. Generally a married woman whose husband is paying tax will have less to gain from an annuity if she has less than £2,335 of other pensions or earnings, because the taxable part of the income from an annuity counts as investment income, meaning that she cannot set the remainder of her Wife's Earned Income Allowance against it.

If the pension from your scheme is one which increases each year (by 3% or 5%, say), you should compare it with an annuity which increases at the same rate. If it is an employer's pension, find out whether it is the firm's policy to give discretionary cost-of-living increases to pensions from time to time. If so, you should be wary of giving up much of your pension as you will miss out on these increases if you do.

Choosing the type of pension

With many employers' pensions, you can choose to take a smaller amount of pension in return for a pension being paid to someone else after your death. You can arrange for this to be paid at the same rate as you get or at a lower rate (half or two-thirds, say).

With personal pensions, there are usually wider options. You can normally transfer the whole of the pension fund that has built up for you to whichever insurance company is paying the highest pensions. You can then choose between a level pension and one which starts lower but increases each year (see page 308 for advice on this). You can give up part of your pension in return for a pension being paid to someone else after your death. And you can choose a pension which is guaranteed to be paid for a minimum period (e.g., 5 or 10 years) even if you do not live that long.

How pensions are paid and taxed

State pensions are normally paid by giving you a book of orders which you can cash each week at a post office.

You can choose instead to have your pension paid directly into a bank or building society account every 4 or 13 weeks. This may be more convenient but you have to wait much longer for your money. If you want your pension paid direct, choose 4-weekly periods, not 13-weekly ones.

The amount of state pension you get is the total you are entitled to in basic, additional and graduated pensions, any extra you have earned by deferring or cancelling your retirement, any increases you are entitled to for dependent children, and any invalidity addition you are entitled to. The total amount will be increased each year by the Government in line with rising prices. The amount you get will also include any cost-of-living increases due to any Guaranteed Minimum Pension you get from a previous employer.

No tax is deducted from your state pensions before they are paid to you. However, if the total amount of your state retirement pensions is more than your tax allowances, you will have to pay tax on the excess.

Pensions you get from your former employers (and, if you are widowed, from your husband's former employers) normally have tax deducted from them under the Pay-As-You-Earn (PAYE) system in the same way as wages. But your Tax Inspector may use this system to collect any tax that is due on other income of yours.

Sometimes the pension scheme will arrange for the pension to be paid by an insurance company, and this pension may still be taxed under PAYE. But it may have basic-rate tax deducted from the full amount. In this case, if your income from all sources is less than your total tax allowances, ask the company if they have an arrangement where they can pay the pension in full with no tax deducted. If they have not, you can ask your tax office to repay the excess tax to you in instalments during the tax year.

Personal pensions are usually paid every month or three months, and usually have a straight deduction of 29% tax made from them. If this comes to more than you actually need to pay, you can claim back the excess from your tax office at the end of the tax year or ask them to pay it in regular instalments during the tax year (see page 355).

If you get a **pension from abroad**, you are normally taxed on 9/10 of the amount you received in the preceding tax year. For more information, ask your tax office for leaflet IR.25.

IF YOU ARE MARRIED

With the two exceptions below, all the pensions above are counted by the Inland Revenue as earned income, so your **Wife's Earned Income Allowance** can be set against them. This means there will be no tax to pay on the first £2,335 of pensions you get in the 1986–87 tax year. If you get more than this, the excess is added to your husband's income, all your other allowances are subtracted and you pay tax on what is left.

There are two cases when you cannot set Wife's Earned Income Allowance against certain pensions you get:

- if part (or all) of your state basic pension is based on your husband's National Insurance contributions, that part counts for tax purposes as your husband's income, not yours

- if you did not get tax relief on all the payments you made into a personal pension plan, some of the pension will be counted as investment income, not earnings, which means it will be treated as your husband's income.

IF YOU DO SOME WORK

Pensions from employers' and personal schemes are not affected by work you do while you are receiving them. Nor are the amounts of state additional or graduated pensions affected, nor widow's benefits or pensions, nor basic pension once you are 65. But before you are 65 your state basic pension (whether based on your own or your husband's contributions) will be reduced for any week in which you earn more than £75 (for what counts as earnings, see DHSS leaflet NP.32). For each *10p* you earn over £75 you lose 5p pension; but you lose 5p pension for each *5p* you earn over £79. This means that if you qualify for a full basic pension of £38.70, it will be reduced to nothing if you earn over £115.70 a week. These limits change from year to year, but stay much the same in value. It may well pay you to defer or cancel your state pensions (see page 300) if your basic pension is going to be substantially reduced by your earnings (you have to defer *all* your state pensions, even though only your basic pension is affected by earnings).

If you are married and under 60 and your husband gets an increase to his pension for you, he will get no increase for you at all in any week in which you earn more than £30.80. If your husband is going to be working regularly after he is 65 and losing pension because of it, it may be worth his while to defer or cancel his basic pension until he stops working or reaches 70. You can get your own pensions in this period, but you cannot get any basic pension you are entitled to on *his* contributions until he decides to start drawing his own.

THE HALF-TEST

Women who were born before 6 April 1919, and who were married when they reached 60, used to have to satisfy a condition known as the half-test before they could get any pension based on their own contributions. The half-test has now been abolished, meaning that some of these women can now get a pension. If you are in this position and you have not been contacted by the DHSS, you should contact your social security office or get DHSS leaflet NI.256 and a free stamped envelope from a post office and send off the form enclosed.

Other sources of income in retirement

Annuities

An annuity is a scheme where you hand over a lump sum of money to an insurance company and in return they pay you an income. There are two main types:

- a **temporary annuity**, where the income is for a set number of years, at the end of which it stops
- a **life annuity**, where the income is paid to you until you die.

It is the second type we are most interested in here, because you are guaranteed an income for life. The insurance company takes the risk that if you live to a ripe old age it will have to pay you a lot of money. On the other hand if you die young, *you* will lose out. So the better your health, the more sense a life annuity makes. The advantage of life annuities are that you can often get a higher income than from other safe investments and this income will never run out. The disadvantage is that once you have handed your money over you cannot ever get any of it back.

The amount of income you get for each £1,000 you hand over depends on:

- your age – the older you are, the more you will get (because the insurance company reckons it will not be paying out for so long)
- how much profit the insurance company thinks it can make by investing the money you hand over
- the type of annuity.

At the time of writing, the best companies were paying women around £140 a year for each £1,000 handed over at age 65, around £155 at age 70 and around £210 at age 80. It is generally better to invest your money elsewhere before you are 70 or so, and only then consider an annuity.

There are several types of life annuity you can get:

- **level annuity**, where the income paid out is the same each year
- **increasing annuity**, where the income starts lower but increases each year by a fixed amount (e.g., 5%)
- **unit-linked annuity**, where the income varies according to the value of the fund your money is invested in
- **joint life annuity**, where the income continues as long as you *or* someone else is alive
- **annuity with guaranteed payments** – if you die within 5 years or before the income paid out has equalled the amount you paid over, the company will pay the balance to your heirs.

Options like these will mean you get a lower income than from a level annuity. But there are also **deferred annuities**, where the income does not start to be paid until a certain period has passed – e.g., 5 or 10 years. The longer the period, the higher the pension that will be paid.

The problem with a simple level annuity is that even if the amount of income you get is adequate at the outset, rising prices will mean it will eventually lose its value. As you may be drawing the income over a good many years, you will soon begin to feel the pinch if inflation goes high. So it would be nice if we could recommend an increasing annuity, but these are really only worthwhile if you reckon you have a good chance of living to a ripe old age. The problem is that because the income starts quite a bit lower, it is a long time before you will have received as much income in total from the increasing annuity as you would have done from a level one. For example, if you buy an increasing annuity when you are 70 you will not have received the same total until you are about 84. Only after that are you better off.

The income you get for each £100 you invest varies quite a bit between insurance companies. And each company changes its annuity rates fairly frequently. Obviously, the higher the rate you can get, the better. If you are thinking of buying an annuity, it is a good idea to start looking at the rates a while beforehand. You can find them in magazines such as *Money Management* and *Savings Market* in your library, or you can consult a life insurance broker. Try to pick a time when the rates are high, and ask your broker to find the highest rate for a woman of your age.

For tax purposes, part of the income you get from an annuity is regarded as repayment of the money you originally handed over, so this is tax-free (the tax-free amount is fixed by the Inland Revenue and does not vary between insurance companies). The rest of the income is taxable and is treated as investment income, not earned income. This means that if you are married you cannot set your wife's earned income allowance against it.

The insurance company will normally deduct basic-rate tax from the *interest* part of each payment and hand it to the Inland Revenue. But if you are not liable to that much tax and would have to reclaim it, you can ask the company if they have an arrangement whereby they can pay you the full amount with no tax deducted.

Because the average woman lives about four years longer than the average man, you will get a smaller income from an annuity than a man of the same age, *and* less of what you get will be tax-free. You will generally get about the same income as a man four or five years younger. So women should generally wait that much longer than a man before buying an annuity.

Extra income from your home

You may be able to use your home to increase your income in retirement. One way is to sell it and buy another smaller home or perhaps move in with relatives or share a home with a friend. Any of these may also save on running costs. But do take into account the high costs of selling and buying property.

Another way is to consider taking in lodgers or converting part of your home into a self-contained flat that you can let. You may even be able to get a grant to cover some of the cost. See Chapter 9 for what you will need to consider.

A third way is to take advantage of a **home income plan**. If you are at least 70 and your home is freehold (or has at least 50 years to run on its lease), these schemes allow you to use your home as security for a loan to buy an annuity. The way a scheme works is this:

- You take out a mortgage on your home (up to about ⅗ or ⅘ of the value of your home).
- The money you borrow is used to buy you an annuity (sometimes some of it can be used for improvements or repairs).
- The annuity pays you an income for life, but the interest on the mortgage is deducted from each income payment before you get it.
- When you die, the mortgage loan is repaid out of your estate (this may mean the home being sold).

For example, if you are 75 and your home is worth £35,000, you might get a loan of £20,000 to buy an annuity. After interest has been deducted you would get a yearly income of around £1,650 if you do not pay tax, or £1,250 if you do.

These schemes are especially valuable if your income is in the band where your age allowance is currently reduced (see page 312). If you take out one of them, you are likely to find that your age-allowance is increased, so there is *less* tax to pay on the rest of your income. However, this benefit may not last more than a few years (because the thresholds for tax allowances generally increase each year).

You get the usual government subsidy on the mortgage interest you pay on up to £30,000 of loans you use for buying the annuity. This means there is much less advantage in borrowing more than £30,000. But you get the subsidy on this £30,000 *in addition to* up to £30,000 of loans you have taken out for buying or improving the home.

The fact that the loan has to be repaid out of your estate when you die is of less concern if your estate is large enough for

Inheritance Tax to be payable (see page 321), as the loan will be deducted from your estate and will thus reduce the amount of tax to be paid.

Three of the schemes available are run by the Abbey National Building Society, the Halifax Building Society (ask at local branches) and Hambro Provident (tel. 01-499 0631). Hambro Provident may provide a larger loan, but the building society schemes will usually provide a bigger income for the same size loan. Avoid schemes which involve selling your home rather than mortgaging it.

Before going ahead with a home income plan, do make sure you understand all the implications. Remember that, however long you live, you do not pay any of the loan back and the full amount will have to be repaid to the company out of your estate. If you decide to sell the home, *you* will have to repay the loan from what you get. And watch that the extra income does not affect any social security benefits you get.

Covenant payments

If your income is too low to pay tax, and someone who does pay tax (or whose husband does) is giving you money on a regular basis to help out, you could suggest to them that there would be a substantial advantage if they gave you the money under a deed of covenant. For every £71 they give you, you will be able to claim £29 from the Inland Revenue. The procedure is fairly simple – see page 205. But if you get any social security benefits, covenant payments may reduce the amount of benefit you get – which voluntary payments will not.

Housing benefits

This is financial help you can get from your local council with paying your rates and, if you are a tenant, your rent. It is much the same as what used to be known as rate and rent rebates. There is no fixed limit to the amount of income you can have and still qualify – so it can be well worth applying. To claim housing benefits, ask your local council for the application form and return it to them. If you have no more than £3,000 in savings and are not in full-time work, you should also go to the DHSS and apply for a supplementary pension (see below) – even if you think you may not qualify for it. More information on housing benefits is given on pages 56 and 57.

Supplementary pensions

If you are finding it hard to make ends meet, you may qualify for a supplementary pension. This is a social security benefit, virtually identical to supplementary benefit, paid to people over state pension age. The amount of pension you get is the difference between the income the Government thinks you need and your actual income. But you cannot get a supplementary pension if you have savings of over £3,000 (ignoring the value of your home) or if you work for more than 30 hours a week (25 hours if you are disabled). It is very complicated working out whether you are entitled to a supplementary pension, so it is best to leave this to the DHSS. The golden rule is that if you think you may qualify, claim. Simply get a form SB.1, called *Cash help*, and a free stamped envelope from a post office. You only need to fill in your name and address on the form and send it off. The procedure is then the same as for supplementary benefit (see page 50). If you get a supplementary pension, you should also apply to your local council for housing benefits.

You will find a very full coverage of housing benefits and supplementary pension in *Your rights for pensioners* published by Age Concern (see page 341).

Age allowance

If you are 64 or more at the start of the tax year, you receive a higher personal tax allowance called **age allowance**, meaning that more of your income each year can be free of tax. A married couple get **married age allowance** which can be set against any of their combined income once either of them is 64. For the 1986–87 tax year, you qualify for the allowance if you (or your husband) were born before 6 April 1922. For a single person, the amount of the allowance in the 1986–87 tax year is £2,850 and for a married man it is £4,505.

The age-allowance trap

Age allowance is reduced if your total income is more than a certain amount, which in 1986–87 is £9,400. If you are single and your total income is £10,173 or more, you will only get the ordinary **single person's allowance** of £2,335. If you are married and your combined total income is £10,675 or more, your husband will only get the normal married man's allowance of £3,655.

If your total income is between these amounts, the allowance is reduced on a sliding scale. For each extra £3 of income above £9,400, your allowance is reduced by £2. This means you pay tax on an extra £5, which is £1.50 tax. So exactly half your extra £3 income has gone in tax.

Diagram 5: **The effect of losing age allowance**

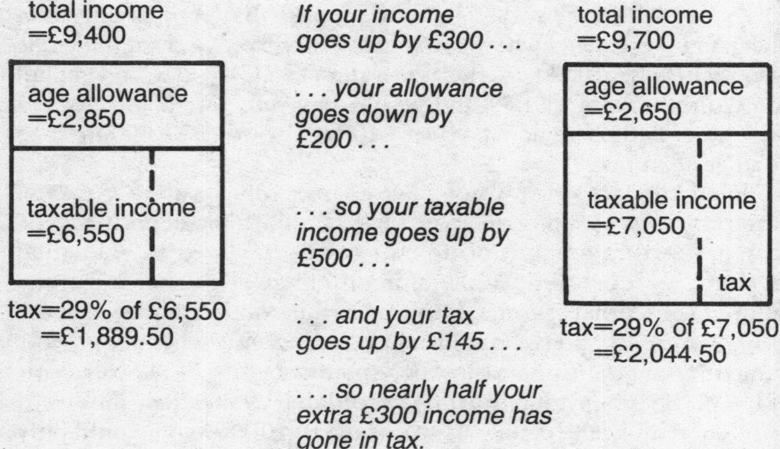

For the same reasons, if your total income were £9,700 but you could reduce it to £9,400 (e.g., by switching to tax-free investments) you would pay £145 *less* tax.

Your **total income** means your income from all sources (*except* tax-free income but *including* the gross amount of interest from building societies, banks and deposit takers), *less* the gross amount of outgoings you make which qualify for tax relief. Details of these payments are given on pages 356 to 361.

How to escape from the trap

If your total income is in the band where you are losing age allowance, half of some of that income will be going in tax. So it is worth exchanging income which comes from a taxable or tax-paid source for income which is **tax-free**. For example, if you transfer money from a building society into National Savings Certificates, this will mean you get more age allowance and so pay less tax on the rest of your income. The only sources of income which are safe are those in the **completely free of tax** list on page 344.

To make this clearer, suppose you are single and get £9,000 in pensions and £1,000 interest from National Savings Income Bonds (which is taxable). If you have no outgoings, your *total income* is £10,000 and your age allowance is reduced to £2,450. So you pay tax on £10,000 minus £2,450 which is £7,550 and your tax is 29% of £7,550 which is £2,189.50. Now suppose that your savings had been in investments where the return is tax-free: your total income would now be £9,000. As this is less than £9,400, you would get full age allowance of £2,850 and would pay only £1,783.50 tax – a saving of £406. Previously, over £400 of the other £1,000 interest had gone in tax.

Even though you do not have to pay any basic-rate tax on interest from building societies, banks and other deposit takers, the grossed-up amount of this interest is included in your total income, so it can reduce the amount of age allowance, meaning more tax on other income. Suppose in the example above that the £1,000 interest had come from a building society. To find the gross amount, you multiply this by 100 and divide by 71 – the answer is £1,408. So your total income would be £9,000 pensions plus £1,408, which is £10,408. As this is over £10,173, you would only get the ordinary single person's allowance (£2,335) to set against your pensions. You would be taxed on £9,000 *less* £2,335, i.e., on £6,665, which is £1,932.85 tax. But if around ¾ of your building society money had been in an investment which was tax-free, your total income would have been under £9,400. You would then have had the full age allowance of £2,850 to set against your pensions, leaving tax on £6,150, which is £1,783.50 tax. This is a tax saving of £149.35.

INSURANCE COMPANY BONDS

Your age allowance can also be reduced if you get money from a non-qualifying life insurance policy (e.g., a single-premium bond) or if you have a qualifying policy which you cash in (in whole or in part) or make paid-up in its first ten years (or within three-quarters of its term, if that is shorter). Some insurance company income and growth bonds are technically policies of this type. You should ask the insurance company if a taxable gain will arise and, if so, how much. The gain will normally be the amount you get back less the premiums you have paid. The gain is added to your total income and so can easily eradicate your age allowance. So it is best to avoid policies of this type which will come to an end after you are 64.

IF YOUR INCOME IS FAIRLY CONSTANT

If most of your income does not increase much from year to year (e.g., because only a small part comes from state pensions), you will gradually move out of the age-allowance trap because the income limits are normally increased by the Government each year.

HOME INCOME PLANS

As described on page 310, a home income plan can not only provide you with extra income, but can also increase your age allowance, meaning less tax to pay. This is because only the **taxable** part of the annuity income you get is added to your 'total income', but the **grossed-up** amount of the mortgage interest you pay is subtracted from your 'total income'. As the amount subtracted is generally a lot more than the amount added, your 'total income' is reduced and your age allowance is thus increased.

MAKING COVENANT PAYMENTS

If your income is in the band where your age allowance is being reduced, and you regularly give money to someone else who does not pay tax (a grandchild, perhaps), there is a special advantage in making these payments under a deed of covenant. For each £71 you hand over, the Inland Revenue will give the recipient a further £29 *and* they will reduce your tax bill by £19. So while you are only £52 worse off, the recipient is £100 better off. This is because the Revenue allow the recipient to reclaim the £29 tax you have 'deducted', and they allow you to deduct the £100 gross amount of the covenant payments from your total income, meaning your age allowance goes up by £67, saving 29% of £67, i.e., £19 in tax. Of course, you should not agree to hand over money you cannot afford purely to reduce your tax bill, and there is less advantage in making covenant payments once you have reduced your total income to £9,400.

Investing in retirement

There is no simple recommendation for your investments in retirement. The information in Chapter 5 should help you select suitable investments for your needs. We look here at particular points which may affect you in retirement.

Before committing yourself, you should think very carefully about what you want to achieve from your investments. It is not sensible to put all your money into one investment, however high your hopes for it, so you must plan carefully.

One thing is likely – that your retirement is a long one. If you retire at 60, you have a 50:50 chance of living to be 81. And the bugbear of such long periods is inflation. Today things cost *six times* as much as they did 20 years ago. Some of your invested money should be protected against inflation by being invested in index-linked National Savings Certificates or index-linked British Government stock. The latter is the *only* investment where the value of your capital is protected against inflation *and* the income rises in line with inflation – though the income is of course only a small percentage of the capital (2% or 2½%). And some of your money should be in investments like unit trusts which, though more risky, do have more chance of giving you a good return over a long period than simple savings like building society accounts.

Your choice of investment will also be affected by whether your main need is for a lasting income or whether you can put some of your money where it will grow and you will be able to draw an income from it later or pass it on to your heirs. If income is all-important, you will normally get the highest return from an annuity (e.g., around 13% after tax if you are 70) – see page 307. The table on pages 76–83 shows which other investments are most suitable for producing an income. Remember that investments like National Savings Certificates, which can be easily cashed in, can be used to provide an income in this way.

Even if you have been paying tax previously, your lower income in retirement may mean that you can now avoid it altogether. This is even more likely once you are 64 and get age allowance. If you do not pay tax, it is worth transferring money from banks or building societies (where tax is deducted and you cannot reclaim it) to National Savings investments where no tax is deducted (like National Savings Investment Account, Income Bonds and Deposit Bonds).

If you are considering an insurance company guaranteed income bond or guaranteed growth bond, and it will come to an end after you are 64, avoid bonds which are technically a life insurance policy producing a taxable gain, as they will reduce your entitlement to age allowance (see page 315).

Once you are 64, remember that if your age allowance is being reduced by the fact that your total income is over £9,400, it would be well worth transferring some of your money to tax-free investments (like National Savings Certificates and Yearly Plan) – see page 314.

While investments you make which qualify under the **Business Expansion Scheme** qualify for tax relief (see page 74), they do *not* increase the amount of age allowance you get.

21

Passing Your Money On

Thinking about who you want your possessions to go to after your death is not a subject reserved for the morbid or the elderly rich. Anyone of any age should make sure that their possessions go to the people they want to have them when they die, and this nearly always means making a will. And you do not have to have amassed a fortune to find that what you leave will be liable to Inheritance Tax – the value of your home alone could mean tax for someone to pay when you die. You need to know if your estate is likely to be liable to tax, because there are steps you can take to reduce the tax quite considerably – so that your heirs end up with more.

In this chapter we also cover the business of making large gifts during your lifetime – something which people do in the hope of avoiding tax when they die, but which should only be done after careful consideration.

If you are married, you should have your own will, and (unless you live in Scotland) it must be made *after* you married (because outside Scotland any will you made before marriage no longer counts). Marriage does *not* mean you jointly own everything with your husband; anything which you owned before your marriage, or which you inherited, were given, won or bought with your own money, is yours alone and you can leave it to whoever you like in your will (except in Scotland – see page 328). Most things you *do* own jointly will automatically go to your husband when you die, but in England and Wales there are special rules for jointly-owned homes – see below.

If you are married or live with someone as a couple, it is equally important to you that your partner has also made a will. Your partner is not under any obligation to tell you what he intends to leave to whom, but it is important that he realises who will have his possessions if he does not make a will. If you are married and live in England or Wales you may only get the first £40,000 of your husband's estate (which may all be tied up in your home, so no ready cash). If you are not married you will inherit nothing from your partner (except in Scotland) and your only recourse will be to the courts. So give your partner this chapter to read too (your partner may need to read 'he' for 'she', 'wife' for 'husband' and so on, but the rules are the same). It is best if you can decide everything together, as you must consider what will happen if *you* die first, if *your partner* dies first and if you die at pretty much the same time.

In Scotland there are different rules about who inherits what if you do not leave a will (see page 330) and about who you can leave things to in your will (see page 328).

What are you worth?

It is worth getting an idea first of the total value of what you own and thinking about which of these things you want to pass on to specific people. So make a quick list of your assets:

- homes or land you own
- your car, furniture, jewellery and other possessions
- any businesses you own
- anything you have a right to use, even though you do not own it – e.g., your home if your husband owns it
- your savings and investments (except annuities)
- life insurance policies on your life
- any money you are owed.

The things in this list are called your **estate**. Beside each item, write down its approximate value in a column headed *Value*:

- With the material things, the value is what they would fetch if you sold them.

- If you own something jointly with anyone or have a right to use it (e.g., a home or a business or a joint savings account), write down the value of your share (assume shares are equal unless you have agreed otherwise).

- With savings and investments, the value is the amount you would get if you cashed in the investment now.

- With life insurance, the value is the amount the policies will pay out on your death – but do *not* include any policies which are **written in trust** (because the benefits go immediately to the person you have named and do not form part of your estate – see page 325), nor money your dependants will get from a pension scheme where the trustees technically have discretion as to who the money is paid to.

Add up all the figures in the *Value* column and write the total at the bottom.

If you owe any money (e.g., on a mortgage or bank loan), it will have to be repaid out of your estate when you die, so subtract the total you owe. Your funeral will be paid for out of your estate, so deduct £500, say, for that. The figure you are now left with is probably the total value of the things you can leave in your will, but in England or Wales it may not be if you own your home jointly. If you live in Scotland or Northern Ireland, or if you are the sole owner of your home (ignoring mortgages), or if you do not own a home, skip to *Tax on things you give away and pass on*.

IF YOU OWN YOUR HOME JOINTLY (ENGLAND AND WALES)

If your home is in joint names, what happens to your share when you die depends on the kind of joint ownership. You can find this out from the deeds of your home. If you are **joint tenants** (usual for married couples), each share in the home automatically passes to the other joint owner, and nothing you say in your will can change this. However, if you are **tenants-in-common** you can each leave your share to anyone you like in your will (your partner could, however, dispute this after your death). It is possible to change from one type of joint ownership to the other. Don't do so without serious consideration.

If you have discovered that you are joint tenants and are intending to remain so:

- **If the joint tenant is your husband,** cross out the amount you entered in the *Value* column for your home and reduce the total by this amount. The reason for this is that your will can ignore your share in the home, and anything which passes to your husband on your death will be exempt from Inheritance Tax.

- **If the joint tenant is not your husband,** leave your *Value* column as it is, because the transfer is not exempt from Inheritance Tax. But make a mental or written note that your will can ignore your share in the home.

Tax on things you give away and pass on

If the total value of your estate – i.e., the things you leave when you die (other than to your husband, registered charities and certain other institutions) – is more than a certain amount, your heirs may have to pay **Inheritance Tax** on the excess. In the 1986–87 tax year the threshold for this tax is £71,000. The higher the value of your estate above this, the higher the proportion that goes in tax, for example:

if you left:	*the tax would be:*
£71,000	nil
£80,000	£2,700
£100,000	£8,950
£150,000	£27,500
£250,000	£74,000

However, even if you are very wealthy, you may be able to avoid tax completely by leaving £71,000 (or whatever the current threshold is) to whoever you like and the rest to charities and, if you are married, to your husband. But leaving a lot to your husband will mean a big tax bill when *he* dies, so the tax may only be deferred in this case – more about this later.

Giving things away in your lifetime

If this were the end of the story, another way you could avoid Inheritance Tax completely would be to give away everything except £71,000 worth of possessions while you are still alive. But the Government is not silly enough to let people avoid tax so easily, and the value of most things you give away in the seven years before you die will be added to your estate and tax will be based on the total. But none of the following are counted:

- gifts between husband and wife, and gifts for the maintenance of your separated or ex-husband
- gifts for the maintenance or education of your children, step-children, adopted children and wards
- transfers of property to your ex-husband which are part of the divorce settlement
- wedding gifts (up to certain limits)
- gifts to your mother or mother-in-law if she is widowed, separated or divorced
- gifts to help support a relative who is elderly or in poor health
- regular gifts of money you pay out of your income
- one-off gifts of up to £250 to as many people as you like in each tax year
- gifts to charities, political (up to £100,000) parties and certain national institutions (e.g., national museums)
- gifts of heritage property.

In addition to all these, you can give away another £3,000 (possibly up to £6,000) in any tax year completely tax-free. All these gifts are ignored for Inheritance Tax purposes. Any other gifts you make in the last seven years of your life are potentially taxable, though the rate of tax is scaled down for things you gave away more than 3 years before your death, down to nothing for gifts made more than 7 years before. There are also special rules for lifetime gifts of family businesses, farms, farmland and woodlands which will normally mean less than the usual amount of tax will be payable.

Unfortunately there is yet another trap – **Capital Gains Tax** (**CGT**) – but you can probably sidestep this one too. CGT is primarily a tax on the profit you make when you sell something, but it also applies if you give something away which is worth more than it was when you acquired it. For example, if you give away something which was worth £15,000 when you acquired it but is now worth £25,000, there may be CGT to pay on the 'gain' of £10,000. But:

- gifts between husband and wife are exempt
- your own home is normally exempt unless you have used it for purposes other than for living in (see page 138)
- cars and things worth less than £3,000 are exempt
- gifts of money are exempt (though shares and certain investments are not)
- the first £100,000 of the increase in value of a business is exempt if you give it away after age 60.

The increase in value of most other things you sell or give away in the tax year is only liable to CGT if the total increases in value of all of them in the periods you have owned them is more than a certain amount (£6,300 in the 1986–87 tax year). So, a bit like Inheritance Tax, it is possible to avoid CGT altogether by making use of the exemptions and spreading taxable gifts over the years. Remember that while Inheritance Tax is worked out on the total value of the gift, CGT is based only on the amount the item has increased in value over the period you have owned it.

Although it is best to avoid CGT altogether if you can by using the exemptions, there is an unusual condition applying to things you give away rather than sell: you and the recipient can simply agree not to pay any CGT – not at the time, anyway. If you do this you should tell your tax office about the gift (there is a space on the Tax Return) and say you want to claim **roll-over relief**. But if the item is valuable, this can put the recipient in a bit of a trap. If they keep the item until they die, then there could be Inheritance Tax to pay on it (but no CGT). If they get rid of it in their lifetime, then CGT will be based on the increase in value since *you* acquired it. If they give it away, they can claim roll-over relief again, but this only makes matters worse for the next recipient – unless the taxes happen to have been cut back by then.

So the problem of handing valuable things on without saddling the recipients (or your heirs) with a tax bill has no simple solution. You would have to work out how much tax would be payable if you did things in different ways on the assumption that the tax system will remain much the same – which is probably not a very safe bet. Think carefully and take advice before making major decisions.

Don't endanger your financial security (and your partner's after your death) by giving away too much to other people in your lifetime.

For more about Capital Gains Tax and other exemptions, see page 364.

Tax when you die

On death, there is no Capital Gains Tax at all. But if the total value of:

- your estate, apart from the following: things you leave to your husband or wife, to charities, political parties (up to £100,000), to certain national institutions, and certain money that comes from life insurance and pension schemes (there are one or two other minor exceptions)

plus:

- the value of gifts you have made in the last seven years of your life (apart from the gifts listed on page 322)

Comes to more than £71,000, there may be Inheritance Tax to pay on the excess.

Diagram 6 shows how the amount on which Inheritance Tax is charged when you die is worked out.

Steps to take in your lifetime

We give here a checklist of things to do and think about in order to make sure that as much as possible of what you have goes to the people you want it to with the minimum amount of delay and without causing hardship:

- Make a will if you haven't yet done so. Make a new will if you haven't made one since 1975, since you married, or since you moved between Scotland and elsewhere in the UK. See page 327 for what to consider.

- Review your will from time to time to make sure it covers your current circumstances. If you are well off, work out what the tax consequences of it are and what provision needs to be made for tax.

Diagram 6

How the amount on which Inheritance Tax is charged is worked out.

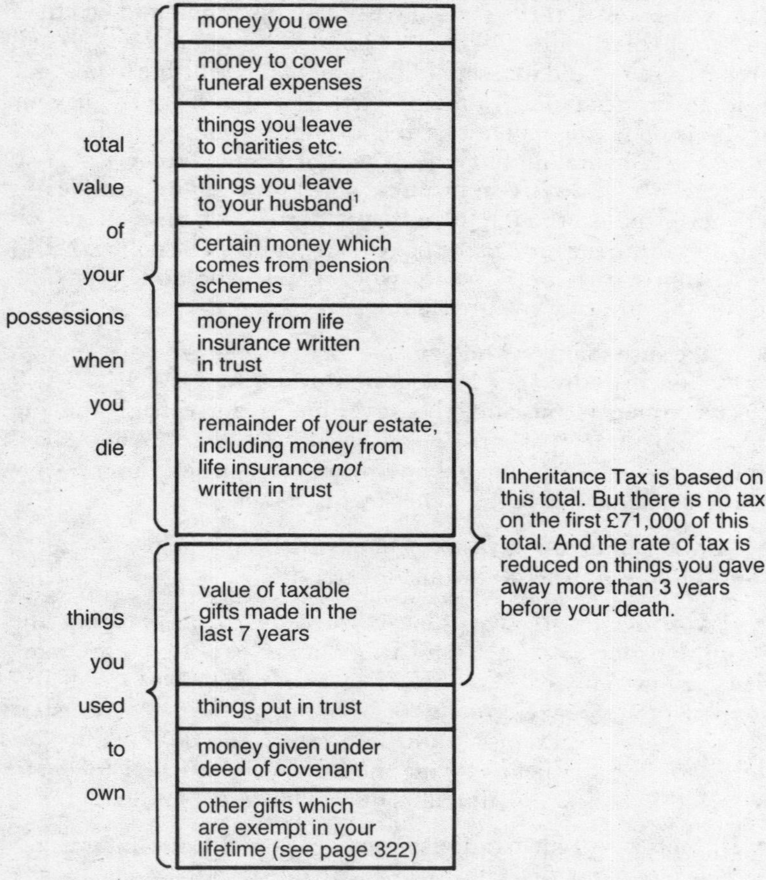

[1]In England and Wales this will automatically include your share in the home if you and your husband are joint tenants (see page 320).

• If you want the proceeds of a life insurance policy to go to a particular person, have the policy **written in trust**. The proceeds do not then become part of your estate so they are exempt from Inheritance Tax *and* the beneficiary can get the money very quickly without waiting for probate. If you have an existing policy which is not written in trust, it can be changed – ask the insurance company.

- If you know that the tax bill when you die is going to be large, and particularly if – to pay it – your heirs would have to sell property you would like kept in the family, it is sensible to take out a life insurance policy to pay the tax. If you are elderly or your health is poor you may not be able to afford a policy which would cover the full amount, but at least part of it could be covered. You really want **whole life insurance** which pays out on your death, whenever that is, though **term insurance** (which pays out only if you die within the term of the policy) is cheaper. The policy should be written in trust for the person who is going to be liable to pay the tax on the property you are leaving.

- Make sure that you and your partner are going to have enough to live on in retirement by checking up on how much you will receive from pensions and other investments, and consider paying more into these (perhaps by selling, rather than giving away, things you own). Money paid out from pension schemes on your death is usually free of tax – check with the scheme.

- Be wary of giving away anything which may help to increase your (or your partner's) income in later life.

- If you decide to give things away, try to keep within the exemptions for both CGT and Inheritance Tax. If you are married, you get only one lot of CGT exemptions between you. But you *each* get the exemptions for Inheritance Tax. As transfers between you are exempt from both taxes, one of you can give things to the other before giving them away if this will help you to keep within the exempt amounts during life or when you die.

- If you (or your husband) pay income tax and you want to make regular payments to a charity or to anyone who does not pay tax (e.g., an elderly relative, a grandchild or a niece, but not your own children under 18 unless they are married), write out a **deed of covenant** and send it to your tax office. Then the amount you give will not only be exempt from Inheritance Tax, but you will also get tax relief on the payments – meaning the recipient gets £140 for every £100 you give. See page 205 for details.

- If your total possessions (apart from what you intend to leave to your husband or charity) are worth a lot (over £150,000, say), ask your solicitor if it is worth your setting up a trust to which you may be able to transfer some of these while retaining some control (but not the right to use them) during your life.

Making a will

Considerations in making your will

- When leaving things to your husband or partner, it is sensible to include the condition that he outlives you by more than a certain period (e.g., 30 days) and that if he does not, the things are to go to someone else you name. Then if you both die within a short space of time (e.g., as a result of the same accident) you and your partner's estates will *each* get a £71,000 tax-free allowance. Otherwise your possessions would go to your partner and then straight on to a third party, and only £71,000 of your *joint* possessions would be tax-free on the second transfer.

- If you are considering leaving a substantial amount to your partner and this will mean that your partner's estate becomes large enough to involve a big Inheritance Tax bill when he dies, it is worth considering leaving some of your possessions directly to other people – your children or grandchildren, perhaps. The first £71,000 of what you leave to other people will be tax-free (but if you are not married, the £71,000 includes what you leave to your partner). But do not endanger your partner's financial security after your death by leaving too much to other people just to reduce the tax bill on the second death – the tax-free limits may be much higher by then, or the tax may even have been abolished for all you know.

- Because you do not know how much your estate is going to be worth at the time you die, it is usual in a will to make **specific gifts** (e.g., 'I give £50,000 to my son Charles') and then to say who is to get the remainder of your estate – called the **residue**. If your estate is large enough for tax to be payable, the tax will normally all come out of the residue, unless you say otherwise in your will. It is sensible either to make a specific gift to the main beneficiary as well as leaving them the residue (e.g., leave your husband £50,000 plus the residue), or to say that large gifts of money are to bear their own tax (i.e., the tax will be deducted from the gift). Again consider the consequences: if the gift is a home or something else valuable, its high value may mean that the recipient has to sell it to pay the tax.

• Ask your solicitor for advice on whether it is worth setting up a **trust** – this can be done simply by wording your will in a certain way. There could be advantages.

• It is possible for your heirs to agree within two years of your death to rearrange your estate between themselves – called a **deed of family arrangement**. This can be useful if they can decide on a more appropriate distribution or can save tax.

In Scotland, you do not have a free choice about how much you leave to whom. If you are married or live with a man as his wife, you must leave him at least one-third of your estate (one-half if you have no children). If you have children you must leave them at least one-third of your estate (one-half if you have no husband or common-law husband). You can leave the remainder to whoever you like.

HOW TO MAKE A WILL

It is sensible to ask a solicitor to draw up your will for you after discussing with him or her what you have to leave and who you would like it to go to. A solicitor is unlikely to charge much more than £25 for drawing up a fairly straightforward will, and you can then feel certain that it does say what you want it to say. You can write your will yourself, but there are a lot of pitfalls for the unaware. A solicitor will also be able to give you advice on Inheritance Tax and on trusts. For how to choose a solicitor, see page 338.

You will need to choose an **executor** (**executor nominate** in Scotland) – i.e., someone who takes over your possessions, pays your debts and any tax which is due and sees that your wishes in the will are carried out. You can have several executors – two is a wise choice – and you should check that they are willing. It is sensible if one of your executors is your husband or partner and one is quite a bit younger than you – e.g., one of your children. You can name a substitute in case one of your executors dies or emigrates. You can ask your solicitor or your bank to be an executor but they will, of course, make a charge, meaning your heirs get less.

If you have children under 18, you should say who you would like to be their guardian if their father is not still alive when you die. Money for children under 18 has to be held **in trust** for them until they are 18, so you will need to appoint trustees to look after the money until then.

If you are married or live with someone as a couple, it is obviously sensible if you sort out your wills together and make sure that both wills express both your wishes and your partner's.

There are important rules about how your will is set out, signed and witnessed, so make sure these are followed. Keep your will somewhere safe – it is sensible if your solicitor or bank keeps a copy. Make a list of the organisations which will need to be contacted on your death, and keep it in the same place as your will. Tell your next-of-kin where these documents are.

IF YOU DO NOT MAKE A WILL

If you die without leaving a will, your possessions are distributed according to the **intestacy rules**. In England and Wales, **if you are not married at the time of death** your possessions are divided equally:

- between your children (including adopted children, step-children and illegitimate children)
- if no children, between your parents
- if no parents, between your brothers and sisters
- if no brothers and sisters, between your grandparents
- if no grandparents, between your uncles and aunts
- if no uncles or aunts, everything goes to the Crown.

If you are married at the time of death:

- if your estate is worth less than £40,000, everything goes to your husband
- if your estate is worth more than £40,000 and you have children, your husband gets your personal belongings and the first £40,000. Half of the rest is divided between your children. The remainder will go to your children when your husband dies, but he can use it and get any income from it while he lives

• if your estate is worth more than £40,000 and you have no children, your husband gets your personal belongings, the first £85,000, and half of the rest; the other half goes to your parents, but if neither parent is still alive it is divided between your brothers and sisters; if you have no parents, brothers or sisters it all goes to your husband.

In Northern Ireland there are slight differences if, at the time of death, you are married and have children and your estate is worth over £40,000.

In Scotland it is all quite different. Your husband gets the home (if it is worth less than £50,000; otherwise he gets £50,000) and the first £10,000 of its contents. If there are children, he gets the next £15,000 plus one-third of the rest; the remaining two-thirds is split between the children. If there are no children he gets the next £25,000 and half the rest; the remaining half goes to the nearest relatives. A common-law husband or wife is normally in the same position as a married person.

FOR REFERENCE

22

When You Need More Help

In many parts of this book we have referred you to particular sources of further information. If you are not sure where to find out more about your particular problem, your first two ports of call should be:

- **your library** Many libraries keep a welter of information. But in some areas branch libraries are less well stocked, and you may need to visit the central library

- **your Citizens Advice Bureau** (CAB) can provide information and help with all sorts of problems. You can be sure of a private talk with someone who knows the ropes and will do what they can to help. The service is free and you do not need to make an appointment (though it is a good idea to, to make sure you can see the person who knows most about the area concerned). Most CABx are particularly good with helping you make claims and fill in forms (e.g., for state benefits, Legal Aid or on insurance policies). Even if the CAB cannot help directly, they will be able to give you the name and addresses of various organisations who can. They will also be able to tell you whether you can handle your problem yourself or whether you need professional help, and what the outcome is likely to be.

In a few areas there are **Money Advice Centres**, **Consumer Advice Centres** and **Law Centres** which may be able to give more specialised advice in these areas. Your library or CAB will be able to give you the addresses and phone numbers of these.

Where to get money advice

Where to go depends much on your financial situation. Most professional advisers (apart from solicitors) are not really interested in people who do not have a lot of money to spend or invest. So if your resources are fairly modest you will probably get the best advice from one of the sources above. If you want a professional adviser, then the main people to ask are your bank manager, an accountant, a solicitor, an insurance broker, a stockbroker or an investment consultant. Finding a good one is not easy; probably the best thing is to ask other people if they can recommend an adviser they use.

Unfortunately, money advice is frequently not as good as it should be. There are two main reasons:

- The adviser is likely to be a specialist in particular areas, and may not know sufficient about other areas to be able to advise you satisfactorily.

- If the adviser is paid by an institution or gets commission from selling its products, he may be less unbiased than he should be if he is to act purely in your interests.

By far your best safeguard against poor advice is to read as much as you can about the subject yourself, and check up on any recommendations before deciding – after all, it is your money and you will be more concerned than anyone else about what happens to it.

Problems with professionals and financial services

If you are dissatisfied with the service you get from anyone or any organisation, always take the matter up with them first and give them a chance to put matters right. If you do not get very far, take the matter up with a senior person in the organisation. Write stating all the facts clearly, and ask what they propose to do about it (or say what you think should be done). If you are still dissatisfied, you can go to the organisations below.

It is worth finding out if there is a code of practice for the profession or organisation concerned – if your library does not have this it will be able to give you the address of the professional association or trade association to write to. If you can show that the code has been broken, you have a stronger complaint.

Accountants Write to the accountants' professional body (it will normally be shown on their notepaper).

Banks At the time of writing, a Banking Ombudsman was being established to deal with complaints that are not resolved between the bank and the customer. If you have a complaint that is still unresolved after taking it to the bank's head office, ask the bank or your CAB for details of the Ombudsman scheme.

Building societies If you have taken up the matter with the society's head office and are still dissatisfied, write giving full details to The Building Societies Association, 3 Savile Row, London W1X 1AF. The Government has proposed setting up a Building Societies Ombudsman – ask your society or your CAB for details.

Credit If you get no joy from the company, ask the Trading Standards Department of your local council for advice. In certain cases they will refer complaints to the Office of Fair Trading.

Estate Agents You can complain to your local Trading Standards Department (who are responsible for dealing with breaches of the Estate Agents' Act). If the agent is a member of the National Association of Estate Agents, you can complain to them at Arbon House, 21 Jury Street, Warwick CV34 4EH (tel. 0926 496800). If the agent is a chartered surveyor, see *Surveyors*.

Finance companies Discuss the matter with staff at your Trading Standards Department. You can also write to the Finance Houses Association, 18 Upper Grosvenor Street, London W1X 9PB.

Insurance Complain to the company's senior management. If you get nowhere and you arranged the insurance through a building society, bank or insurance broker, ask them to take it up on your behalf. Otherwise ask if the company is a member of the Insurance Ombudsman Bureau (31 Southampton Row, London WC1B 5HJ, tel. 01-242 8613) or the Personal Insurance Arbitration Service (75 Cannon Street, London EC4N 5BH, tel. 01-236 8761); if so, you can ask to have your complaint referred to them (it costs nothing). Otherwise you can write to the Association of British Insurers, Aldermary House, Queen Street, London EC4N 1TU, or, if you insured through a Lloyd's broker, to the Advisory Department at Lloyd's, London House, 6 London Street, London EC3R 7AB.

If your complaint is about an **insurance broker**, take it up first with the British Insurance Brokers' Association (BIBA), Fountain

House, 130 Fenchurch Street, London EC3M 5DJ. If you are still dissatisfied, write to the Registrar, Insurance Brokers' Registration Council, 15 St Helen's Place, London EC3A 6DS.

Solicitors The Law Society (113 Chancery Lane, London WC2A 1PL, tel. 01-242 1222) publishes a free leaflet about its procedure, *Complaints to the Law Society about Solicitors*. In Scotland, the Law Society of Scotland will investigate complaints (26 Drumsheugh Gardens, Edinburgh EH3 7YR, tel. 031-226 7411). In Northern Ireland contact the Incorporated Law Society of Northern Ireland, Royal Courts of Justice, Belfast BT1 3JZ (tel. 0232 231614).

Surveyors You can write to the Professional Practices Department of the Royal Institution of Chartered Surveyors, 12 Great George Street, Parliament Square, London SW1P 3AD (tel. 01-222 7000).

Complaints about central government departments and local authority services Who you take up a complaint with depends on the department concerned and the nature of the complaint. Ask at your local CAB, or look in *Which? Way to Complain* (see books listed on page 341).

Problems in your job

If you belong to a trade union or staff association, a representative should be able to help you deal with problems that arise. If you do not, or if you would rather talk about the problem with someone outside your workplace, then contact the Advisory, Conciliation and Arbitration Service (ACAS). You can simply ring their regional office and get advice over the phone, or make an appointment for a half-hour interview to discuss the problem in detail with an expert who will be able to explain your rights, what courses of action are open to you and the likely outcome. The service is completely free, and no one will know you have been. A conciliation officer can help you pursue your complaint if you want them to. You can get the address and phone number of the regional office from a CAB or Jobcentre.

Discrimination

Sex discrimination If you think you have been unfairly discriminated against, contact the Equal Opportunities Commission

(EOC) for free general advice and help on a specific complaint. They can advise you on pursuing your case, and will occasionally take up a case on your behalf. Addresses are: Overseas House, Quay Street, Manchester M3 3NH (tel. 061-833 9244); Caerwys House, Windsor Place, Cardiff CF1 1LB (tel. 0222 43552); 249 West George Street, Glasgow G2 4QE (tel. 041-226 4591) and Chamber of Commerce House, 22 Great Victoria Street, Belfast BT2 2BA (tel. 0232 242752).

Race discrimination The Commission for Racial Equality (CRE) provides a very similar role to the EOC (see above). Address: Elliot House, 10–12 Allington Street, London SW1E 5EH (tel. 01-828 7022) or ask your CAB for the address of the regional office.

Where to go for advice on:

Consumer problems Trading Standards Department of your local authority; Citizens Advice Bureau; Consumer Advice Centre.

Domestic violence, family break-up National Women's Aid Federation (England), 374 Gray's Inn Road, London WC1X 8BB (tel. 01-837 9316); Welsh Women's Aid, Incentive House, Adam Street, Cardiff (tel. 0222 388291).

Housing rights SHAC (the London Housing Aid Centre), 189a Old Brompton Road, London SW5 0AR (tel. 01-373 7841); local Housing Aid Centre; Citizens Advice Bureau.

Legal problems Rights for Women, 374 Gray's Inn Road, London WC1X 8BB (tel. 01-278 6349); local law centre or Citizens Advice Bureau.

One-parent families, separation and divorce National Council for the Divorced and Separated, 13 High Street, Little Shelford, Cambridge CB2 5ES; National Council for One-Parent Families, 255 Kentish Town Road, London NW5 2LX (tel. 01-267 1361); Gingerbread (Association for One-Parent Families), 35 Wellington Street, London WC2E 7BN (tel. 01-240 0953).

Pensions and Retirement Age Concern, 60 Pitcairn Road, Mitcham, Surrey CR4 3LL (tel. 01-640 5431); Help the Aged, 32 Dover Street, London W1A 2AP; Occupational Pensions Advisory Service, Room 327, Aviation House, 129 Kingsway, London WC2B 6NN.

Welfare benefits Child Poverty Action Group (CPAG), 1 Mack-

lin Street, London WC2B 5NH (tel. 01-242 3225); local authority welfare rights officer; Citizens Advice Bureau.
Widowhood National Association of Widows, Chell Road, Stafford ST16 2QA (tel. 0785 45465); Cruse (the national organisation for the widowed and their children), Cruse House, 126 Sheen Road, Richmond, Surrey TW9 1UR (tel. 01-940 4818).

Where to get legal advice

It is sensible to start at your local Citizens Advice Bureau, who will be able to tell you if your problem is one they can deal with or, if not, what you will need to do to pursue it. In many areas, CABx have set times each week when you can talk to a qualified solicitor free of charge. If you decide you need a solicitor, the CAB will be able to recommend one who is experienced in problems of the same kind, and will be able to help you apply for Legal Aid (see below).

If your problem arises from the fact that you are a woman, it would be worth getting in touch with Rights for Women, 374 Gray's Inn Road, London WC1X 8BB (tel. 01-278 6349) who will be able to give you more advice.

If the problem is basically a consumer one, *Which?* Personal Service gives advice and assistance in pursuing claims against suppliers of goods and services (e.g., writing letters for you and threatening legal action) but excludes most financial services. It costs £20 a year. Details from Department BJJ, Consumers' Association, 14 Buckingham Street, London WC2N 6DS.

Ask at your library if there is a Law Centre or Legal Advice Centre in your area (they are listed in the *Directory of Legal Advice and Law Centres* published by the Legal Action Group, 28a Highgate Road, London NW5 1NS).

Using a solicitor

As various firms of solicitors tend to specialise in certain areas of the law, it is best to look in the *Solicitors' Regional Directory* or the *Legal Aid Solicitors List* to find a suitable one (these are kept at most libraries and advice centres). It is also worth following up any firms who are recommended by friends who have had problems in the same area.

One of the most useful schemes is the **fixed fee interview**. For

£5 (sometimes less) you can have half an hour's discussion with a solicitor, in which he will be able to tell you whether it is worth pursuing your complaint, how to go about it, what you are likely to get out of it and how much it will cost. This is valuable because you will not have lost much if you decide not to press ahead.

The directories mentioned above also show which solicitors operate the Legal Aid schemes. There are basically two schemes:

- **The Green Form Scheme** This allows people on lowish incomes to get free legal assistance up to £50 (£90 in cases of undefended divorce). The solicitor will give you advice, write letters, negotiate for you, get a barrister's opinion and prepare a written case for a court or tribunal, but the scheme does not cover the solicitor's court costs – so you will normally have to present your case yourself. The scheme has few formalities – you tell the solicitor about your income and resources and he works out on the spot whether you qualify and whether you will have to pay part of the cost. If you are eligible for supplementary benefit or family income supplement, you will normally qualify for free advice. (In Scotland, this is known as the Pink Form Scheme.)

- **Legal Aid** This is a more formal scheme, under which you can get a much higher amount of legal costs paid, including court costs. The amount you get depends on your income and resources – the higher they are, the less you get. You can qualify for Legal Aid even if your resources are too high to qualify under the Green Form Scheme. The solicitor helps you complete the application forms, after which you will be sent a form to fill in giving details of your finances. You should wait until you hear the result of your application before asking the solicitor to proceed, or you will be liable for all his costs until your application is passed. In very urgent cases, it is possible to get Legal Aid immediately – ask the solicitor about this.

For more information on these schemes, ask your CAB for the free leaflets *Legal Aid guide* and *Legal Aid – financial limits*.

Suing in the County Court

County Courts have a relatively informal way of settling disputes which involve claims for money arising from poor quality goods or services. For example, you may be trying to get your money back on a duff washing machine or a chaotic holiday, or to get compensation from a garage that has made such a mess of your car that you have had to get someone else to put it right. Or *you* may be sued if you refuse to pay a bill on the grounds that the goods or services were substandard (see below).

If the amount claimed is under £500, the procedure is straightforward and is very cheap to initiate. The only cost is your own time and the court fee of up to £28; even if you lose, you do not have to pay the other side's legal costs. Quite often the issue of a summons does the trick and the other side either pays in full or offers an acceptable amount. If the case goes to arbitration, there is no need for you to engage a solicitor, as it is quite normal for ordinary people to present their own case.

Full information is given in the booklets *Small claims in the County Court* and *Enforcing money judgments in the County Court* which you can get from the County Court or CAB.

If you are sued

When the summons arrives, your first reaction will probably be to panic and wonder what the neighbours will think when your name is in the paper. Well, don't. If you have been withholding money you know you owe for no good reason at all, then all you have to do is to pay it into the court (and pay the court fee as well). But if you are certain you have a good reason for refusing to pay, then stick to your guns and do not be intimidated. Remember, the only reason you have been sent the summons is that you are lucky enough not to have paid already; if you had, *you* would be issuing the summons to get your money back. But you *must* follow the instructions on the summons and respond with the required documents within the stipulated times. Get the booklets mentioned above from the county court and read them carefully. If you need more help, call at your CAB.

Books you may find helpful

Women:

Women's Rights, Anna Coote & Tess Gill (Penguin, £3.95).
Living Together, Clare Dyer & Marcel Berlins (Hamlyn, £1.50).

Complaints, disputes and legal advice:.
Small Claims in the County Court (free from County Court or CAB).
Taking your own case to Court or Tribunal (Consumers' Association, £5.95).
Which? Way to Complain, Ian Hooper (Consumers' Association, £5.95).
Your home:
Rights Guide for Home Owners, Joe Tunnard & Clare Whately (SHAC, £2.50).
Renting and Letting (Consumers' Association, £5.95).
Which? Way to Buy, Sell and Move House (Consumers' Association, £8.95).
Building Societies and House Purchase (free from Building Societies Association, 3 Savile Row, London W1X 1AF, tel. 01-437 0655).
Consumer rights, buying and borrowing:
Fair Deal – a shopper's guide (Office of Fair Trading, 95p).
A Handbook of Consumer Law, National Federation of Consumer Groups (Consumers' Association, £5.95).
Divorce:
Divorce and Your Money, W. M. Harper (Unwin, £1.95).
Divorce: legal procedures and financial facts (Consumers' Association, £5.95).
Undefended Divorce (free from County Court or CAB).
Social security:
National Welfare Benefits Handbook, Ruth Cohen & Beth Lakhani (Child Poverty Action Group, £4).
Rights Guide to Non-Means-Tested Social Security Benefits, Roger Smith & Mark Rowland (Child Poverty Action Group, £4).
Insurance:
Value-for-Money Insurance, British Insurance Brokers' Association (Flame Books, £2.95).
Investment:
Which? Book of Saving and Investing (Consumers' Association, £10.95).
Tax:
Which? Book of Tax (Consumers' Association, £12.95).
Retirement:
Your Rights for Pensioners, Rose Moreno (Age Concern, 70p).
Your Housing in Retirement, Janice Casey (Age Concern, £1).
Moving Home in Retirement, Lorna Gordon & Rose Moreno (SHAC, 85p).

Your Taxes and Savings in Retirement, Joe Irving (Age Concern, £1.50).

Addresses are on pages 335–8 except for Consumers' Association, Castlemead, Gascoyne Way, Hertford, SG14 1LH.

23

Your Taxes – Income Tax and Capital Gains Tax

What is taxable?

In any year you may get money from a number of different sources. The Government raises most of its money by making people pay tax on some of the money they get. In some cases, they make the person paying you dock the tax from what you get and hand the tax over to the Government. You can't avoid tax by asking someone to give you a thing rather than money, because the rules invariably say that the amount of tax will then be worked out on the value of the thing instead of on the amount of money.

There are volumes of complex rules which decide whether or not you have to pay tax on money you get, and how the tax is worked out. It all depends on how you come by the money:

Prizes from competitions, lotteries, premium bonds or gambling are yours to keep in full – the Government does not even want to know about them.

Money or things you borrow have no effect on the tax you pay. But if you pay interest (e.g., on a bank loan) or charge interest to someone you have lent money to, the amount of interest paid can affect your income tax.

Money or things you are given as a present or which you inherit are generally yours to keep in full. But there are three points to watch:

- Only genuine gifts are ignored by the tax people. If you have done something in return, you could be said to have earned the money – and earnings are taxable.

- If the other person *has* to pay you because of a legally binding agreement (like a deed of covenant or a court order), the money they pay you counts as your income and is taxable.

- If the person who gave you the money (or things) dies within 3 years of giving them to you, and the total value of everything they give away or leave is more than £71,000, there could be **Inheritance Tax** to pay. See Chapter 21 for details.

Certain other money you get is completely free of tax. This includes money from:

- most social security benefits (see page 357)
- most grants and scholarships for education or training
- grants for improving or insulating your home (see page 132)
- the value of certain fringe benefits you get from your job (see page 225)
- strike and unemployment pay from a trade union
- certain payments you get when you leave a job (see page 226)
- cashing in National Savings Certificates, National Savings Yearly Plan, Save-As-You-Earn schemes
- a lump sum or income paid out by most life insurance policies (see page 361)
- money paid out by insurance policies after you have claimed, as long as you use the money to repair the damage
- interest credited to a National Savings ordinary account (up to £70)
- dividends from a credit union
- interest on a tax rebate.

If you sell something and make a profit, this profit is what the tax people call a **capital gain**. Each year they add up the profits you have made on things you have sold. If these come to more than £6,300, you may have to pay **Capital Gains Tax** on the extra. For example, if you have made gains of £8,000, you will have to pay 29% tax on £1,700, which is £510 tax. You cannot avoid Capital Gains Tax by giving something away, because if you do, the tax is based on what the item was worth. But there are certain things you can sell or give away without fear of any tax. The main ones are:

- your own home (except in certain circumstances – see page 138)
- cars
- most items (or sets of items) worth less than £3,000 each
- anything with a predictable life of less than 50 years
- British Government stock ('gilts') and many corporate bonds (see page 81)
- shares bought under the *British Expansion Scheme* after 18 March 1986
- collections of British coins
- anything which a husband and wife give to each other – unless they are separated
- anything you give to charity or certain national institutions
- anything you leave to other people when you die (though there may be Inheritance Tax to pay – see Chapter 21).

Even if an asset is not exempt, there are lots of rules which can reduce the tax you have to pay. One of the main ones concerns selling or giving away a business when you are 60 or over. Details of Capital Gains Tax are on page 364.

Most other money you get is called **income** by the tax people. It includes earnings, business profits, pensions, interest from investments, rents, maintenance payments, certain social security benefits and covenant payments. We look at this in detail on the following pages.

The tax system

The tax you have to pay is based on the income you get (and the capital gains you make) in a **tax year**. Tax years are not the same as calendar years. Each tax year runs from 6 April one year to 5 April the next (due, quaintly enough, to a church decree in the twelfth century that the year should begin on 25 March, followed by a calendar adjustment of twelve days in 1753!). Some of the rules and the figures change each year as a result of the Chancellor of the Exchequer's March Budget. All the tax information in this book refers to the Chancellor's proposals for income and capital gains which are being taxed in the 1986–87 tax year, which runs from 6 April 1986 to 5 April 1987.

The Government department which administers the income tax (and Capital Gains Tax) system is the Inland Revenue. Your own affairs will be dealt with by a tax office with a Tax Inspector and other staff. If you have a query you want to talk to someone about, you can call at a local tax enquiry office (look in the phone book under *Inland Revenue*).

Once your tax office has a file on you, they will not need to ask you everything about your circumstances and your income, but only about any changes in these. They will also get information direct from other sources – like your employers, your bank, your building society. This makes it much harder to cheat the tax system.

Tax Returns

Your tax office may send you a Tax Return each year. This is a form which asks for details of your income, capital gains and certain outgoings over the past year. It also has a section for you to claim the personal allowances you are entitled to in the *coming* tax year. Most people with simple finances (e.g., a job and a building society account) only get a Tax Return every few years. If you regularly have to claim back tax, you may be sent a form called a Tax Claim instead. Whether or not you are sent a Return, you still have to tell your tax office about any income you have. The latest you should tell them is by the end of the tax year after the one in which you received the money. So if you received money in January 1986, you should tell the tax office before April 1987.

If you are married, it is normally only your husband who will be sent a Tax Return and it is his responsibility to give details of both his and your income, outgoings and allowances. If you have some savings of your own which you do not want your husband to know about, the only way is to put your money into tax-free investments which he does not have to enter on his Tax Return. However, if you want to receive your own Tax Return (and be responsible for paying your own tax), you should ask your tax office for **separate assessment** (see page 157 and Inland Revenue leaflet IR.32). Your husband does not then have to give any details of your income on his Tax Return, though he will still be able to work out roughly how much income you have (apart from tax-free income).

Income tax

How income is paid to you

Of the income you get, some may be:

- **tax-free** Examples are in the list on page 344. Tax-free income is paid to you in full without any tax deducted, and is completely ignored when working out your income tax.

- **tax-paid** Interest you get from building societies, banks, finance companies and deposit takers is *treated* as though basic-rate tax has already been paid. So you do not have to pay any basic-rate tax on it. If you have a very high income, you may have to pay some higher-rate tax on what you get.

- **with basic-rate tax deducted** from what you get. The people paying will make a straight deduction of 29% from the amount they are paying. They pay this 29% to the Inland Revenue, and give you 71%. Examples are company share dividends, unit trust dividends, personal pensions you get, maintenance payments of more than £48 a week (or £208 a month), covenant payments, interest payments on local authority investments and British Government stock you bought through a stockbroker.

- **with tax deducted under the Pay-As-You-Earn system (PAYE)** If you have a job or get a pension from a former employer, your tax office will tell your employer how much tax to deduct from each paycheque or pension payment. The tax will not be a set percentage of your earnings. The system is designed to collect the tax you owe for the year in roughly equal instalments.

• **with no tax deducted** Some income is paid to you with no tax deducted, even though it is taxable. Examples are state retirement pensions, widow's benefits, unemployment benefit, small maintenance payments, interest payments on British Government stock bought through the post office, interest on National Savings Investment Account, interest on National Savings Income Bonds and Deposit Bonds, rents you get from letting property, profits from your business. If your income is low, you may not have to pay tax on this income. If you do have to pay tax on it, you may be sent a demand for it during the year or, if you have a job or get a pension, the tax due may be collected through the PAYE system.

So during any tax year, you will receive a certain amount of income and will have paid a certain amount of tax. The PAYE system is the only one in which any attempt is made during the year to collect the correct amount of tax *for you*. So it is quite likely that over the year the amount of tax you have paid is too high or too low. This is why it is sensible to check your income tax each year.

Tax relief

You do not have to pay tax on the income you use to make certain payments called **outgoings**, so these payments are said to give you relief from income tax. For example, if you make a payment of £100 which qualifies for tax relief, £100 of your income which would have been taxed will now be tax-free. If that £100 would have been taxed at the basic rate of 29%, you will have saved £29 tax. So the cost to you of paying that £100 is effectively only £71.

Relief from basic-rate is given in three different ways:

• **by handing over less money** This happens with the interest you pay on nearly all mortgages and home improvement loans, covenant payments you make and certain maintenance payments (including all those over £48 a week or £208 a month). For each £100 you are liable to pay, you only hand over £71. The recipient claims the other £29 from the Inland Revenue if they are entitled to it.

• **by reducing your tax demand** This may happen if you have paid for certain things which are essential for your work, paid contributions to a personal pension plan, made small maintenance payments or paid interest on certain types of loan. The amount of these payments is simply deducted from your income before working out how much tax is due on it.

- **through the PAYE system** Contributions to your employers' pension scheme will be allowed for in the PAYE system, so that no tax will be taken from the part of your earnings used to make these payments. The PAYE system can also be used to give you tax relief on any of the payments in the previous group.

Relief from higher rates of income tax is always given in one of the last two ways.

How your income tax is worked out

Each year, the income you get from various sources is added up. You are allowed to have a certain amount of income without paying any tax – how much depends on your personal circumstances. Then there is no tax to pay on income you use to pay qualifying outgoings. But you have to pay tax on each extra £ of income you get. For example, if you are allowed to have £2,500 without paying tax, and your income in the year is £7,500, you will have to pay tax on £5,000. The basic rate of tax is 29%, so you will have to pay 29% of £5,000 which is £1,450 tax.

If your taxable income is more than a certain amount (£17,200 in the 1986–87 tax year) tax starts being charged at a series of higher rates running from 40% to 60%. Very few people pay these higher rates – you would need an income of over £43,500 to be paying any tax at 60%.

There are a number of different ways of working out your income tax liability. Tax offices tend to do it in one way, accountants in another, but we think the simplest is to look at basic-rate tax and higher-rate tax quite separately. In each case you add up the income liable to tax in the tax year, subtract your outgoings and allowances, and tax is due on what is left. Details of each category are given on pages 356 to 364.

Income taxable at the basic rate	**Income taxable at higher rates**
earnings from jobs	earnings from jobs
pensions	pensions
certain social security benefits	certain social security benefits
taxable profits from business	taxable profits from business

freelance earnings	freelance earnings
rents from letting property	rents from letting property
dividends on company shares and unit trusts	dividends on company shares and unit trusts
interest on investments (*except* tax-paid interest from banks, building societies and other deposit takers)	interest on investments (*including* interest from banks, building societies and other deposit takers)
maintenance payments	maintenance payments
covenant payments received	gains made when cashing-in life insurance policies

From this income you can deduct:

expenses in your work	expenses in your work
pension contributions	pension contributions
payments into personal pensions	payments into personal pensions
half amount paid in Class 4 NI contributions (self-employed)	half amount paid in Class 4 NI contributions (self-employed)
interest paid on certain loans (but *not* loans on which you have already had basic-rate tax relief under MIRAS)	interest paid on certain loans (*including* loans on which you have already had basic-rate tax relief under MIRAS)
small maintenance payments you have made in full (without deducting any tax)	*all* maintenance payments you have made
	covenant payments to charities
amount invested under the Business Expansion Scheme	amount invested under the Business Expansion Scheme
your personal allowances	your personal allowances
	you also deduct £17,200

Basic-rate tax will be payable on the amount of income that is left in the left-hand column. The tax due will be 29% of this amount. If the outgoings and allowances come to more than the income, you are not liable to any tax and can claim back any that has been deducted.

If there is any income left in the right-hand column after you have made all the deductions there, you will have to pay higher-rate tax on what is left. As you have already worked out how much basic-rate tax you have to pay, you only have to add on the extra over the basic rate. This means:

11% tax on the first £3,000
16% tax on the next £5,200
21% tax on the next £7,900
26% tax on the next £7,900
31% tax on anything more.

Net amounts and gross amounts

It is always the *gross* amount of income and outgoings that you use for your calculations. This is the amount of the payment *before* any tax is deducted. The *net* amount is the amount actually handed over after tax has been deducted.

If you have received income from which tax has been deducted at the basic rate, you can work out the gross amount by multiplying the amount you received by 100 and dividing by 71 (if you have a calculator, simply divide by 0.71). For example, if you have received £71, multiplying by 100 gives £7,100 and dividing by 71 gives £100. So a net amount of £71 is equivalent to a gross amount of £100. You must always do this with interest from building societies, banks and deposit takers.

Similarly, if you have made outgoings and given yourself basic-rate tax relief by paying a lower amount (e.g., with the interest on a mortgage), you work out the gross amount by multiplying the amount you have actually paid by 100 and dividing by 71.

If you are married

A married couple are together treated much like a single person for tax purposes. The income of both husband and wife are added together, the outgoings they both pay and the allowances they both get are subtracted, and the husband is responsible for paying all the tax due. The amount he has to pay will take account of any tax that has been deducted from income paid to you – like tax deducted under PAYE from earnings or pensions, and the tax credits you get with company share dividends.

In certain circumstances you will be taxed individually, in the same way as a single woman:

- in the tax year in which you get married (see page 159)
- if either of you lives abroad or is abroad for the whole tax year
- if you are separated and the separation is likely to be permanent.

There are two other ways in which you can choose to be taxed:

- **separate assessment** The tax bill on your and your husband's joint income is split between you according to a set of complicated rules. You each get your own Tax Return and are each responsible for paying your own tax. The total tax you pay between you is not affected.
- **having your earnings taxed as if you were a single person** This is a different way of calculating the tax, and will affect the total amount payable. It will mean more tax to pay if your combined income is less than £26,500, but could mean less tax to pay if your combined income is more than that.

You can, if you want to, choose both these options. More details of them are in Chapter 11. Even with these options, it is still impossible to check that your income tax is correct without knowing full details of your partner's income (except tax-free income) and outgoings.

How tax is collected

The two ways your tax office gets you to pay the correct amount of tax are through the PAYE system (if you have a job or get a pension) and by sending you a tax demand or a tax rebate.

PAY-AS-YOU-EARN (PAYE)

The PAYE system works like this. At the beginning of the tax year, your tax office writes down the outgoings and allowances they think you are entitled to on a form called a **Notice of Coding**. They add these up, then subtract from them the amount of any untaxed income they expect you to get over the tax year (e.g., state retirement pensions). The amount that is left is the amount of income you may receive from the job or pension without paying any tax. This figure is converted into a PAYE code (by knocking off the last digit and inserting a letter). The Notice of Coding is sent to you so that you can check it, and the Code is sent to your employer along with a set of Tax Tables. Together, these tell your employer exactly how much tax to deduct from each paycheque or pension payment. As long as your code is correct (unfortunately many are not), and your circumstances do not change, the correct amount of tax will be deducted over the year.

Tax offices usually start sending out Notices of Coding around January – before the tax year has started. This means:

- they may have to estimate some of the figures on your Notice of Coding – e.g., your income from certain sources or expenses in your job. If you think any of these estimates is wrong, write to your tax office and say so.

- they do not yet know the amounts of personal allowances for the coming tax year – because the Chancellor's Budget is normally in March – so they use the previous year's allowances for the time being. However, the letter in your PAYE code tells your employer what allowances you get so that, when the new allowances are known, the necessary adjustment can be made without your tax office having to issue a new Notice of Coding. The new higher code should then appear on your payslips. The letters used are:

  L – you get single person's allowance or Wife's Earned Income Allowance (£2,335)

  H – you get single person's allowance plus the additional personal allowance for a child which comes to £3,655 (**H** is also used for married men)

  P – you get full age allowance for a single person (£2,850)

  The letter **T** is used if the tax office has to work out your new code and tell your employer. This may be because you get a reduced amount of age allowance, or because you do not want your employer to know what allowances you are getting.

  If your PAYE code starts with the letter **F**, it means that your employer has to deduct tax at more than 29% from what he pays you. This will be done to collect tax due on untaxed income you get, if this comes to more than your total personal allowances and outgoings.

Your tax office may make other adjustments in working out your PAYE code. They may, for example, use your code to:

- collect tax owing from a previous tax year

- collect higher-rate tax due on income you get which has been taxed at the basic-rate only

- give you relief from higher rates of tax on mortgage interest, maintenance payments or covenant payments to charities.

If your circumstances change during the year (e.g., you become entitled to a new allowance), write to your tax office and ask for your code to be increased. Less tax will then be deducted from your pay or pension. You should really inform the tax office of any change which would mean a decreased code, but if you leave this until the end of the tax year, the tax office will normally adjust your code for the *following* tax year – meaning you pay the extra tax later.

At the end of the tax year, your employer gives you a form P.60 (or equivalent) which shows how much pay or pension you have received over the tax year (after deducting any contributions you have paid into the firm's pension scheme) and how much tax has been deducted under PAYE. Use this form when checking your tax.

Tax demands and rebates

If you pay tax under PAYE and you end the tax year owing some tax, your tax office will normally collect it through the PAYE system by reducing your PAYE code the following year. But if you are self-employed or have income from property or a high income or more complicated affairs, the tax office will send you a demand for the tax you owe. And if you have overpaid tax during the year, they will send you a rebate.

A demand or rebate is normally accompanied by a **Notice of Assessment** showing how your tax liability for the year has been calculated. If your income is high and from a number of sources, these forms can be very complicated. If you do not understand it, ask your tax office (or a local tax office) to explain it. If you do not agree with the assessment, you must write and say so within 30 days of the date on it. Even if you do this, with some assessments you may still have to pay the tax demanded within 30 days unless you also ask for it to be postponed. Assessments have instructions and forms telling you how to go about this.

An assessment may not cover all your income – so you may need to wait until you have all the assessments for a year before you can check your tax.

If your tax office are asking you to pay tax owing from a tax year earlier than the previous one, due to a mistake or oversight on their part, you may not have to pay all the tax owing if you have kept your affairs in order and were not aware that you owed them money. If your gross income in the year in which you receive the demand is no more than £8,500, you will not have to pay any of it. If it is between £8,501 and £10,500 you will only have to pay one-quarter of what you owe. If your income is between £10,501 and £13,500 you will have to pay one-half, between £13,501 and £16,000 you pay three-quarters, between £16,001 and £23,000 you pay 9/10. If your income is above £23,000 you have to pay all the tax owing. But if you are 65 or over or receive a state retirement pension or widow's pension, all the income limits are increased by £2,500.

If you cannot agree with your tax office about your tax liability, there is an appeals procedure which is described in Inland Revenue leaflet IR.37, *Appeals*, which is free from tax offices.

CLAIMING A REBATE

If you think that too much tax has been deducted from your income, write to your tax office explaining what you think is wrong. This is not at all unlikely – large numbers of PAYE codes and Notices of Assessment are wrong every year. It will probably be a few weeks before you hear from your tax office, but if you have overpaid tax you should eventually get a rebate.

You do not have to wait until the end of the tax year to claim a rebate – for example, if you have given up your job to have a child or have received all the investment income you are due in the tax year. Write to the tax office telling them what income you have received to date and what other income you expect to receive in the tax year.

If you regularly receive income from which tax has been deducted and which you are entitled to reclaim (e.g., maintenance payments or income from investments), you can ask to have the tax repaid to you in instalments over the tax year.

If you discover that you have paid too much tax in earlier tax years, you can claim back the excess for any of the last 6 complete tax years. For years before the previous tax year, you may also get interest on the rebate if it is more than £25.

Income, outgoings and allowances

In this section we tell you in detail how different types of income are taxed, and about the outgoings and allowances you can claim.

Tax is normally based on the amount of income you receive (and the amount of outgoings you pay) in the whole tax year, unless:

- you were married for the whole tax year, in which case your husband's income and outgoings are included with yours
- during the tax year you were widowed or separated from your husband. In either of these cases, the tax year is split into two at the date of death or separation, and each period is treated like a separate tax year. See page 184 (widowed) or page 166 (separated) for more details.

Income

EARNINGS FROM EMPLOYMENT

You are taxed on the amount you are paid in the tax year. This includes overtime payments, bonuses, commission, tips, holiday pay, statutory sick pay, maternity pay and any share in the profits. The amount (except for tips) will usually be shown on the P.60 form your employer gives you at the end of the tax year. You should deduct the amount you have paid in contributions to your firm's pension scheme (including any Additional Voluntary Contributions) if these have not already been deducted.

You are also taxed on the **taxable value** of any fringe benefits you get – such as a company car, BUPA subscription or luncheon vouchers of more than 15p a day (see page 225). You can ask your employer to tell you the taxable value of any benefits that you get.

If your employer pays you any money to cover expenses, you should include the amount you have received in your income (unless the firm has a **dispensation** for them). But you can deduct from your income the amount you have spent on expenses which are tax-deductible. In many cases the two figures will balance out. Some trade unions have agreed a standard allowance for expenses for people in certain jobs – if so, you can deduct this instead.

If you belong to a scheme your employer runs for paying up to £100 a year out of your salary direct to a charity, the amount you pay is subtracted from your salary before working out the tax on it.

You may be able to deduct part of the amount you pay to a trade union or friendly society for sickness or pension benefits or part of any compulsory payments for dependants' pensions: check with your employer or trade union. If you belong to a professional body recognised by the Inland Revenue, you can deduct the annual subscription from your earnings. Ask your tax office if any organisation you subscribe to qualifies.

Certain payments you may have received when you left a job (e.g., redundancy payments) are normally tax-free and do not have to be included in your income for tax purposes (see page 227).

PENSIONS

You should include in your income the gross amount of pensions you have received in the tax year from previous employers, state retirement pensions (including any invalidity addition, but not Christmas bonus nor additions for dependent children nor the increases paid between July 1986 and April 1987) and pensions from personal pension plans. If your state pensions are paid 4-weekly or quarterly, the correct amount to include in your income is the amount you would have received if it had been paid weekly.

SOCIAL SECURITY BENEFITS

The only social security benefits which are taxable are:

- unemployment benefit
- supplementary benefit, but only if it is paid as a result of being unemployed, on short-time working or on strike
- widow's allowance
- widowed mother's allowance
- widow's pension
- industrial death benefit
- invalid care allowance.

All other social security benefits are tax-free and should not be included in your taxable income, nor should any additions for dependent children, paid with any of the benefits above. (This assumes that statutory sick pay is included with your earnings, and any invalidity allowance paid with your state retirement pension in with your pensions.)

You will normally need to include the full amount of these benefits that you have received in the tax year in your income. But in certain cases you will not have to pay tax on the full amount of unemployment benefit or supplementary benefit you have received. The benefit office will tell you the *taxable amount* when your claim ends or at the end of the tax year. Inland Revenue leaflets IR.41, IR.42 and IR.43 explain how the taxable amount is worked out.

TAXABLE PROFITS FROM YOUR BUSINESS

You should include in your income the amount on which tax is being assessed in this tax year. This will normally be the taxable profits from your business in the accounting year ending in the *previous* tax year, but there are special rules for the opening and closing years of a business. See page 264 for details.

FREELANCE EARNINGS

You should include in your income any fees you have received from freelance work you have done which your tax office is including in the current year's tax assessment. You can, of course, deduct your allowable expenses from this income.

INCOME FROM LETTING PROPERTY

You are taxed on the rents you receive in the tax year, plus any profits on gas or electricity supplies, less your allowable expenses and any interest you have paid on loans to buy or improve the property. See page 136 for details.

INVESTMENT INCOME WITH BASIC-RATE TAX DEDUCTED

This includes dividends from company shares and unit trusts, interest payments from British Government stock bought through a stockbroker, interest on loans to local authorities, and part of the income from annuities. In each case you must include the gross amount in your income (before tax was deducted). With dividends from company shares and unit trusts the gross amount is the dividend (the actual amount you received) *plus* the tax credit.

INVESTMENT INCOME WITH NO TAX DEDUCTED

This includes interest from National Savings Investment Account,

National Savings Income Bonds and Deposit Bonds, interest on Co-operative Society deposits and interest on British Government stock bought through the Bonds & Stock Office. In the first two tax years in which you get interest from one of these sources, you pay tax on the amount you get in the normal way. In the third tax year you can choose whether to pay tax on the amount you get that year or the amount you got in the previous tax year – choose whichever is lower. In the fourth and subsequent years, you pay tax on the amount of interest you received in the *previous* tax year. So you may need to check when you got your first interest payment to see whether it is this year's income you are now being taxed on or last year's.

MAINTENANCE PAYMENTS

You should include in your income the gross amount of maintenance payments you have received in the tax year. Only include enforceable payments (e.g., made under a court order), not voluntary ones. Include payments made to you *for* a child, but not payments *to* a child. If tax has been deducted from what you get, be careful to include the *gross* amount in your income (see page 351). There is more information on maintenance payments on page 170.

COVENANT PAYMENTS

The gross amount of covenant payments you have received in the tax year is to be included in your income taxable at the basic rate (but not at higher rates).

Outgoings deductible for basic-rate tax

EXPENSES IN YOUR WORK AND PENSION CONTRIBUTIONS

These can be deducted from your earnings – see page 356. If they have already been deducted, they do not need to be deducted again.

PAYMENTS INTO PERSONAL PENSION PLANS

Include in your outgoings the amount you have paid in premiums into personal pension plans or **Section 226A life insurance policies** (see page 289). This includes any amount you have paid to use up tax relief unused in previous years. But do not include any amount which you have paid this year but which you have asked to be treated as though you paid it last year.

HALF THE AMOUNT PAID IN CLASS 4 NATIONAL INSURANCE CONTRIBUTIONS

If you are self-employed, include in your outgoings half the amount of Class 4 National Insurance contributions you have paid in the tax year.

INTEREST PAID ON CERTAIN LOANS

Do not include here any loan on which you have already had basic-rate tax relief under the MIRAS system by making lower payments to the lender. So do not include a building society or bank mortgage on your own home.

Include in this category the interest you paid in the tax year on any loan on which you have not already had tax relief by making reduced payments, which you used for:

- buying or improving your own home, the home you live in most of the time or a home occupied by your mother or mother-in-law (if she is widowed, divorced or separated), your ex-husband or separated husband, or any other relative who is unable to work because of old age or permanent illness or disablement and who pays you nothing for living there (up to £30,000 of loans)
- buying an annuity (e.g., a home income plan), if you are over 65 and the loan is secured on your only or main home (up to £30,000 of loans)
- paying Inheritance Tax (for up to 12 months)
- buying a share in a partnership or close company, or lending money to it
- buying plant or machinery used by a partnership or in your job
- buying a share in an industrial co-operative or employee-controlled company.

SMALL MAINTENANCE PAYMENTS YOU HAVE MADE

If you have paid maintenance to anyone under a court order for less than £48 a week or £208 a month, include the amount you have paid in the tax year with these outgoings.

BUSINESS EXPANSION SCHEME

You can get tax relief on the amount you have invested which qualifies under the Business Expansion Scheme.

Other income (affecting higher-rate tax only)

INTEREST FROM BANKS, BUILDING SOCIETIES AND DEPOSIT TAKERS

The amount of interest which is paid to you or credited to your account is treated as though it was what was left after basic-rate tax had been deducted. For example, if you got £71 interest, you are regarded as having had a gross amount of £100 from which £29 tax has been deducted. Include the gross amount in your income liable to higher-rate tax.

GAINS ON LIFE INSURANCE POLICIES

All the money you get back from most life insurance policies will be free of tax. With all policies, what you get is free of basic-rate tax. But if the policy is not a qualifying policy, or if you cash in a qualifying policy or make it paid-up within 10 years (or within three-quarters of its term, if that is less) the *gain* you make is liable to higher-rate tax in the same way as other income. The gain is normally the difference between the premiums you paid in and the amount you get back – but check with the insurance company. You may not pay as much higher-rate tax on this gain as you would on other income because there is a special relief called **top-slicing relief**. The effect of this is usually that the whole of the gain is taxed at whatever is your highest rate of tax at present, instead of causing tax at even higher rates.

Other outgoings (affecting higher-rate tax only)

INTEREST ON MORTGAGES, ETC. PAID NET OF TAX UNDER MIRAS

MAINTENANCE PAID AFTER DEDUCTING TAX

COVENANT PAYMENTS TO CHARITIES

With these payments, you have already given yourself relief from basic-rate tax by paying a reduced amount to the recipient. You get your relief from higher-rate tax by counting the gross amount as an outgoing.

Allowances

Tax allowances are not money which is paid to you, but amounts of money you can have without paying any tax. It is worth claiming all you are entitled to because each £100 of allowances you get means £29 less tax to pay.

The personal allowances you can claim depend on your marital status at the *beginning* of the period being assessed (getting married during the period makes no difference). The period is the whole tax year, unless you separated from your husband or were widowed during the tax year. In either of these cases there are two periods in the tax year – the first (up to the date of death or separation) which you started married, and the second which you started separated or widowed.

SINGLE, SEPARATED OR DIVORCED AT THE START OF THE PERIOD

The allowances you can claim are:

- **single person's allowance** (£2,335) You get this automatically. But if you are over 64 at the start of the tax year you get the higher **single person's age allowance** (£2,850) instead, though the amount of this allowance will be lower if your income is above a certain limit (see page 312).
- **additional personal allowance** (£1,320) You can claim this if you have a child living with you who is your own child, your step-child, a child you have legally adopted or any other child under 18 whom you look after at your own expense. If the child is over 16 at the start of the tax year he or she must be in full-time education or on a full-time training course lasting at least 2 years.
- **dependent relative allowance** (£145) You can claim this if you help to support your mother (if she is widowed, divorced or separated from her husband), or any relative who is unable to work and is over 64 or permanently ill or disabled. The allowance is reduced if you contribute less than £75 a year other than by deed of covenant (unless the relative lives with you) or if the relative's income is more than a single person's basic state retirement pension (£38.70 a week). If you support more than one relative, you can claim an allowance for each of them. If another relative helps to support the dependant, the allowance is divided between you. Note that if you get this allowance, you (or the relative) would benefit if you gave the money you pay under a deed of covenant (see page 205) – except for £75 a year if the relative does not live with you.

• **blind person's allowance** (£360) You can claim this allowance if you are on the local authority Blind Persons' Register. You do not have to be totally blind to register.

• **son's or daughter's services allowance** (£55) You can claim this allowance if you were over 64 at the start of the tax year or are permanently ill or disabled, and you support your son or daughter who lives in your home to look after you. You cannot get this allowance as well as blind person's allowance.

WIDOWED AT THE START OF THE PERIOD

The allowances you can claim are identical to someone who was single at the start of the period, with two possible additions:

• **widow's bereavement allowance** (£1,320) If this period is the latter part of the tax year in which you were widowed, or the tax year following that, you should get this allowance automatically. If it is not given to you, write to your tax office to claim it.

• **housekeeper allowance** (£100) You can claim this allowance if you have a relative or employee living in your home acting as your housekeeper. But you cannot claim it if you get additional personal allowance. And if you get housekeeper allowance, you cannot get son's or daughter's services allowance.

MARRIED AT THE START OF THE PERIOD

Unless you have asked for your own earnings to be taxed as if you were a single person (see page 158), the allowances you and your husband can claim are:

• **married man's allowance** (£3,655) This allowance is normally given to your husband, though it can be set against any of his or your income. So if his income is less than £3,655, the unused part of the allowance can be set against income of yours. If either you or your husband are 64 or over at the start of the tax year, he will get the higher **married man's age allowance** (£4,505) instead, though the amount of this allowance will be lower if your combined income is over a certain limit (see page 312).

• **Wife's Earned Income Allowance** (£2,335) You get this allowance automatically. But it can only be set against income of yours that is classed as **earned income**. This comprises your earnings from jobs and freelance work, the profits you make in your business and money you draw from it, pensions you get from your previous employers and from your payments into personal pension plans, state pensions you get based on your own National Insurance contributions (or the amount you are entitled to on your own contributions if you get a pension based on your husband's contributions because it is higher) and unemployment benefit you get based on your own NI contributions. In certain cases, income you get from letting property can count as earned income (for details see page 136). Your allowance is normally £2,335, but cannot be more than the total of these earnings. If your earnings in the tax year are less than the amount of the allowance, there will not be any tax to pay on them but the rest of the allowance is lost.

- **additional personal allowance** (£1,320) Your husband can claim this allowance only if, for the whole of the tax year, you are unable to look after yourself because of permanent illness or disability. Your husband must also have a child living with him who meets the same conditions as a child living with a single woman claiming this allowance (see above).

- **dependent relative allowance** (£100) The same conditions apply as for a single woman (see above) except that the amount of the allowance is £100 and you and your husband can claim an allowance for each of your relatives, or his relatives, that you support.

- **blind person's allowance** (£360) You can get this allowance if either you or your husband is on the local authority Blind Persons' Register. If you are both registered you can get two allowances.

- **son's or daughter's services allowance** (£55) Your husband can claim this allowance only if both of you were over 64 at the start of the tax year or are permanently ill or disabled, and you support your son or daughter who lives in your home to look after you. You cannot get this allowance as well as blind person's allowance.

Capital Gains Tax (CGT)

This is a tax on the profit you make when you sell (or give away) something valuable. But unless you are fairly wealthy, it is not a tax to worry about. Your most valuable possessions are probably your home and your car, and both are normally exempt from CGT. Anything worth less than £3,000 when you sell it is exempt. And you are allowed to make a profit on other things you sell of up to £6,300 in a tax year before you start to pay Capital Gains Tax. This means you can often avoid CGT simply by not selling or giving away vast amounts in one year.

A list of the main things which are exempt from CGT is given on page 345. The most likely things you are going to be caught for are:

- a second home or a home which you have not used purely for domestic purposes (see below and page 138)
- land (apart from your garden, unless it is huge)
- a valuable family heirloom
- a business (see page 368)
- company shares, unit trusts, local authority stocks and yearling bonds.

You do not actually need to sell something or make a profit to become liable to CGT. You need only cease to own it. If you give something away or sell it for less than it's worth, the tax will be based on the increase in value during the time you owned it instead of on the profit you made.

Of course, it is very likely that part of the increase in value or profit you make will be due to inflation. Until 1982 you were taxed on inflationary increases in value as well as genuine profit. Since then, values have all been expressed in today's money. But this does not apply to money you spent before March 1982, so the rules are slightly different for things you first owned before then – see below.

The following method will tell you very closely how much Capital Gains Tax you have to pay in the tax year (but see below for things you owned before March 1982). Figures for the Retail Price Index are on page 370.

- For each thing which is not exempt and which you have disposed of during the tax year, write down the amount you paid for it (including any costs you incurred in buying it, like auctioneer's commission) or, if you were given it or inherited it, its value at the time.

- Multiply that amount by the Retail Price Index (RPI – see page 370) for the month you disposed of it and divide by the RPI for the month you acquired it. This gives the cost of buying it in today's money.

- If you spent money on the asset in order to increase its value (e.g., extending a house), multiply the amount you spent by the RPI for the month you disposed of it and divide by the RPI for the month the money became due and payable. This gives the cost of the expense in today's money. Add these costs to the cost of buying the asset in today's money.

- Now add to this amount any costs you incurred in selling the asset (e.g., legal or agent's fees) and subtract the total from the amount you sold it for (or, if you gave it away, from its value at the time).

- The amount you now have is the **taxable gain** for each asset or, if you are left with a minus number, the **taxable loss** for that asset. Add up all the taxable gains and subtract all the taxable losses. You can also subtract any losses you have carried forward from earlier years.

- If the amount you now have is less than £6,300, there is no CGT to pay this year. You can carry over to next year any losses which reduce your total taxable gains below £6,300.

- If the amount you now have is more than £6,300, you pay tax on 29% of the excess. You do not have any losses to carry forward.

You may find that the answer you get using this method is a few pounds different from your Tax Inspector's because the Inland Revenue has a more long-winded method which includes set ways of rounding the numbers in the calculations.

IF YOU OWNED THE ASSET BEFORE MARCH 1982

You can choose between two ways of working out the taxable gain. You can either follow the method above, using the RPI for March 1982 (313.4) for any month prior to that when you spent money on the asset. Or you can leave out the inflation adjustment for any expenditure before March 1982 and then subtract from the final answer the amount the asset is assumed to have increased in value since March 1982. You work out the amount to subtract by:

- subtracting 313.4 from the RPI in the month you disposed of the asset
- multiplying by the value of the asset on 31 March 1982 (you may need a professional opinion – the higher the valuation the better)
- then dividing by 313.4.

You can choose which method you like to work out the taxable gain. Generally the second method will produce a smaller gain, meaning less tax to pay.

IF YOU OWNED THE ASSET BEFORE 6 APRIL 1965

Capital Gains Tax started in April 1965, so you do not have to pay any tax on the part of the gain that is assumed to have accumulated before that date. Again, you can choose between two methods for working out the taxable gain. This time the first method will normally produce a smaller taxable gain, though you usually have to use the second method for quoted shares, unit trusts and land with development value:

Method 1: Work out the gain in the usual way, multiply by the number of complete months between 6 April 1965 and the date of disposal and divide by the number of complete months you owned the asset. But if you first owned it before 6 April 1945, count only the number of complete months since that date.

Method 2: Work out the gain in the usual way, but as though you bought the asset on 6 April 1965 and the amount you paid was its value on that day.

Your home

If you own only one home, it will normally be exempt from Capital Gains Tax, but there are some circumstances in which some of the gain you make when you sell can become liable (see page 138). A home which you own which is occupied by a dependent relative can also be exempt, whether you own another home or not. Apart from that, if you own more than one home only one of them can be exempt from CGT. This is the one you select as your 'main' home – it does not *have* to be the one you live in most of the time(though you will need to live there quite a bit), nor the one on which you get tax relief on a mortgage. You simply write to your tax office and tell them which of your homes is to be treated as your main home for CGT purposes (you can backdate your choice by up to two years). You should choose the home on which you are likely to make the largest taxable gain, and should make your choice within 2 years of acquiring a second home – if you have had two homes for longer than that, do it straightaway. The home you choose will then be exempt from CGT unless one of the circumstances on page 138 applies, but other homes you own (apart from one occupied by a dependent relative) will not be exempt.

Your business

There is no Capital Gains Tax on the profits you make from trading, nor when you sell minor business assets. But if you sell or give away land, buildings, fixed plant or machinery there will be a capital gain or capital loss for CGT purposes. Also if you sell or give away the business (or part of it, e.g., some shares in it) and part of the selling price or value is attributable to these assets or to good will, there will again be a capital gain or loss for CGT purposes.

However, if within three years you spend the money you get on new business assets (it does not have to be the same business) you can choose not to pay any CGT at the time – called **roll-over relief**. When you finally sell assets and do not replace them, the gain or loss is worked out much as if you had owned one business asset all along.

But if you are 60 or over when you sell business assets (or if you have been forced to retire earlier through ill-health), you can claim **retirement relief**. £100,000 of the gains you make can then be free of Capital Gains Tax (less if you have owned the business for less than 10 years). See page 301 for more details.

The effect of these rules is that if, during your working life, you always reinvest most of the money you get from selling business assets in new business assets and do not dispose of the business until you are 60, you can then make gains of £100,000 completely free of Capital Gains Tax.

Shares and unit trusts

There are a number of special rules for shares and unit trusts which can get extremely complicated. See sources of further information below.

Gifts

When you give something away, you and the recipient can agree to **roll-over** the gain. This means that there will be no capital gain or loss when you give the asset away, but when the recipient comes to dispose of the asset it will be treated much as if they had owned it all along.

If you are married

The limit for tax-free gains (£6,300 in the 1986–87 tax year) is the same for a married couple as for a single person – you do not get an allowance each. Anything which you give or sell to each other is exempt from Capital Gains Tax. You can only have one home exempt from Capital Gains Tax plus one home which is occupied by a dependent relative (see page 139). Normally all the taxable gains you both make in a tax year are added up and all the losses you both make are subtracted to arrive at your net taxable gains. But if one of you has a net loss and the other a net gain which is less than £6,300, the one who has made the loss should ask for it to be carried forward and set against their own gains (only) in future years. Otherwise it will be set against the partner's gains in the same year and will be wasted. You must request this within three months of the end of the tax year (for 1986–87 this means before 6 July 1987).

Normally your husband will be responsible for giving the Inland Revenue details of both his and your gains and losses on his Tax Return. If you want to give details of your own affairs yourself and be responsible for paying your own Capital Gains Tax, you should ask to be **separately assessed** for CGT. You should do this within 3 months of the end of the tax year (i.e., before 6 July 1987 for the 1986–87 tax year). Separate assessment will continue until you ask to be jointly assessed.

You are treated as married if you are living with your husband at the start of the tax year. If you are separated from your husband at the start of the tax year, you are treated as a single person if there is a decree of judicial separation or a separation deed, or if maintenance is payable under a court order, or if the separation has lasted for a year or more or is likely to be permanent.

FURTHER INFORMATION

For more about Capital Gains Tax, see Inland Revenue leaflets CGT.4, *CGT: owner-occupied houses*, CGT.11, *CGT and the small businessman* and CGT.12, *CGT: Indexation*, and the horrendously complicated CGT.8, *Capital Gains Tax* and its supplements. A more readable account covering most aspects of CGT is given in *The Which? Book of Tax* (£12.95 from Consumers' Association or bookshops) which you should be able to get at your local library.

RETAIL PRICE INDEX (RPI) FROM MARCH 1982

Year	Jan	Feb	Mar	Apr	May	Jun	Jul	Aug	Sep	Oct	Nov	Dec
1982			313.4	319.7	322.0	322.9	323.0	323.1	322.9	324.5	326.1	325.5
1983	325.9	327.3	327.9	332.5	333.9	334.7	336.5	338.0	339.5	340.7	341.9	342.8
1984	342.6	344.0	345.1	349.7	351.0	351.9	351.5	354.8	355.5	357.7	358.8	358.5
1985	359.8	362.7	366.1	373.9	375.6	376.4	375.7	376.7	376.5	377.1	378.4	378.9

Index

ANTHONY SAMPSON

THE MONEY LENDERS

THE MONEY LENDERS reveals for the first time the power, the workings and the personalities of the money men who make the world go round:
The Superbankers – including Chase's David Rockefeller, Citibank's Walter Wriston, Lloyd's Sir Jeremy Morse and Robert McNamara.
The debt-ridden regimes of Poland and Iran, Brazil, Zaire and Pakistan.
The Medicis, the Rothschilds, the Barings, the Barclays whose banks have transformed the economic map of the world.

THE MONEY LENDERS tells the full story of the world banking crisis: as The Guardian review confirmed 'Anthony Sampson has said it all. There's nothing else to say'

ANTHONY SAMPSON

THE CHANGING ANATOMY OF BRITAIN

'Anthony Sampson's field of vision is enormously wide . . . everyone who reads this book, however well-informed, will learn something.'

THE ECONOMIST

Twenty years ago Anthony Sampson's unique bestseller, ANATOMY OF BRITAIN, became the essential, definitive guide to the workings of British power. Now Sampson has surpassed that achievement with THE CHANGING ANATOMY OF BRITAIN, the remarkable book that holds the key to who really runs Britain today.

How much have British institutions really changed? What happened to the promises of reform? How effectively have the old elites fought back against the challenge from the new? The author analyses the hopes and promises of change and the failure to reverse Britain's decline over the last two decades. Packed with exclusive interviews – ranging from Mrs Thatcher to Moss Evans, from the Prince of Wales to Michael Edwardes, THE CHANGING ANATOMY OF BRITAIN is essential reading for anyone interested in Britain today.

'*A tour de force* . . . whether it's press lords or politicians, public schools or social democrats, merchant bankers or monarchy, diplomats or doctors, Sampson has something fascinating to say.'

NEW SOCIETY

CORONET BOOKS

HOWARD DAVID DEUTSCH

GETTING INTO AMERICA

How do you get the coveted 'green card'?

What kind of visa do you need in order to study, set up a business, work as a domestic, perform, or write in the United States?

Why should your records with the various immigration authorities – the Immigration and Naturalization Service, the Department of Labor, the State Department – be absolutely consistent?

When does it make sense to enter on a temporary visa and apply later for a change of status?

When do you need a lawyer and what should you ask before hiring him?

These are some of the many questions posed by anxious potential immigrants to the United States. GETTING INTO AMERICA answers them all, without resorting to legal and bureaucratic jargon. This book is the first accessible and comprehensive guide to immigration, and will prove an invaluable aid to immigrants themselves, to relatives, employers and others who want to petition on their behalf, and to lawyers in the speciality.

GETTING INTO AMERICA provides practical solutions to immigration problems, tells how to take advantage of government red tape, and spells out perfectly legal short-cuts that can save you thousands of dollars and years of waiting.

HOWARD DAVID DEUTSCH, an acknowledged expert in immigration law has travelled more than half a million miles in recent years representing people from more than twenty countries who wish to enter the United States. Whatever your situation may be, GETTING INTO AMERICA will tell you how to do just that: get into (and stay in) the United States.

CORONET BOOKS

JOEL MAKOWER

PERSONAL COMPUTERS A–Z

Everything you need to know about computers – and nothing you don't

Finally, a book for non-computer experts.

From acoustic couplers to Z-80 microprocessors, PERSONAL COMPUTERS A–Z introduces you to the key terms you need to make your introduction to personal computing painless – and even enjoyable. In clear, non-technical terms, here are the basics of BASIC and no-nonsense explanations of RAM and ROM, modes and modems, formats and FORTRAN, and much more.

PERSONAL COMPUTERS A–Z also features valuable information about the care and feeding of your personal computer, from cleaning disc drives to dealing with dealers to deducting your computer from your taxes.

Whatever computer your own – or are thinking of owning – PERSONAL COMPUTERS A–Z is your road map to the world of personal computing.

CORONET BOOKS

RAY HAMMOND

THE WRITER AND THE WORD PROCESSOR

Word processors and computers reduce the labour of writing; they enhance composition and they offer editing power which cannot be achieved by other means.

THE WRITER AND THE WORD PROCESSOR is the indispensable guide to choosing a word processor system suited to your own specific needs. Clearly and entertainingly written, the author has used his own experience and that of other writers to provide a comprehensive manual that a writer needs to enter the computer age. It includes:

The hardware – what it does and what a writer needs.

The programs – how to choose a good word processing program.

How to choose a printer.

How to choose automatic dictionaries and grammar checkers.

How to use the telephone lines to tap into libraries and the world's electronic store of information.

Portable word processing: how to choose a machine which lets you work anywhere.

How to buy a word processing system on a shoestring budget.

Writers talking about their experiences with computers, with exclusive interviews with Len Deighton, Dorothy Dunnett, Tom Sharpe and Terence Feely.

CORONET BOOKS